How to Use Emotional, Cultural, and Spiritual Intelligence to Mentor Doctoral Learners

Best Practices and Tools to Help Mentors and Doctoral Learners Navigate the Dissertation Process

by Walter R. McCollum, PhD
Foreword by Marilyn K. Simon, PhD

Published by

McCollum Enterprises, LLC

Walter R. McCollum, PhD

Fort Washington, Maryland

ISBN 978-0-9791406-5-5

All Rights Reserved, Copyright 2014

No part of this book may be reproduced or transmitted in any form or by any means, graphic, electronic, or mechanical, including photocopying, recording, taping, or by any information storage retrieval system, without permission in writing from the publisher.

Dedication

Iron sharpeneth iron; so a man sharpeneth the countenance of his friend. —Proverbs 27:17

Thank you God for equipping me with Emotional, Cultural, and Spiritual Intelligence and for showing me what it means to sharpen the countenance of learners around the world!

This book is dedicated to all academicians who are changing the lives of doctoral learners by guiding them through the dissertation process and aiding them in becoming scholar-practitioners.

To all doctoral learners who are dedicated, committed, and focused on completing the dissertation process.

This book is also dedicated to those who mentored me through my doctoral journey.

Acknowledgments

To Dr. Marilyn Simon, who mentored me through the dissertation process over a decade ago and demonstrated what mentoring excellence looks like. I am indebted to you forever.

To the doctors and doctoral learners whom I've had the opportunity to mentor at various universities, thanks for such a profound experience and for the opportunity to mentor you.

Special thanks to my editor, Toni Williams. Thank you so much for supporting this book project. You are a gem! I am very grateful.

Table of Contents

Preface ix
Introduction 1
1 Emotional Intelligence Is the Heart of Mentoring Doctoral Learners 9
2 Using Cultural Intelligence as a Critical Success Factor to Mentor Doctoral Learners 35
3 Aligning Spiritual Intelligence Principles With the Dissertation Process 57
4 16 Best Practices for Doctoral Learners to Navigate the Dissertation Process 73
5 Steven LaFalce, PhD 93
6 Dereje Tessema, PhD 108
7 William Quisenberry, DBA 130
8 Daniel Hansen, Doctoral Candidate 163
9 Tom Butkiewicz, PhD 181
10 William Dzekashu, PhD 195
11 Markus Shelton, PhD 213
12 Gladwyn Sandiford, PhD 227
13 Lewis Saunders, PhD 245
14 Scott Evans Willette, PhD 262
15 Phillip R. Neely, PhD 279

16 Madhu Rao, Doctoral Candidate 293
17 B. Bernard Ferguson, PhD..309
18 Gary Lee Lucy, Sr., PhD 321
19 Richard T. Brown, Jr., PhD 331
20 Jodi M. Burchell, PhD 346
21 Kim Tran, PhD..362
22 Verna L. Velez, PhD...375
23 Lisa R. Brown, Doctoral Candidate............................388
24 Jennifer Perkins, PhD, MPH, CHES 403
25 Victoria B. Buck, Doctoral Candidate........................417
About the Author 438

Preface

Most top athletes, top musicians, top actors, and top executives have excellent mentors who also serve as coaches and cheerleaders to assist them in achieving their best. Doctoral students need top-notch mentors to perform the same roles.

I have known Dr. McCollum for over 15 years, first as a member of his doctoral committee and then as a colleague and friend. I was his unofficial mentor and have had the pleasure and honor of seeing this mentee pay it forward and become the best mentor I know.

There are numerous books and resource materials for mentoring in the business section of bookstores, but few exist that are specifically designed for graduate faculty to mentor doctoral students. This book will explain how it's done and what outcomes are possible. By writing this book, Dr. McCollum contributes authentic information that fulfills a necessary role for doctoral students and their mentors in a variety of ways. The literature for the business world is designed to help people become better leaders and advance in their careers. This book is designed to help faculty gain insights that will enable them to do the same with their doctoral students, whether the degree program is on ground or online.

Dr. McCollum's andragogy combines Emotional Intelligence, Cultural Intelligence, and Spiritual Intelligence to enable mentees to achieve their goals and to maximize their professional and personal potential. In order for mentors to help mentees develop and shape the mentoring characteristics, Emotional, Cultural, and Spiritual Intelligence must be integrated into the dissertation mentoring process. This exemplar method is explained in exquisite detail.

—Marilyn K. Simon

Introduction

Give a man a fish and you feed him for a day. Teach a man to fish and you feed him for a lifetime.
—Chinese Proverb

The focus of this book is to show that Emotional, Cultural, and Spiritual Intelligence are critical factors used to help both mentors and doctoral learners successfully navigate the dissertation process together. I will also provide 16 best practices that I have used to mentor doctoral learners effectively over the past decade. As a result of instituting these practices, I've been able to increase my doctoral learner graduation rate by 50% each year. Additionally, I will share proven tools and tips from doctors and doctoral candidates who have been successful in the dissertation process. Both mentors of doctoral learners and mentees will benefit from this book.

Many scholars have conducted research on the paradigm of mentoring doctoral learners. Doctoral education has a history of individual mentoring of students as a means of guiding them through their research, inducting them into the academic community, and often introducing them to professional networks and launching their academic career through a supportive and personal relationship (Anderson & Shore, 2008; Davis, 2007; Forehand, 2008; Hu, Thomas, & Lance, 2008, Paglis, Green, & Bauer, 2006). Although scholars have conducted research on doctoral mentoring, the concepts of mentoring doctoral learners have been informed largely by practical advice drawn from observation and experience.

Different concepts of research on mentoring exist in the academic world. These concepts include (a) perceptions of mentoring, (b) mentoring doctoral dissertations, (c) mentoring students in online programs, and (d) specific mentoring characteristics that include, but are not limited to, Emotional, Cultural, and Spiritual Intelligence. Although there are many concepts on doctoral mentoring, mentors have varying perspectives about those concepts. In this book, I provide perspectives from both mentors and mentees.

Most existing research focuses on mentee perceptions and very little research focuses on mentor perceptions. In research conducted by Norton and Hathaway (2008), learners were asked to report on their experience as mentees after different kinds of learning activities. In the one-on-one context, mentors were perceived as a positive influence when they were knowledgeable about content and technology; adjusted their responses and activities to meet individual needs; were prompt in responding to students; asked evocative questions; provided encouragement, compliments, and positive feedback; and maximized opportunities to relate with mentees. Jones (2001) conducted a study on mentor perceptions in which mentors of practicing teachers in both England and Germany provided their perceptions of the mentoring process. There was strong agreement among the mentors from both countries that the role of the mentor included constructive and critical advising, honest support, and being a role model, although there was a clear recognition that there were serious limitations to being seen in that role. A comparison of the studies by Norton and Hathaway and by Jones indicated that faculty members see mentoring more in terms of improving student work, whereas students see it more in terms of personal encouragement.

The second concept of research is on mentoring doctoral dissertations. Kearns, Gardiner, and Marshall (2008) developed the premise that three self-defeating behaviors make writing a dissertation a difficult and sometimes unsuccessful task: overcommitment, procrastination, and perfectionism. Their findings indicated that coaching programs and cohort or peer mentoring models addressing these behaviors can bring about significant changes, but mentors also need to be appropriately responsive for the coaching to work well, which might include having regular contact, giving timely feedback, and allowing open negotiation of responsibilities. I have instituted a cohort model at various universities with my doctoral learners and have proven that doctoral learners can minimize the self-defeating behaviors of overcommitment, procrastination, and perfectionism when learners within the cohort hold each other accountable for meeting milestones. In another study of students in a counseling doctoral program, Protivnak and Foss (2009) identified several qualities of positive mentoring: genuine caring, quality time with mentees, joint research projects, serving as role models, and offering holistic mentoring that includes both personal and professional lives. This is something that I have incorporated into my mentoring model: spending quality time with my doctoral mentees and working on joint research projects with them. I spend quality time with them by getting to know them outside of the dissertation process and mentoring them holistically on a personal and professional level. I also invite many of my mentees to collaborate with me on research initiatives such as book projects or international projects.

The third concept of mentoring is mentoring students in online programs. Williams (2008) compared face-to-face mentoring with online mentoring for undergraduate students and revealed a significant overlap of mentoring qualities identified by instructors and students: (a) a student-centered program, (b) a humanistic learning orientation, (c) creating a context conducive to adult learning, (d) grounding learning objectives in an analysis of students' needs, and (e) facilitating the learning process. In addition, a uniquely online factor emerged that had not appeared in studies of face-to-face environments: maintaining a constant presence in the student's school life. This quality of constancy, Williams noted, is "being reliable, loyal, and never too busy" (p. 204) and "being completely there and engaged in a constant way during each step and between them" (p. 204). Williams suggested that the lack of face-to face contact can be compensated for with the regular use of telephone and e-mail communications shaped around the particular needs of the student at each stage of the study.

The fourth concept of research focuses on mentoring characteristics. Dua (2008) developed a Mentoring-Friendliness Scale of 26 items that she used to explore the mentoring climate of various departments with women students. She devoted at least eight out of 26 items to the notion of induction, including a faculty member's willingness to "provide information about educational programs," help students to "understand educational bureaucracy," "train students into the profession," "sponsor students," "socialize students into the institutional culture" and the "department culture," "inculcate professional values/ethics," and "engage in joint research/publications" (p. 311). Mentors' role is not to create clones of themselves but "to maximize their [mentees'] professional and personal potential" (Fletcher, 2007, p. 78) and nurture a growing sense of independence in the mentor–mentee relationship so that the mentee ultimately can exercise "personal and professional autonomy" (Anderson & Short 2008, p. 7). The whole focus of the doctoral experience is for the doctoral learner to become a scholar-practitioner, embrace individual scholarly identity through branding, and determine his or her value and worth as a new doctor. In order for mentors to help mentees develop and shape the mentoring characteristics, Emotional, Cultural, and

Spiritual Intelligence must be integrated into the dissertation process. Chapter 1 provides context around Emotional Intelligence being the heart of mentoring doctoral learners.

References

Anderson, D., & Shore, W. (2008). Ethical issues and concerns associated with mentoring undergraduate students. *Ethics & Behavior, 18*, 1-25. doi:10.1080/10508420701519577

Davis, D. (2007). Access to academe: The importance of mentoring Black students. *Negro Educational Review, 58*, 217-231.

Dua, P. (2008). The impact of gender characteristics on mentoring in graduate departments of sociology. *American Sociologist, 39*, 307-323. doi:10.1007/s12108-008-9053-y

Fletcher, S. (2007). Mentoring adult learners: Realizing possible selves. *New Directions in Adult and Continuing Education, 114*, 75-86. doi:10.1002/ace.258

Forehand, R. (2008). The art and science of mentoring in psychology: A necessary practice to ensure our future. *American Psychologist, 63*, 744-755.

Hu, C., Thomas, K., & Lance, C. (2008). Intentions to initiate mentoring relationships: Understanding the impact of race, proactivity, feelings of deprivation, and relationship roles. *Journal of Social Psychology, 148*, 727-744.

Jones, M. (2001). Mentors' perceptions of their roles in school-based teacher training in England and Germany. *Journal of Education for Teaching, 27*, 75-94. doi:10.1080/02607470120042555

Kearns, H., Gardiner, M., & Marshall, K. (2008). Innovation in PhD completion: The hardy shall succeed (and be happy!). *Higher Education Research & Development, 27*, 77-89. doi:1080/07294360701658781

Norton, P., & Hathaway, D. (2008). Exploring two teacher education online learning designs: A classroom of one or many? *Journal of Research on Technology in Education, 40*, 475-495.

Paglis, L. L., Green, S. G., & Bauer, T. N. (2006). Does advisor mentoring add value? A longitudinal study of mentoring and doctoral student outcomes. *Research in Higher Education, 47*, 451-476.

Protivnak, J., & Foss, L. (2009). An exploration of themes that influence the counselor education doctoral student experience. *Counselor Education & Supervision, 48*, 239-256.

Williams, L. (2008). *Mentoring online adult undergraduate learners* (Unpublished doctoral dissertation). Union Institute and University, Cincinnati, OH.

1
Emotional Intelligence Is the Heart of Mentoring Doctoral Learners

Adult learning theories provide a deeper understanding of how adults process their learning. Each learning theory explains that adults require interaction with their environment and with other individuals to learn. Establishing social interaction between doctoral learners and their peers, who have different frames of reference, requires a certain level of Emotional Intelligence for doctoral learners to communicate their ideas, thoughts, stories, and mental models effectively with their peers.

Emotional Intelligence is the catalyst that brings the doctoral mentoring experience together. As indicated in its label, Emotional Intelligence is comprised of emotions and intelligence. Mayer, Salovey, and Caruso (2000) explained, "Emotions are internal events that coordinate many psychological subsystems including physiological responses, cognitions, and conscious awareness" (p. 267). Mayer, Salovey, and Caruso (2004) defined Emotional Intelligence as "the capacity to reason about emotions and of emotions to enhance thinking" (p. 197). The thinking aspect of emotions involves cognition. Several Emotional Intelligence models have been developed over time to help explain the connection of emotion to cognition.

Researchers have varying perspectives on Emotional Intelligence models. Measuring Emotional Intelligence may include the areas of mood regulation, interpersonal skills, internal motivation, empathetic response, and self-awareness (Barbuto & Burbach, 2006). Goleman (2000) provided an emotional competence framework consisting of personal competence, empathy, and social skills. The results of over 300 investigations across a wide range of professions, including academia, demonstrate that emotional competence is weighted more heavily than cognitive ability through all these professions (Goleman, 2000). Emotional Intelligence has an impact on doctoral learners' knowledge sharing in cohort models and is, therefore, important to measure.

Howard Gardner described seven: Verbal/ Linguistic, Logical/Mathematical, Visual/Spatial, Musical, Bodily/Kinesthetic, Interpersonal, and Intrapersonal Intelligences (Smith, 2008). The interpersonal and intrapersonal dimensions of Gardner's multiple intelligences model relate closely to Emotional Intelligence, but Mayer et al. (2000) coined the term *Emotional Intelligence* as an individual's ability to perceive and manage the emotions of him or herself and others. Mayer et al. developed the Emotional Intelligence ability tests called the Mayer-Salovey-Caruso Emotional Intelligence Tests (MSCEITs). These tests identify a person's ability to perceive emotions of others. Goleman (2000) wrote a bestselling book on Emotional Intelligence and noted, "If we look at sets of different variables such as persistence, warmth, optimism, and so forth, we can predict important life outcomes" (p. 174). This holds true for mentoring doctoral learners: When integrating Emotional Intelligence in the dissertation process, mentors can predict that learners will have positive life-changing results after completing the doctoral degree. Goleman developed an instrument that tests different Emotional Intelligence competencies and can be used with individuals or groups.

Another study on Emotional Intelligence is Reuven Bar-On, who developed a self-report instrument on Emotional and Social Intelligence. In 1985, he coined the term *EQ*, which stands for emotional quotient (Emmerling, 2007). Bar-On created the Emotional Quotient Inventory (EQ-i), one of the most widely used test of Emotional

Intelligence. Over 1 million EQ-i assessments have been conducted worldwide (Emmerling, 2007). In evaluating both Goleman's and Bar-On's assessment tools on Emotional Intelligence, I prefer Goleman's tool because it appears to better align with assessing the Emotional Intelligence of both mentors and doctoral learners in a learning environment.

Emotional Intelligence is a critical component in the process of mentoring doctoral learners and is crucial to the personal and professional development of mentees in the dissertation process. Below are the five components of Goleman's Emotional Intelligence model.

Self-Awareness	The ability to recognize and understand your moods, emotions, and drives, as well as their effects on others
Self-Regulation	The ability to control or redirect disruptive impulses and moods; the propensity to suspend judgment to think before acting
Motivation	A passion to work for intrinsic reasons that go beyond money or status a propensity to pursue goals with energy and persistence
Empathy	The ability to understand and relate to the emotional makeup of other people skill in treating people according to their emotional reactions

Social Skill   Proficiency in managing interpersonal relationships and building interpersonal networks an ability to find common ground and build rapport with others

In mentoring doctoral learners, it is advantageous for the mentor to have high Emotional Intelligence and to demonstrate the characteristics from the five components of this model. From my experience, doctoral learners may begin to develop their own Emotional Intelligence skills and competencies through modeling their mentor's behaviors. All five components in Goleman's Emotional Intelligence model can be aligned to effective mentoring of doctoral learners as described below:

1.   *Self-awareness.* Having the ability to understand one's emotions and moods and how they impact others is critical in mentoring doctoral learners. In establishing relationships between mentors and doctoral learners, mentors set a certain tone set that has an influence on the bidirectional communication exchange between the mentor and mentee. A mentor who is moody or has an emotional stance could impact the relationship between the mentor and the doctoral learner and could impact the progress that the learner makes in the dissertation process. It is paramount for mentors of doctoral learners to be self-

aware of their moods and emotions and make necessary adjustments to keep the mentoring relationship on task. It's equally as important for mentees to be self-aware of their disposition and how they relate to their mentor, as this may impact the mentor's responsiveness. When learners are overbearing, arrogant, and disrespectful, I tend not to focus as much of my energy on them. The mentoring relationship is more effective when there is an understanding of mutual respect between both the mentor and doctoral learner.

    2. **Self-regulation.** Having the ability to redirect disruptive impulses, to suspend judgment, and to think before acting are some of the more difficult components to which a mentor and mentee should adhere. When working with doctoral learners, mentors must be skilled in redirecting disruptive impulses when there may be a conflict or a disagreement that has escalated out of control. This sometimes happen between the mentor and the doctoral learner when there are two strong personalities and both parties stand firmly on their positions. Suspending judgment to think before acting can de-escalate the situation to be more manageable and controllable. Both the mentor and the doctoral learner must take a step back, decompress, and take the emotion out of the situation. It's ultimately the mentor's responsibility to set boundaries in situations like this and to begin the process of diffusing the situation. This could be a teachable moment for a learner and an opportunity for the learner to develop Emotional Intelligence competencies in self-regulation.

    3.   *Motivation.* It's important for mentors of doctoral learners to be motivated about the work they are doing to support the learners while coaching them through the dissertation process. Intrinsically, mentors need to be excited and have the energy and commitment to help doctoral learners reach their academic goals, rather than only collect a fee for service for their mentoring work. Learners can certainly feel when mentors are making a true investment in their learning experience, rather than just going through the motions and collecting a paycheck. It's also just as important for learners to be motivated and excited about embracing the doctoral process, providing the highest level of quality in their dissertation, and growing and developing in the process. As a mentor, I am more inclined to go the extra mile and stand up for the learner who is motivated and produces high-quality work. Based on the growth and development I've assessed from the learner, I'm more eager to provide them with leadership opportunities like appointing them as a peer mentor or cohort leader of other doctoral learners, which in turn helps

the learner begin to embrace their scholarly identity and also provides them with experience in mentoring doctoral learners. From my experience in mentoring doctoral learners over the past 9 years, most of the learners I have appointed to peer-mentor other doctoral learners have been able to transition into academia within the first 3 months of completing the doctoral program. This is an incentive for learners to remain motivated in the dissertation process.

  4. *Empathy.* Being able to feel and relate to what doctoral learners are going through is critical! Life happens, and there are often extenuating circumstances such as financial issues, health issues, divorce, and even death in the family. Mentors need to have compassion for doctoral learners and be flexible with them while they are going through situations. Some doctoral learners have learning disabilities or physical disabilities and need additional support. Mentors need to be sensitive to these situations and be willing to empathize with the learners and provide them with the necessary resources available to them while providing them with needed support. Learners also need to be sensitive to the obligations and schedules of their mentors. Mentors have the same life situations as learners, and learners need to be sensitive to this. In many instances, mentors are also working with other learners and providing the same level of mentoring to those learners. When learners are not considerate of my time and try to push me, I generally wait until the very last date to respond or conduct a review of their work. They are not going to get through the dissertation process any faster by pushing me. In fact, it will probably take them longer to complete the process. When learners embrace the process, follow instructions, and pay attention to detail, I will do anything in my power to take the least amount of time possible to conduct reviews of their work. Empathy needs to go both ways.

5. *Social skill.* Managing interpersonal relationships and building networks is critical for doctoral learners to grasp early in the dissertation process. Mentors can help learners develop these skills by conducting workshops on networking. Mentors can also help learners to build relationships by creating a student-led cohort model and providing learners with the necessary resources to support their progress while empowering them to facilitate the meetings and bond as a group. Another way to help learners develop their social skills is to provide them with opportunities to present their research in the cohort among other doctoral learners or encourage them to present at doctoral dissertation consortia or professional

conferences where they will have the opportunity to exchange with academics, other professionals, and other doctoral learners and receive feedback on their research. The social skill component of Goleman's model is critical to doctoral learners' transition from a learner into the sea of scholars. I spend a lot of time helping my learners become more engaged and connected to industry professionals, professional organizations, and other academics. Many of my learners partner with me on research initiatives and have even accompanied me on social change and international development trips to South Africa, Costa Rica, and Haiti. My goal is to provide them with as many outlets and connections that will aid them in becoming the scholar-practitioner they are aspiring to become.

It really pays off when mentors have high Emotional Intelligence and can use it in the process of mentoring doctoral learners. When mentors model Emotional Intelligence characteristics in the dissertation process, learners have many opportunities to develop their Emotional Intelligence competencies and skills. It's also good for mentors to know which components in Goleman's Emotional Intelligence they need to improve upon themselves and how to go about doing so. A few years ago, I became a certified Emotional Intelligence mentor and as part of the certification process, I had to take the Emotional Intelligence assessment and Personality Inventory based upon Goleman's Emotional Intelligence model. The results from my assessment and inventory appear in the next sections.

Emotional Intelligence Assessment Results

My score on the Emotional Intelligence assessment was analyzed and is depicted in the graphics below. My score is shown in gray and the average score for each subscale is shown in orange. The error bars represent an average score. If the score falls above or below the error bars, I scored high or low for that subscale, respectively. If I choose to raise my Emotional Intelligence, the subscales of Emotional Intelligence on which I scored the lowest should be the focus of my development.

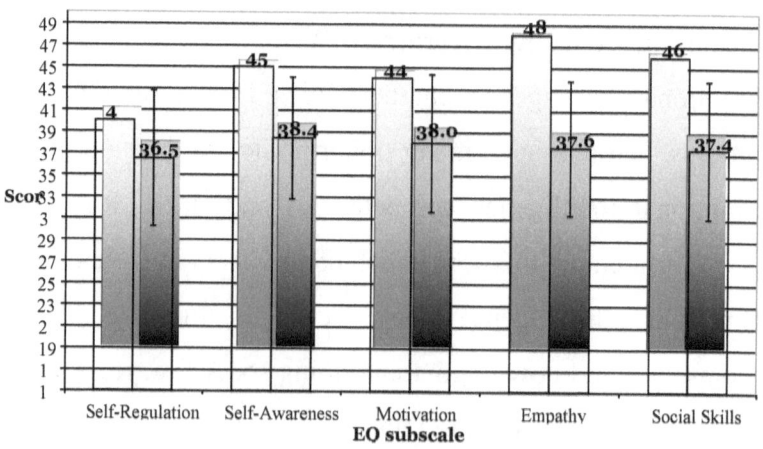

Scoring Information

Self-Regulation, Self-Awareness, and Motivation subscales add up to represent my Intrapersonal Emotional Intelligence Score. The Empathy and Social Skills subscales add up to represent my Interpersonal Emotional Intelligence Score. My level of Emotional Intelligence was calculated by summing the Intrapersonal and Interpersonal Scores.

Score:	Scale:
40	Self-Regulation
45	Self-Awareness
+ 44	Motivation
129	Intrapersonal Emotional Intelligence
48	Empathy
+ 44	Social Skills
94	Interpersonal Emotional Intelligence

129 + 94 = 223   Emotional Intelligence

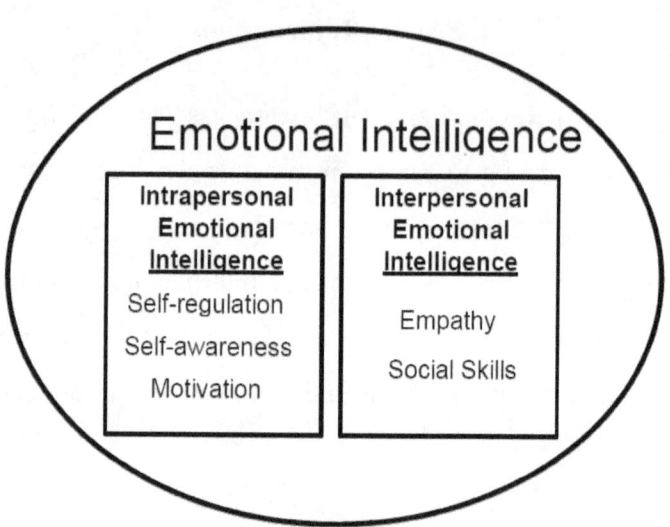

Scoring Interpretation

The higher one's score, the higher one's Emotional Intelligence is. This instrument can help identify areas of relative weakness and target specific areas for improvement. The highest score for each subscale is 48. I scored a 48 on the Empathy subscale. The lowest score for each scale is 0. Because there are five subscales, the total Emotional Intelligence score is out of 240 points. My Emotional Intelligence score is 223, and I consider Emotional Intelligence one of my strong suits.

Emotional Intelligence

Emotional Intelligence is the ability to sense, understand, and effectively apply the power and acumen of emotions to facilitate high levels of collaboration and productivity. One's overall score indicates the level of overall Emotional Intelligence. The higher the number, the more emotionally intelligent a person is!

Intrapersonal Intelligence

Intrapersonal Intelligence is a component of Emotional Intelligence that refers to the ability turned inward. This is the ability to understand oneself. It is a capacity to form an accurate concept of oneself and to be able to use that concept to operate effectively in life. The higher a person's number, the more Intrapersonal Intelligence that person has!

Self-Regulation:

Self-regulation, a component of Intrapersonal Intelligence, is the ability to control or redirect disruptive impulses and moods and the propensity to suspend judgment and think before acting. Self-regulation is characterized by trustworthiness and integrity, comfort with ambiguity, and openness to change. Although people cannot choose when to be emotional, individuals who score high on self-regulation tend to be able to choose how long that emotion lasts.

Self-Awareness:

Self-awareness, a component of Intrapersonal Intelligence, is the ability to recognize and understand one's moods, emotions, and drives, as well as their effect on others. Self-awareness is characterized by self-confidence, realistic assessment of the self, and a self-deprecating sense of humor. Persons scoring on the low end of self-awareness may find it hard to make decisions or express their emotions.

Motivation:

Motivation, a component of Intrapersonal Intelligence, is a passion to work for reasons that go beyond money or status and a propensity to pursue goals with energy and persistence. Those scoring high on motivation have a strong drive to achieve, are optimistic even in the face of failure, and have a strong sense of organizational commitment. Optimistic thinking is the key to this persistence; those individuals scoring on the low end of the motivation subscale tend to have a pessimistic approach, often thinking thoughts along the lines of "I failed again."

Interpersonal Intelligence

Interpersonal Intelligence is the ability to understand other people. This component of Emotional Intelligence enables a person to relate effectively to other people. One who is Interpersonally Intelligent can understand what motivates others, how they work, and how to work cooperatively with them. The higher a person's score, the more Interpersonal Intelligence that person has!

Empathy:

Empathy, a component of Interpersonal Intelligence, is the ability to understand the emotional makeup of other people. Those scoring high in empathy have a skill in treating people according to their emotional reactions, are expert in building and retaining talent, are sensitive to others of different cultures, and provide great service to both clients and customers. The extremes of the empathy spectrum are clearly differentiated. Those with high scores tend to experience emotion when they see someone else suffer, and as a result, tend to be quite altruistic. Persons with the lowest scores do not have strong emotions and will experience a similar response when observing both mundane and shocking events.

Social Skill:

Social skill, a component of Interpersonal Intelligence, is a proficiency in managing relationships and building networks. Those scoring high in social skill have an ability to find common ground and build rapport with others, are persuasive, are effective in leading change, and are expert in building and leading teams. Those individuals scoring low on social skills may find interactions with others awkward and difficult.

If one scored lower than expected, there is hope; Emotional Intelligence can be learned and increased. Emotional Intelligence is independent of one's level of general intelligence; Emotional Intelligence and IQ are two different paths to success. When a person possesses both, that person maximizes the chances for success!

Personality Inventory

My score on the personality inventory was analyzed and is depicted in the following graphics. Each personality trait exists on a bipolar spectrum, with low scorers displaying opposite characteristics than high scorer. As the score is an average, those with average scores tend to use each pole equally or do not have a strong preference.

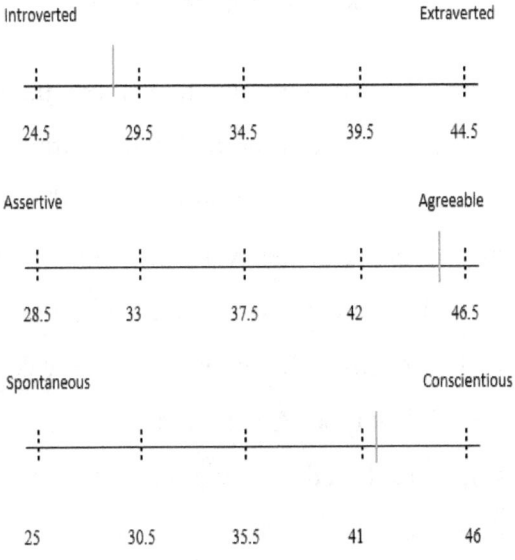
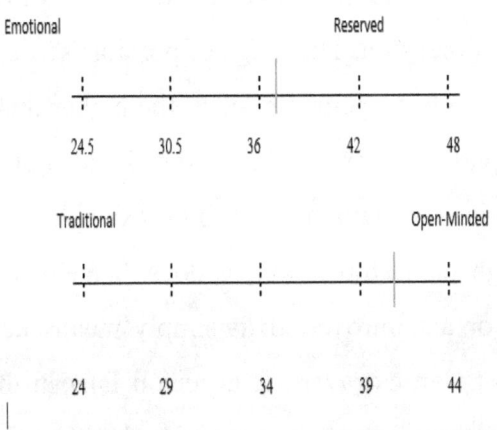

Scoring Interpretation

One's personality is a stable disposition that remains consistent over time and across situations and that affects your thoughts, emotions, and behavior. A personality scale can be very helpful in raising self-awareness. This scale can give a person a deeper understanding of his or her strengths and weaknesses based on his personality type. A person's reactions and responses to stressors are based on two determinants: his or her personality and the situation. In many cases, it is an interaction of the two, with either playing a bigger role. Understanding one's personality can help self-awareness and can make self-regulation easier.

A higher number indicates that one is high on that particular dimension. The range of possible scores is from 9 to 45. The higher a person's score, the higher that person is on that particular trait. Each trait is a preference for behaving in a certain manner. For example, if a person scores high on Extraversion, it doesn't mean that he can never be or act introverted; it simply means he naturally prefers to be an extravert. If a person falls in the middle, that person experiences the best of both worlds by tending to experience both sides of the spectrum equally. If a person scores high on Introversion, it means that person naturally prefers to be an introvert.

Introvert vs. Extravert

The Extraversion subscale measures the tendency to experience positive emotions. A high score indicates the propensity to be sociable, gregarious, assertive, talkative, and active. Extraverts tend to like working in teams and tend to make natural leaders. Those scoring low on the scale are likely to be Introverted: quiet, low key, and deliberate. A person who scores low on Extraversion does not tend to experience positive emotions as often. This is termed introversion. Introverts would rather have their own office than work in an open environment with excessive noise. Extraverts feel energized during and after social activities whereas introverts get their energy from ideas.

Assertive vs. Agreeable

Agreeableness measures an individual's concern with cooperation and conformity. Individuals scoring high on the Agreeableness subscale value harmony and getting along with others and are considerate, generous, helpful, compliant, tolerant, flexible, and friendly. They tend to believe that other people are good, honest, decent, and trustworthy. They also tend to be more interested in others than in themselves. Individuals scoring low on the Agreeableness subscale place their self-interests above the interests of others. Skepticism about motives leads them to be suspicious, unfriendly, and uncooperative. They are seen as argumentative and opinionated.

Spontaneous vs. Conscientious

Conscientiousness measures the way people control and regulate their impulses. Conscientiousness entails the need for achievement and dependability. Those scoring high tend to engage themselves in purposeful planning, avoid trouble, and generally achieve much success. One with an extremely high score on this scale may be considered a perfectionist, workaholic, stuffy, or even boring. They like to have a plan for everything. Those on the lower end of the spectrum are more spontaneous. They are likely considered lazy, sloppy, or unreliable. They may be underachievers not living up to their fullest potential.

Emotional vs. Reserved

The Emotionality subscale measures a tendency to experience negative emotions. A high score is associated with a calm demeanor and freedom from persistent negative feelings. An emotionally stable individual will generally be highly optimistic and quick to rebound from stressful situations. Individuals with low scores have tendencies to be depressed, anxious, angry, embarrassed, emotional, worried, or insecure. Those scoring low have more intense emotional reactions than do most people. They may be quick to take offense or react angrily if they do not regulate these emotions properly.

Traditional vs. Open-minded

The Openness subscale distinguishes imaginative and creative people from down-to-earth and conventional people in terms of beliefs. Sometimes this subscale is termed Intellect or Culture. Those with a high score on the Openness subscale are likely to have an appreciation for art and strong intellectual curiosity and may hold unconventional and individualistic beliefs. Those high on this scale seek complexity, accept innovation, and tend to be creative. Those scoring low on this scale are likely to have narrow, common interests; be conservative; and prefer familiarity and simplicity, and they may be resistant to change.

How to Best Work With Each Personality Style

An awareness of the various personality components will not only enable a person to understand him or herself better, but will also help that person work with other people. People who receive an extreme score on a subscale have very strong preferences for their interactions and lifestyle; these preferences may or may not complement others' style. Recognizing those who tend to score either very high or very low can help with communication and teamwork. The following is a guide for how to best work with people who score on the extreme ends of the personality dimensions spectra.

EXTRAVERSION	HIGH: Extravert	Extraverts are generally talkative and easy to start a conversation with. Because they seek interaction with other people and tend to be involved in many activities, they do their best work collaboratively.
	LOW: Introvert	Introverts tend to get overwhelmed when exposed to sensory stimulation from people and social situations. They prefer to work alone and are private regarding personal matters. Note that this does not mean they are shy or lacking in social skills.
AGREEABLENESS	HIGH: Agreeable	Those individuals scoring on the extreme end of Agreeableness are friendly and easy to get along with. Their highly agreeable nature usually manifests itself as people-pleasing behavior. When they agree with you or follow your instructions, they may be doing so to avoid confrontation. Make sure they know that you welcome respectful disagreement and debate.
	LOW: Assertive	Those individuals scoring very low on the Agreeableness dimension will likely confront you quite bluntly and directly about most matters. Even though they may seem uncooperative and opinionated, you can usually take their words as constructive criticism.
CONSCIENTIOUSNESS	HIGH: Conscientious	Extremely conscientious individuals prefer rigid structure and control. You can count on them to be very dependable and achievement-oriented. They have a low tolerance for ambiguity and sloppiness. If you answer their questions incompletely or are late, they may be annoyed with you.
	LOW: Spontaneous	Those extremely low in conscientiousness are quite spontaneous and, at times, unreliable. They do not like to schedule their time and are very relaxed about handling responsibilities.

EMOTIONAL STABILITY	HIGH: Reserved	Since emotionally stable individuals tend to respond to stressful situations in a calm, steady, and secure way, they are generally easy to interact with without miscommunication. Keep in mind that this extreme group may not be as emotionally expressive.
	LOW: Emotional	Realize that those very low in emotional stability may react to stressful situations through negative thought processes, a heightened intensity of emotions, and/or exhibiting out-of-character behavior. Thus, be aware that he or she may need an extra minute or two to self-regulate, as opposed to those who do so naturally. A positive aspect of neurotics is that they tend to worry more than those who are emotionally stable, leading to great achievements and attention to detail.
	HIGH: Open-Minded	Persons on the extreme high end of openness tend to be unconventional and seek new ways of doing things. Since they are likely to be creative and innovative, they will do their best work when they have the freedom to pursue tasks as they see fit.

OPENNESS	LOW: Traditional	Persons on the extreme low end of openness prefer expert ideas and opinions as well as traditional beliefs. They prefer simplicity, so clear instructions work best.

Emotional Intelligence is a critical component in the doctoral mentoring process. Mentors with high Emotional Intelligence will typically be successful in mentoring doctoral learners and will provide opportunities for learners to develop their Emotional Intelligence skills and competencies in the process, through their own modeling of Emotional Intelligence characteristics. When mentors use Emotional, Cultural, and Spiritual Intelligence as critical success factors for mentoring learners, outcomes are affected in the areas of student retention rates and graduation rates. Since using these critical success factors, I have increased my doctoral learner graduation rate by 50%. I encourage mentors to take Goleman's Emotional Intelligence Assessment and Personality Inventory and compare your results with the averages on both the assessment and inventory to see which areas need improvement. This could serve as a means to serve doctoral learners more effectively. I also encourage doctoral learners to take the assessment and inventory and use the results as a means to develop Emotional Intelligence skills and competencies. In the next chapter, I will show how to use Cultural Intelligence as a critical success factor to mentor doctoral learners.

References

Bar-On, R. (2007). The reliability of the Bar-On psychometric model. Retrieved from http://www.reuvenbaron.org/bar-on-model/essay.php?i=23

Barbuto, J., & Burbach, M. (2006). The emotional intelligence of transformational leaders: A field study of elected officials. *Journal of Social Psychology, 146,* 51-64.

Emmerling, R. (2007). Reuven Bar-On, Ph.D.: Biography. Retrieved from http://www.eiconsortium.org/members/baron.htm

Goleman, D. (2000). *Working with emotional intelligence*. New York, NY: Bantam Books.

Mayer, J., Salovey, P., & Caruso, D. (2000). Models of emotional intelligence. In R. J. Sternberg (Ed.), *Handbook of intelligence* (pp. 396-420). Cambridge, UK: Cambridge University Press.

Mayer, J., Salovey, P., & Caruso, D. (2004). Emotional intelligence: Theory, findings, and implications. *Psychological Inquiry, 15*, 197-215.

McGraw, K., & Harbinson-Briggs, B. (1989). *Knowledge acquisition, principles and guidelines*. Englewood, CA: Prentice Hall.

Smith, M. K. (2008). Howard Gardner and multiple intelligences. Retrieved from http://www.infed.org/thinkers/gardner.htm

Smith, K., Collins, C., & Clark, K. (2005). Existing knowledge, knowledge creation capability, and the rate of new product introduction in high-technology firms. *Academy of Management Journal, 48*, 346-357.

2
Using Cultural Intelligence as a Critical Success Factor to Mentor Doctoral Learners

Academia, too, has cultures in both the faculty and the learner populations, which are often very distinctive. Anyone who joins a new faculty cadre spends the first few weeks deciphering its cultural code, and anyone who is accepted into a doctoral program spends the entire time in the program trying to decipher the cultural code. Within doctoral programs, there are sparring subcultures as well: the first-year students are too frightened to reach out to the all-but-dissertation learners, and the learners working on their dissertation proposal lose patience with the learners still working on course work. Each of these subcultures has a constellation of manners, histories, and values that will confuse the interferer and cause him or her to stumble—unless he or she has a high Cultural Intelligence. Cultural Intelligence is related to Emotional Intelligence, but it picks up where Emotional Intelligence leaves off (Earley & Mosakowski, 2004). The ability to interact effectively in multiple cultures was recently labeled Cultural Intelligence. Cultural Intelligence is a "multifaceted competency consisting of cultural knowledge, the practice of mindfulness, and the repertoire of behavioral skills" (Thomas & Inkson, 2004, pp. 182-183). The competencies are critical for mentors to use in mentoring doctoral learners from different ethnicities, countries, and other diversity dimensions.

Cultural Intelligence is a capability that allows individuals to understand and act appropriately across a wide range of cultures. According to Ang, Van Dyne, and Koh (2006), Cultural Intelligence is a person's capability to adjust to diverse cultural situations and effectively adapt to various cultural settings. Peterson (2004) noted Cultural Intelligence

> is the ability to engage in a set of behaviors that uses skills (i.e. language or interpersonal skills) and qualities (e.g., tolerance for ambiguity, flexibility) that are tuned appropriately to the culture-based values and attitudes of the people whom one interacts. (p. 89)

To be culturally intelligent, an individual needs to know how to suspend judgment of a situation until multiple cues can be assessed, as well as how to integrate and understand the knowledge gained from the situation

(Triandis, 2006). This is much like the self-regulation component in Goleman's Emotional Intelligence model that I addressed in the previous chapter. Similar to the five Emotional Intelligence scales in Goleman's Emotional Intelligence model to measure Emotional Intelligence competencies and skills, there are four scales to measure Cultural Intelligence capabilities.

Cultural Intelligence consists of four parts: metacognition, cognition, motivation, and behavior. High Cultural Intelligence individuals use all four in unison (Ang et al., 2004). A person with high Emotional Intelligence grasps what makes people human and at the same time what makes each person different from one another. A person with high Cultural Intelligence can somehow tease out of a person's or group's behavior those features that would be true of all people and all groups, those peculiar to this person or this group, and those that are neither universal nor idiosyncratic. Below are brief descriptions of the four Cultural Intelligence capabilities theorized by Ang et al. (2004).

Metacognition   The ability to process information and the knowledge of processing it, as well as processing the individual's motives, goals, emotions, and external stimuli

Cognition   General knowledge about the structures of a culture; information gained from experience and education that involves specific norms and practices

Motivation   Enhancement, or wanting to feel good about oneself; growth, or wanting to challenge and improve oneself; and the desire for continuity and predictability in one's life

Behavior   The ability to exhibit the appropriate verbal and nonverbal behaviors when interacting with others from a different cultural background and to generally interact competently with individuals from diverse backgrounds

    All four of these Cultural Intelligence capabilities can be aligned to effective mentoring of doctoral learners. Cultural differences can lead to misunderstanding, and misunderstanding can lead to conflict or unpleasant experiences for both the mentor and the learner. Understanding the variety of cultures should be a priority in academic institutions, as more universities are expanding their mission and vision to support more learners globally. Below, I use an example of how I used Cultural Intelligence to mentor a doctoral learner who was from a different country and found herself in a difficult situation when previous mentors discouraged her, refused to support her, and led her to believe she was not doctoral material and would never make it through a doctoral program.

1.   *Metacognition:* having the ability to process information and the ability to critically evaluate what is being processed and how; having a keen sense to process individuals' motives, emotions, and goals. Also, being aware and able to plan in light of cultural understanding. I demonstrated metacognition in evaluating my learner's situation and recognizing that she was not provided the opportunity to succeed from previous mentors, partly because the mentors did not have a clear understanding of her culture and the support she needed to be successful. From my experience, every person can be mentored, coached, and guided, provided they have the willingness to set goals, put forth the effort to reach those goals, and are open to receiving support from advocates who are willing to support their dreams. In this situation with my learner, I had a keen sense to process her motives, emotions, and goals. I knew she had the potential to complete the doctoral program if given the opportunity and necessary support. I knew that she had embraced the doctoral process, she was excited about learning, and she knew that she had a language barrier and writing issues but was willing to do anything in her power to improve her English and writing.

As her mentor, I was willing to do everything in my power to help her meet her complete the dissertation process.

2. *Cognition:* having knowledge and experience with a structure within various cultures; being able to use one's own experience and education involving specific cultural norms and practices. Also, having a strong understanding of how cultures are similar and different. It was relatively easy for me to use my education and experience from various cultures to understand what my learner must have been experiencing by not receiving the opportunities and necessary support to be successful. Having grown up in poverty and learning to survive the plights of life, living in the Philippines and Turkey while serving in the United States Air Force learning aspects of multiculturalism, and being the only African American male in leadership in many roles most of my professional career with minimal support, I have an affinity for those who have been told they will not be successful or do not receive the opportunities and resources to prove themselves. I immediately had a connection with my learner because I could relate to what she was feeling based on my frame of reference.

3. *Motivation:* wanting to feel good about oneself and wanting to challenge oneself to make the necessary improvements or adjustments to grow and succeed. Also, possessing a high level of interest, drive, and motivation to adapt cross-culturally. This is the catalyst for doctoral learner success. Most doctoral learners want to grow and develop in some way by going through the doctoral experience. In this case, my learner was from the first generation of persons in her family to earn a degree. The opportunity to earn a doctoral degree in her culture was slim to none. I was just as motivated and interested in helping her accomplish her goal as she was to show me that she would succeed if I only gave her an opportunity. The intrinsic reward for me is to get students across the finish line despite their situations, especially those who have had to overcome obstacles throughout their entire life just because they may have cultural differences or diversity dimensions that the majority doesn't understand.

    4. ***Behavior:*** exhibiting nonverbal and verbal behaviors when interacting with others from different cultural or diverse backgrounds. Also, knowing when to adapt and when not to adapt when engaging cross-culturally. This is the most import Cultural Intelligence capability that a mentor can exhibit while mentoring doctoral learners. This is where the rubber meets the road. Through both education and experience, mentors should be able to demonstrate behavior that is multidimensional and inclusive of all learners, no matter the cultural background. After assessing my learner's situation and connecting with her, I made a commitment to her that would change her life forever. I committed to serving as her mentor and provide her with specific resources that would help her meet her educational goals coupled with my support. I suggested she take a Toastmasters course in her community, take a remedial English course at a local community college and work with the university writing center throughout the dissertation process. As I began to see significant improvements in her English and writing skills, I found other opportunities that would be instrumental in further developing her skills. As a result, my learner was able to write a well-written dissertation that we both are proud of. She has also volunteered to accompany me to other countries to affect social change in the communities where others don't have access to education. She is now providing others with opportunities that I provided her. That is my intrinsic reward and the highlight of my experience mentoring doctoral learners using Cultural Intelligence.

    It is critical for mentors to develop their Cultural Intelligence capabilities when mentoring doctoral learners. Heightening one's awareness of another's culture does not necessarily mean learning a second language, studying the political development of a country, or conducting an anthropological study of the culture. It does involve a serious attempt to become familiar with the cultural differences that might be encountered and develop a strategy to deal with them before they become an insurmountable issue. Cultural Intelligence is a learned behavior based on an intrinsic individual desire to interact with others with a different cultural upbringing. This was demonstrated by a woman who took an interest in mentoring me through my doctoral program when I didn't receive the necessary support from my mentor. As an African American male who earned a doctoral degree and experienced obstacles in the process, I have made it my academic mission to increase the number of African American males with doctoral degrees by mentoring them through the dissertation process. Over the past five years, I have chaired close to 40 dissertation committees and served on close to 100 dissertation committees. I'm proud to say that 90% of my doctoral graduates have been African American males.

Shaping African American Doctoral Learner Success Through Mentoring

For many African American doctoral students, progress toward degree completion is a journey wrought with obstacles. Previous research about African American degree attainment has revealed low degree-completion rates at preceding educational levels and an underrepresentation of minority faculty as two primary causes for the slow progression of African Americans doctoral degree completion rates in the United States (Gasman, Hirschfield, & Vultaggio, 2008; Thompson 2006; Willie, Grady, & Hope, 1991). This is especially the case within elite institutions where there is a lack of minority faculty leadership coupled with historical legacies of exclusion that cultivate alienating educational environments. In these educational environments, the stakes for increasing social capital become higher, with fewer African Americans being socialized in the nation's most prestigious and well-resourced institutions (Gasman et al., 2008). Many African American doctoral learners have indicated that if they had the representation and support from more African American faculty, they would progress more in doctoral programs.

Doctoral learners from some cultures feel a sense of connection when they can identify with someone with a similar frame of reference. Doctoral learner development, the transformation whereby graduate students evolve into emerging scholars, is a process where faculty members can have a tremendous influence to enhance the likelihood of success (Gasman et al., 2008). African Americans who press toward doctoral degree attainment may find it difficult to find the right faculty adviser who can mentor their professional development and shape their disciplinary identities during their graduate student socialization experiences (Davidson & Foster-Johnson, 2001; Gasman et al., 2008; Thompson, 2006). In my experience as a faculty mentor of doctoral learners at several universities, I am often the only African American male faculty member present at residencies where doctoral learners have the opportunity to socialize. For that reason, they tend to engage with me more because they are seeking opportunities to connect with someone who has a similar cultural experience and can relate to them and their experiences. Professional identity development at the doctoral level entails the creation of a research agenda and the cultivation of collegial relationships that are important to continued success after degree attainment (Gardner &

Barnes, 2007; Lovits, 2001). Doctoral learners are often interested in conducting research within their own culture and in spending most of their lives affecting change within their own culture or country. It's important for them to feel a sense of connection to faculty members who are interested in helping them shape their professional identity.

The faculty–student relationship plays a huge part in the success of the doctoral learner. For the African American doctoral experience, mentorship has been a common topic when discussing the faculty–student relationship (Davidson & Jounson, 2001; Gasman et al., 2004). Faculty mentoring has been characterized as "activities and interactions that may be related to work, skill acquisition, and social or emotional aspects of the mentor or the protégé" (Davidson & Johnson, 2001, p. 551). This relationship has been addressed as a critical function in the doctoral experience and can be viewed as one of the few formal mechanisms in this process (Nettles & Millett, 2006). The nature of the faculty mentorship is one of the strongest determining factors of African American doctoral degree completion (Willie et al., 1991). I've proven this by developing a relationship with all of my doctoral learners and creating a mentoring model for them to be successful, regardless of race.

There definitely needs to be a diverse cadre of faculty in universities to contribute to enhancement of the learner experience. The lack of minority mentorship has been a concern addressed by many scholars who have asserted that increasing the levels of minority participation with graduate education is directly related to the development of an emerging cadre of diverse scholars who are prepared to progress into faculty roles (Gasman et al., 2001; Moses, 1994; Thompson, 2006). These researchers have found that increased levels of both student and faculty diversification positively affect faculty–student relationships and the socialization experiences of minority doctoral students. However, Gasman et al. (2008) asserted that given the make-up of the professoriate, it's impossible for African American faculty to be solely responsible for mentoring the number of African American doctoral learners (p. 128). This is why my mission in academia is to increase the number of African American doctoral graduates so they can go back into academia to narrow the gap by mentoring doctoral learners. The implication here is that any faculty member who is genuinely interested in a doctoral learner's research agenda, professional development, and degree completion can be important to an African American's degree completion regardless of race.

Preparing and Mentoring International Doctoral Learners

Matriculation into a doctoral program of study can be a difficult transition for many people. Learners transitioning into graduate school have been shown to experience increased feelings of insecurity, decreased self-esteem, and high levels of stress and anxiety (Grant-Vallone & Ensher, 2000). Another gauge of the graduate school experience is persistence, or its negative counterpart, attrition. Although attrition rates vary by institution and discipline, records indicate that attrition from doctoral programs has ranged consistently between 40 and 50% over the past 20 years (Schinke & da Costa, 2001). Because these factors affect doctoral learner success, it is important for mentors to provide doctoral learners with support to make the experience more pleasant.

Students from differing cultural backgrounds typically have challenges adjusting in the doctoral process. While the doctoral experience can be stressful and even bewildering for any learner, it can be particularly so for international learners (Watkins, 1998). International learners are unique because they speak different languages and come from educational systems that are different from those of the United States. Most international learners have different learning styles and cultural backgrounds compared to their U.S. peers. These international learners need to cope with many layers of cultural novelty when pursuing their study in a foreign country. Cultural novelty is a term that reflects the degree to which norms of the host culture differ from those of the internal learner's home culture (Mendenhall & Wiley 1994). Some of the biggest challenges for foreign-born learners include difficulty with the English language, separation from family, social and cultural adjustment, and academic role conflict (Ryan et al., 1998; Zhai 2002). Despite the challenges that international learners may face in doctoral programs, they also experience benefits.

The benefits of recruiting and retaining high caliber international learners in U.S. postsecondary institutions are numerous. International learners with positive experiences in the United States may be effective ambassadors who convey favorable attitudes toward the United States when they return to their countries (Ebersole, 1999). Another potential benefit of having international learners is the long-term connections between the institution and alumni who can facilitate research collaborations and other relationships with overseas organizations (Trice, 2001). In addition, international learners who stay in the United States to work in faculty positions bring much needed international perspectives to the academic culture that may foster the ability of domestic graduates to operate more successfully in an increasingly global community (Association of American Universities, 1998; Trice, 2001). However, with increasing numbers of international learners seeking postgraduate employment in academia, there appears to be little published research addressing academic support mechanisms for international doctoral students in general or for international doctoral learners aspiring to employment as university faculty in particular.

Mentoring is one approach shown to increase graduate student success. Although there is no consensus regarding the definition of mentoring, a mentor may be seen as more than a supervisor, instructor, or coach. Rose (2005) noted, "The two most important things mentors can do for graduate students are to communicate clearly and effectively, and to provide honest feedback" (p. 53). A mentor actively engages their mentee in an educative, personal, and professional sense, thus promoting the mentee's development (Sundli, 2007). The mentor–mentee relationship may be even more vital for international doctoral learners because they are dealing with a high level of cultural adjustment and language barriers, as well as attempting to understand the culture of academia. Several researchers have noted that academic mentoring includes at least three elements: (a) emotional and psychological support, (b) role modeling, and (c) career guidance (Davidson & Foster-Johnson, 2001; Kartje, 1996). In general, research has indicated that mentoring has been beneficial, particularly for doctoral learners of color seeking careers in academia and international learners (Hill et al., 1999; Lamb, 1999). The key is that mentors can help doctoral learners shape their doctoral experience, despite the challenges or obstacles learners may experience.

Mentoring as a Bridge to Cross-Cultural Boundaries

There are strategies that those involved with mentoring doctoral learners can implement to navigate relationships at both the individual and group levels. Mentoring can serve as a bridge at each level—a passageway to gain access to alternative perspectives and insights. At the individual level, one of the most effective competencies to enable mentoring relationships is Emotional Intelligence (Goleman, 1995). To the extent that individuals are aware of and managing their emotions (through self-awareness and self-regulation) and are in touch with the emotions of others (through empathy and social skills), they may find that their mentoring relationships are strengthened. Emotional Intelligence is a useful bridging competency because as mentoring partners are reaching across dimensions of difference, they are likely to face misunderstandings and miscommunications that can devastate a mentoring relationship. But if they have a tool to navigate emotional aspects of mentoring, they stand a better chance of being able to leverage their differences to enhance their mentoring relationship.

At the group level, doctoral mentors may be required to show greater Cultural Intelligence. Cultural Intelligence is the ability to make sense of and fit into unfamiliar contexts (Earley & Mosakowski, 2004). Cultural Intelligence represents the ability to distinguish between which aspects of behavior can be attributed to cultural norms and which aspects are idiosyncratic to understand what is specific versus what is general. Within mentoring relationships, understanding the difference between cultural influence and individual attributes may provide critical guidance to mentors when a mentor is offering feedback to a doctoral learner. If a mentor thinks a doctoral learner is not putting his or her best foot forward because the learner is an introvert, the advice offered might be different than if the mentor believes that the doctoral learner is showing restraint because of a cultural tradition. Thus, the understanding of what is cultural and what is idiosyncratic is an important factor for consideration.

It is paramount for mentors of doctoral learners to use Cultural Intelligence in the mentoring process. Gathering people from many geographic lcoations in a multicultural approach is a mark of inclusivity, increased consciousness, and dialogue (Anzaldua, 2002, p. 3). Given the changing global demographics in both traditional and nontraditional education, how people relate to each other is of immediate practical importance and speaks to the effectiveness of universities, as well as to mentors' abilities to help doctoral learners advance in their dissertation process and to gain satisfaction from their progress. At the same time, differences of nationality require mentors to do some additional work to reach across chasms to build mentoring relationships. In light of the global aspect of academia, the ability to bridge the gaps that separate us will be increasingly critical to the sustained well-being of a diverse academy. Now more than ever, mentoring can serve as a bridge to crossing cultural boundaries.

References

Ang, S., Van Dyne, L., Yee, N. K., & Koh, C. (2004). *The measurement of cultural intelligence*. Paper presented at the 2004 Academy of Management Meetings Symposium on Cultural Intelligence in the 21st Century, New Orleans, LA.

Ang, S., Van Dyne, L., & Koh, C. (2006). Personality correlates of the four factor model of cultural intelligence. Group & Organization Management, *31*, 100-123.

Anzaldua, G. E. (2002). Preface: (Un)natural bridges, (un)safe spaces. In G. E. Anzaldua & A. Keating (Eds.), *This bridge we call home: Radical visions for transformation* (pp. 1-3). New York, NY: Routledge.

Association of American Universities. (1998). *Association of American Universities committee on graduate education: Report and recommendations*. Washington DC: Author.

Davidson, M. N., & Foster-Johnson, L. (2001). Mentoring in preparation of graduate researchers of color. *Review of Educational Research, 71*, 549-574.

Earley, P. C., & Mosakowski, E. (2004). Cultural intelligence. *Harvard Business Review, 82*(10), 139-146.

Ebersole, J. F. (1999). The challenge and the promise of international education. *Continuing Higher Education Review, 63*, 98-106.

Gardner, S. K., & Barnes, B. J. (2007). Graduate student involvement: Socialization and the professional role. *Journal of College Student Development, 48*, 269-387.

Gasman, M., Gerstl-Pepin, C., Aderson-Thompkins, S., Rasheed, L., & Hathaway, K. (2004). Developing trust, negotiating power: Transgressing race and status in the academy. *Teachers College Record, 106,* 689-715.

Gasman, M., Hirchfield, A., & Vultaggio, J. (2008). "Difficult yet rewarding": The experiences of African American graduate students. *Journal of Diversity in Higher Education, 1,* 126-138.

Goleman, D. (1995). *Emotional intelligence: Why it can matter more than IQ.* New York, NY: Bantam Books.

Grant-Vallone, E. J., & Ensher, E. A. (2000). Effects of peer mentoring on types of mentor support, program satisfaction and graduate student stress: A dyadic perspective. *Journal of College Student Development, 41,* 637-642.

Hill, R. D., Castillo, L. G., Ngu, L. Q., & Pepion, K. (1999). Mentoring ethnic minority students for careers in academia: The WICHE doctoral scholars program. *Counseling Psychologist, 27,* 827-845.

Mendenhall, M. E., & Wiley, C. (1994). Strangers in a strange land: The relationship between expatriate adjustment and impression management. *American Behavior Scientist, 37,* 605-619.

Nettles, M. T. (1990). Success in doctoral programs: Experiences of minority and white students. *American Journal of Education, 98,* 494-522.

Peterson, B. (2004). *Cultural intelligence: A guide to working with people from other cultures.* Boston, MA: Intercultural Press.

Rose, G. L. (2005). Group differences in graduate students' concepts of the ideal mentor. *Research in Higher Education, 46*, 53-80.

Ryan, D., Markowski, K., Ura, D., & Liu-Chiang, C. Y. (1998). International nursing education: Challenges and strategies for success. *Journal of Professional Nursing, 14*(2), 69-77.

Schinke, R. J., & da Costa, J. (2001). Considerations regarding graduate student persistence. *Alberta Journal of Educational Research, 47*, 341-352.

Sundi L. (2007). Menoring – A new mantra for education? *Teaching and Teacher Education, 23*, 201-214.

Thomas, D. C., & Inkson, K. (2004). *Cultural intelligence: People skills for global business.* San Francisco, CA: Berrett-Koehler.

Thomas, D. C. (2004). Domain and development of cultural intelligence: The importance of mindfulness. *Group & Organization Management, 31*, 78-99.

Triandis, H. (2006). Cultural intelligence in organizations. *Group & Organization Management, 31*, 20-26.

Trice, A. G. (2001, November). *Faculty perceptions of graduate international students: The benefits and challenges.* Paper presented at the annual meeting of the Association for the Study of Higher Education, Richmond, VA.

Watkins, G. H. (1998, November). *Satisfaction and mentoring: An African-American perspective.* Paper presented at the annual meeting of the Association for the Study of Higher Education, Miami, Florida.

3
Aligning Spiritual Intelligence Principles With the Dissertation Process

Spiritual Intelligence is inherently difficult to define. It is the human capacity to ask ultimate questions about the meaning of life and to experience simultaneously the seamless connection between each of us and the world in which we live. According to Sisk and Torrance (2001), Spiritual Intelligence is the ability to use a multisensory approach to problem solving and to learn to listen one's inner voice. According to Wolman (2003), each of us possesses Spiritual Intelligence and we have the capacity to think with our souls. Zohar (2005) noted Spiritual Intelligence is an ability to access higher meanings, values, abiding purposes, and unconscious aspects of the self and to embed these meanings, values, and purposes in living a richer and more creative life. Signs of high Spiritual Intelligence include an ability to think out of the box, humility, and an access to energies that come from something beyond the ego, beyond just me and my day-today concerns. Spiritual Intelligence is the ultimate intelligence of the visionary leader. It was the intelligence that guided men and women such as Churchill, Ghandi, Nelson Mandela, Martin Luther King, Jr., and Oprah. The secret of their leadership was their ability to inspire people, to give them a sense of something worth struggling for. This same type of intelligence is demonstrative of mentors who mentor doctoral learners through the dissertation process.

Out of the aforementioned definitions of Spiritual Intelligence, the closest one aligned to mentoring doctoral learners is the perspective of Zohar (2005), who believes that all human beings are born with the capacity to use Intellectual Intelligence, Emotional Intelligence, and Spiritual Intelligence to some measure, because each contributes toward survival. A mentor may be strong in one and weak in others, but each can be nurtured and developed. Spiritually intelligent mentoring can be fostered by applying Zohar's 12 principles:

Self-awareness	Knowing what I believe in and value, and what deeply motivates me
Spontaneity	Living in and being responsive to the moment

Being vision and value led	Acting from principles and deep beliefs, and living accordingly
Holism	Seeing larger patterns, relationships, and connections; having a sense of belonging
Compassion	Having the quality of "feeling-with" and deep empathy
Celebration of diversity	Valuing other people for their differences, not despite them
Field independence	Standing against the crowd and having one's own convictions
Humility	Having the sense of being a player in a larger drama, of one's true place in the world
Tendency to ask fundamental "why" questions	Needing to understand things and get to the bottom of them
Ability to reframe	Standing back from a situation or problem and seeing the bigger picture; seeing problems in a wider context
Positive use of adversity	Learning and growing from mistakes, setbacks, and suffering
Sense of vocation	Feeling called upon to serve, to give something back

The qualities of great spiritually intelligent mentorship are underpinned by vision, purpose, meaning, and values. All these qualities are aligned with mentoring doctoral learners. Below is a demonstration of how mentors can use these qualities to successfully mentor doctoral learners:

1. ***Self-awareness.*** This principle differs from Daniel Goleman's emotional self-awareness addressed in Chapter 1, which referred to knowing what we're feeling at any given moment. Spiritual self-awareness means to recognize what one cares about, what one lives for, and what one would die for. It's to live true to oneself while respecting others. Being authentic in this way is the bedrock of genuine communication with our own deeper self and with learners we mentor. It allows us to bring the truth of the inner self into the outer world of action.

In mentoring doctoral learners, it's important for mentors to be connected with what's important to them, what they will stand up for and commit to, and what they are passionate about. For me, that passion is mentorship. In my mentoring paradigm, I create clear expectations, requirements and boundaries based upon my value ethics. Through this self-awareness, I am able to set the tone and example for mentoring that is very clear, without ambiguity. Based upon this, learners know early in the process what is expected and can make a choice regarding whether we are a good fit to work together in the process.

2. ***Spontaneity.*** Being spontaneous does not mean merely acting on a whim. It refers to authentic behavior honed by the self-discipline, practice, and self-control of the martial artist. To be spontaneous means to let go of all of one's baggage—childhood problems, prejudices, assumptions, interpretations, and projections—and be responsive to the moment, appreciating "the power of now." And "spontaneity" echoes "responsibility," which reminds us to use it responsibly in the moment.

When mentoring doctoral learners, it is imperative for mentors to be responsible for helping learners successfully complete the dissertation process, provided the learner dedicates and commits 100% to the process and embraces the process. All other personal problems or distractions that could impede the learner's success should be eliminated from the process. Mentors also need to be responsible enough to provide a framework or environment that will foster learner success and progress in the dissertation process. For example, one thing I've established is a doctoral cohort model that includes all my learners who are working on their dissertation. In this cohort, I have appointed student leaders who are handpicked and trained by me to lead, within boundaries, other doctoral learners. The student leaders conduct weekly facilitated calls with the learners in the cohort to share best practices, lessons learned, risks, and challenges or issues. When doctoral learners can socialize, collaborate, and engage with each other in the dissertation process, they tend to feel a sense of connection and perform at a higher level. Although the cohort is student led, I am engaged in the cohort to deal with issues, to invite and schedule key speakers and presenters, to monitor progress, and to ensure students receive the necessary support to be successful. This model has increased my annual graduation rate by 50%.

    3.   ***Being vision-and value-led.*** Vision is the capacity to see something that inspires us; it means something broader than a company vision or a vision for educational development. It seeks answers to the bigger, more difficult questions, such as why do we want the world to benefit from our brand and why are we trying to impact positive social change?

    When doctoral mentors are being vision- and value-led and demonstrating through action how their actions are inspiring, motivating, and positively changing the lives of others, learners will be more inclined to adopt those same practices and be more eager to make a difference in the world. For example, I'm led by both my vision and the value of impacting positive social change in impoverished countries or underserved communities to provide service, leadership development, and mentorship to young men and women who may not have access to resources or support. My actions and my demonstration of positive social change in various countries and communities have inspired many of my learners to support my initiatives by accompanying me to impoverished countries to work beside me in impacting positive social change. Others have created their own initiatives and use my framework as a point of reference to impact change in the lives of others.

   4.   *Holism.* In quantum physics, holism refers to systems that are so integrated that each part is defined by every other part of the system. What one thinks, feels, and values affects the whole world. Holism encourages cooperation, because as people realize they are part of the same system as everyone else, they take responsibility for their part in it. A lack of holism encourages competition, which encourages separatism. Human enterprises need leaders who can foster cooperation and a sense of oneness to be more effective.

   When mentoring doctoral learners, the ultimate goal is to help them become scholar-practitioners and find their niche in the sea of scholars. It's important to make learners feel like they are part of the same system as other scholars. We do this by providing them with necessary resources to be successful and setting an example through our own integration into the system of scholars. Doing so encourages learners to cooperate and engage in the doctoral process and become responsible for their own progress and performance.

5. *Compassion*. In Latin, compassion is defined as "feeling with." One doesn't recognize or accept others feelings, but feels them. Compassion is actively sympathetic concern for the suffering of others.

Doctoral learners experience life challenges just as we do, which may impede upon their performance and progress. As mentors, we must be compassionate toward our learners and let them know that we feel their struggle. I've coined the following phrase: People don't want anything from you, they just want to feel a little bit of you. The phrase applies to doctoral learners who may be experiencing challenges in their personal lives. They only want to feel that we understand their situation and have compassion for them as they are going through their seasons. A little compassion goes a long way!

6. *Celebration of diversity*. Compassion is strongly linked to the principle of diversity. Many organizations have diversity programs that involve, for example, putting a token woman or African American on the board of directors or ensuring the workforce contains specified percentages of various ethnic groups. But in this context, celebrating diversity means something different. It means we celebrate our differences because they teach us what matters.

We mentor doctoral learners from all walks of life, frames of reference, geographical domains, and different ethnicities. The beauty of the diverse population of learners is that they all bring something unique and special to the mentoring process. Because they all bring something new and fresh to the mentoring process, I learn just as much, if not more, from my mentees than they learn from me. Additionally, their contribution to research or bodies of knowledge is impeccable and should be embraced and supported. Many doctoral learners' areas of research interest are a reflection of their diversity. Mentors should not deter doctoral learners from researching something they are passionate about, but instead should help them shape their topic into something that is researchable, original, and contributory to existing bodies of knowledge.

7.   *Field independence.* Field independence is a term from psychology that means standing against the

crowd and willing to be unpopular for what one believes in. It's a willingness to do it alone, but only after carefully considering what others have to say. Almost by definition, any visionary leader must stand alone sometimes.

Field independence is something that all doctoral learners should be empowered to have, as it provides them with an opportunity to demonstrate their ability as a researcher to formulate their own perspectives based upon existing research. Mentors should step outside of the box of only helping doctoral learners through the dissertation process and be willing to engage with learners in publishing, presenting at conferences, and encouraging them to become more independent in their field.

8. ***Humility***. Humility is the other necessary side of field independence, whereby a person realizes he or she is an actor in a larger play and might be wrong. Humility makes a leader great, not a small one. Humility is a sense of being marked by modesty and meekness.

The doctoral process is humbling and will break learners down to the lowest common denominator if they don't have a humble spirit. Some learners approach the process with a very arrogant disposition, as if they know everything and don't feel their mentor can add value to their growth and development in the process. Learners need to understand that their mentors all hold doctoral degrees, and the learners need to be more humble in the process so they can also hold a doctorate one day. Mentors need to hold doctoral learners accountable to being humble in the process and should choose not to work with learners who appear to have a pompous, arrogant disposition toward the doctoral process. In many instances, mentors can turn this disposition around by demonstrating what humility looks like in their own actions toward learners. One way to do this is to take on a partnership role with learners so they can feel they have a stake in the doctoral process and a voice in shaping their research, rather than taking control of the doctoral process and instructing learners based upon your own personal agenda for their research.

9. *Tendency to ask fundamental "why" questions.* Asking these questions is subversive, and people are often frightened by questions without easy answers. Why are we doing it this way rather than that way? Why am I in this collaboration and why does it exist? Why aren't we doing something else? Answers are a finite game played within boundaries, rules, and expectations. Questions are an infinite game; they play with the boundaries and they define them.

When mentoring doctoral learners, it is important for mentors to help learners shape their critical thinking and analytical skills to ask the right questions to solve their problems in research. It's also important for mentors to help learners understand answers to the basic fundamental questions that may pertain to the dissertation process. Doing so creates an opportunity for learners to be successful in the process.

10. Ability to reframe. Reframing refers to the ability to stand back from a situation and look for the bigger picture. One of the greatest problems in the world today is short-term thinking. Education has also become consumed with short-term thinking. By focusing on exams, schools are trying to measure the progress learners have made at the end of a year rather than cultivating their infinite potential as human beings.

Mentoring doctoral learners is all about reframing and helping learners look at not only the dissertation process, but also at the factors that will be critical after the dissertation process, such as building a scholarly identity, branding oneself, and determining one's value after earning a doctoral degree. Mentors should be engaged in partnership with learners to assist them in becoming the best scholar-practitioner possible. This does not end with completing the dissertation process!

11. *Positive use of adversity.* This principle is about owning, recognizing, accepting, and acknowledging mistakes. How many of us get trapped in courses of action because the initial step we took was a mistake and we didn't want to lose face by admitting it? Rather than having the courage to acknowledge our error, we pursue the mistaken course of action, digging ourselves deeper into the mess. I have learned a great deal from this. Great passion and energy can be released by saying, "I made a mistake. What I did was wrong, and I'm now going to embark on a different course." Great leaders have the confidence to admit mistakes. This also holds true for great mentors.

It's important to share with learners when we have made a mistake and when we don't know something. This helps the mentoring relationship become more real and trusting. When learners can see that mentors make mistakes and can admit to it, the learners tend to have greater respect for mentors in the doctoral process.

12. *Sense of vocation.* This principle sums up Spiritual Intelligence. Vocation comes from the Latin *vocare*, "to be called." Originally, it referred to a calling to

God. Today, it often refers to the professions of medicine, education, and law. For example, in education, universities will become a vocation that appeals to learners with a larger purpose and a desire to make wealth that benefits not only those who create it but also the community and the world.

Successfully mentoring doctoral learners requires mentors to take a vow of service to something higher than themselves by making an investment in the lives of learners to be successful in their academic journey and their communities. As we are changing the lives of learners through our sense of vocation, learners are, in turn, impacting change in the lives of others in their families, communities, and countries around the world.

In *Business Dynamics: Systems Thinking and Modeling for a Complex World*, John Sterman (2000) provides a blueprint for how to make a system work as it should. Most systems have the same failing: human behavior. If we want to change systems, we have to change human behavior. But human behavior is not so easily changed. To achieve real transformation, we have to change the motivations that drive behavior. That is the prime responsibility of a mentor of a doctoral learner.

Today, education, as most systems, is driven by four negative motivations: fear, greed, anger, and self-assertion. When we are controlled by these negative emotions, we trust both ourselves and others less, and we tend to act from a small place inside ourselves.

We can change our motivations to more positive ones if inspired to do so. A mentor practicing Zohar's 12 principles of Spiritual Intelligence can provide that inspiration and the energy it unleashes. When we apply the 12 principles of spiritual transformation to our collaborations with doctoral learners, self-assertion becomes exploration, anger becomes cooperation, craving becomes self-control, fear becomes mastery, and so forth. Our motivations have been raised and this changes our behavior. As our behavior changes, our results change, as well as the whole purpose and meaning of our collaborations with doctoral learners.

References

Sisk, D., & Torrance, E. (2001). *Spiritual intelligence: Delivering higher consciousness.* Buffalo, NY: Creative Education Foundation Press.

Sterman, J. (2000). *Business dynamics: Systems thinking and modeling for a complex world*. New York, NY: McGraw-Hill.

Wolman, R. N. (2003). *Thinking with your soul: Spiritual intelligence and why it matters*. New York, NY: Harmony.

Zohar, D. (2005). Spiritually intelligent leadership. *Leader to Leader, 38*, 45-51. doi:10.1002/ltl.153

4
16 Best Practices for Doctoral Learners to Navigate the Dissertation Process

Very little research has been done on the influence of the opportunity to mentor or be mentored. However, most mentoring literature contends that each member in the dyad seeks a mentoring relationship (Kalbfleish & Davies, 1993; Turban and Dougherty, 2004). If individuals see opportunities for mentoring or positive outcomes for other individuals in mentoring relationships, expectations for a mentoring relationship may become more well-defined and salient.

Mentoring opportunities relate to the perceptions individuals hold about mentoring in doctoral programs. Therefore, it is likely that this factor will shape, to some extent, the expectations both mentors and doctoral learners hold about a mentoring partner and the extent to which mentoring support will be provided. Over the past 8 years, I have mentored countless doctoral learners and have created opportunities for them to be successful by providing them with clear expectations, best practices, tools, and support. Here are 16 best practices that I've shared with my learners to be successful.

1. Mentally prepare yourself for the undertaking. Earning a doctoral degree is very challenging and requires a lot of discipline, determination, tenacity, commitment, patience, humility, and intestinal fortitude. A person must mentally prepare for this arduous undertaking and be willing to make sacrifices for the duration of the doctoral program. In other words, a person must be willing to spend a minimum of 20 hours a week on doctoral work for an average of 3½ or 4 years, but maybe longer, depending on individual situations and the goals the candidates set to complete the program. One reason doctoral learners are not successful in completing the program is because they underestimate the level of effort and the requirements necessary to complete the program.

2. Make the shift from the passenger's seat to the driver's seat. Many doctoral learners have a difficult time making the transition from having faculty drive the car to driving the car themselves and letting faculty navigate the path or learning process. In undergraduate programs and even graduate programs, faculty provides the syllabus or agenda and learners must follow the agenda to the letter to earn a passing grade. In doctoral programs, mentors expect learners to have a certain level of preparedness by taking the initiative to critically and analytically think about creating their own research interest area and inviting faculty to help shape and guide their path to conduct the research. In other words, learners need to have a sense of autonomy and provide faculty with their perspectives, perceptions and questions to begin the research process, rather than ask faculty to lead them to a research topic or problem that is researchable, original, and contributory. There is nothing worse than having a learner approach a faculty member unprepared and not providing his or her own thoughts or questions about what the learner is interested in researching. Learners need to stand up for what they are passionate about researching and take the initiative to become familiar with what is in the literature. To begin, learners need to take the initiative to read at least 10 dissertations, at least 15 peer-reviewed journal articles, and at least 10 books related to the topic. This will help learners begin to become knowledgeable about what is in the literature related to their research interest area. This will also help learners become prepared to have discussions with their faculty mentor about their research interest area.

3. ***Prioritize from the inside out.*** Learners must begin to conduct a self-diagnosis or self-reflection to determine what is cluttering their lives and monopolizing their time. The self-diagnosis includes exploring technical errors, external realities, and psychological obstacles. Technical errors are simple, mechanical mistakes in a person's organizing system that can be easily fixed. This may be as simple as adjusting a schedule to allow time to focus on doctoral work. This is the first category of causes to review because all messes can be attributed to at least one technical error. External realities are environmental realities beyond a person's control that limit how organized he or she can be. An example of this may be caring for an elderly person, going through a divorce, or dealing with an illness. Recognizing these realities will save doctoral learners from having unrealistic expectations of themselves. Lastly, psychological obstacles are hidden, internal forces that make a person gravitate toward disorganization, no matter how much he or she craves control. An example of this is someone who may be a hoarder or who live a cluttered life. Through awareness of this psychological obstacle, a person can find a way to work around these issues and achieve organizing success.

4. Set up an organization system that works for you. Being organized in a doctoral program is critical, especially when organizing and evaluating literature, developing reference lists and annotated bibliographies, and collecting and analyzing data. To begin setting up an organization system, learners should create an office space or work space dedicated to working on their doctoral research. This needs to be a space that has an environment where one can be productive, concentrate, critically think, and write. It also helps to have a filing system of some sort to organize peer-reviewed journal articles and other research relative to completing the dissertation. To manage schedules, it is critical to have a calendar or electronic device that one feels comfortable using to manage tasks, activities, and schedules relative to the doctoral process.

5. Engage your family in the process. Family involvement in the doctoral journey is a must. Doctoral learners make myriad sacrifices and family members often don't really understand what is involved in the process unless they are somewhat involved. Marriages have dissolved and relationships have been broken due to doctoral learners not engaging loved ones in the process. There are many ways to engage family members in the process. Children can become engaged by going to the library with parents who are in the doctoral process and retrieving books or making photocopies of peer-reviewed journal articles. In fact, I have received e-mails from learners who have followed this advice and indicated that this tip has brought their family closer together and has inspired their children to do better in school and earn higher grades. Spouses can become involved by attending academic residencies with their doctoral learner, especially if the academic residencies are international. This could become an academic and cultural experience for the entire family and could be integrated into a family vacation. When family members are engaged in the process, they generally become more supportive of their brother, sister, mother, or father completing the program.

6. Create a favorable and trusting relationship with your dissertation committee chair. The relationship with your dissertation committee chair is the most critical component of completing a doctoral process. The committee chair can make or break you. The chair is part of your team and serves as your champion to advocate getting you to the finish line and walking across the stage. It is in your best interest to form a trusting relationship with your chair and let him or her get to know you and what your capability and potential is related to producing quality work. Also, get to know your chair, find out something you may have in common. Send holiday cards and birthday cards to show your appreciation and thoughtfulness. It is very important to communicate with your chair at the beginning of the process to ensure you understand expectations and requirements and do your best to meet them. Keep in mind, your chair is just as busy as you are and probably will be working with other learners while working with you. If you send a communication to your chair and don't receive a response in a timely fashion, take the initiative to send a reminder. Don't let weeks and months elapse before you communicate with your chair. Remember, this is your journey and your process, and you should be driving the car. The chair is in the passenger seat navigating the learning process. If you don't move from the passenger's seat to the driver's seat, you will probably not make much progress in your doctoral program. Approach your chair with a sense of humility, and demonstrate your ability to transform into a scholar-practitioner. Don't be arrogant and close yourself off from feedback or guidance. This is the worst thing you can do while working with someone who is advocating for you. Remember, the chair has the option not to work with you, just as you have the right to request another chair. The best advice is to build a solid foundation on trust with your chair and enjoy the ride.

7. ***Develop a project management plan to manage program milestones***. There are so many activities and milestones to accomplish in the doctoral process. Developing a formal project management plan and treating the dissertation process as a high priority project that needs to be completed will ensure success. There are review times allotted to all members in the process that learners do not have control over. These review dates need to be taken into consideration and included in the project management plan so there will be a realistic view of how much progress is being made and how much progress is not being made. Establishing a project plan will help learners formulate a clear path from conception to completion in the doctoral process, while monitoring risks and critical paths. It will also be very important to establish an evaluation or monitoring and control system in the project plan to stay apprised of the activities and milestones that might need to be adjusted throughout the process. Life happens! Extenuating circumstances happen! By having a project plan in place, it will be relatively easy to get back on task and continue making progress on the dissertation should something derail the plan a bit. Learners can use the project

management plan as a guide to have progress discussions with their chair. By creating a project plan, both the learner and the chair will always have a holistic view of the learner's progress and what specific activities have been completed and need to be completed to ensure the learner meets his or her graduation date. Remember, a person who fails to plan plans to fail!

8. *Join a student network group or cohort.* Completing a doctoral degree can be a lonely journey. Learners may feel isolated or may not have the momentum and drive necessary to make progress in completing the dissertation. They may even have writer's block. Although the committee chair is the most important person on the learner's team and provides support, other learners can provide additional support that may energize and encourage a learner who may feel stuck. Student network groups and cohorts are good for keeping learners focused, accountable, and motivated. In some online doctoral programs, the only face-to-face interaction learners may have with faculty or other learners is when they attend a residency. In traditional programs, face-to-face interaction may not be an issue. Research shows that doctoral learner engagement and socialization with other learners is a critical component to learner retention and performance. Some faculty members

create cohorts as a means for learners to engage and collaborate with each other continuously throughout the doctoral process. Learners often form their own network groups comprised of peer learners. Whether the cohort or network group is formed by the faculty or by learners, the content provided and the environment to support a positive learning experience is the most important. Some ideas for content may include, but not be limited to, having speakers from the Writing Center support the cohort, identify reputable statisticians and professional editors to present in the cohort meetings, and provide an opportunity for learners to conduct mock orals to help them prepare for their proposal and dissertation defense. In many instances, this has increased learners' graduation rates, quality of writing, and presentation skills. Learners have also been known to embrace their scholarly identity and become more closely connected to their responsibility of stewardship to academia .

9. *Familiarize yourself with the university's dissertation process, templates, and forms.* There are certain standards and guidelines that learners must follow to get through the dissertation process. University processes, templates, and forms change frequently, and it is the learner's responsibility to ensure they are using the most up to date documents as they are completing their proposal and dissertation. It will be helpful for learners to become prepared by learning which resources are available and each step in the process to have a seamless experience. The dissertation chair will expect learners to know the process in order to navigate it. When learners are ill-prepared and don't know the steps in the dissertation process, they are at risk of missing key milestones, making necessary progress, and possibly missing their graduation date. The best tip to ensure preparedness is to develop a checklist of some sort with all the steps within the dissertation process mapped to deliverables required for each step. This will help learners conduct a self-check at every step in the process prior to submitting documents to their chair.

    10. Work with the university's writing center, library, and a professional editor. Most universities have a writing center with skilled staff to help learners develop their writing skills. Writing a dissertation is no easy feat and it requires a lot of practice to develop one's scholarly voice. Writing centers have a repository of webinars, tools, and resources to assist learners with different aspects of writing such as American Psychological Association (APA) style, passive voice, anthropomorphism, and grammar. It's also important for learners to use the library to become well versed in literature search strategies and to know what databases are available to help them search for peer-reviewed journal articles or books related to their research topic. It's also good to work with university librarians when particular documents are needed but can't be obtained through normal channels. Librarians may be able to assist in obtaining documents through other means. Lastly, using a professional editor for the proposal and dissertation is paramount. The dissertation needs to be written with the highest level of quality and scholarship. A professional editor can help by providing an additional set of objective eyes that are not so close to the research. It helps tremendously when the professional editor is an APA expert or an expert in whatever style the university requires. The proposal is written in future tense, but the tense has to be changed after the data are collected and analyzed. The final dissertation needs to be written in past tense. A professional editor familiar with the doctoral process and working with doctoral learners will know this and can help learners with the necessary modifications, along with form and style issues.

11. ***Consult with a professional statistician or analysis tool expert.*** Data collection and analysis are the heart of developing a reputable research product that can contribute to the existing body of knowledge. Many learners are not skilled in statistical techniques and data analysis unless they are a statistician or have conducted some form of data analysis on their jobs or in some other capacity. If learners use a statistician consultant, it is paramount to ensure the consultant is skilled in the statistical technique used in the research project. It is also important for learners to work closely with their consultant to learn exactly how the data were analyzed so they can confidently explain the data analysis process in the proposal or dissertation defense. Learners should also be knowledgeable about statistical tools such as NVivo for qualitative research or SPSS for quantitative research. If learners don't have expertise in this area, it is encouraged that they work with a professional statistician or analysis tool expert in conjunction with the methodologist on the dissertation committee. Both the dissertation chair and methodologist on the committee expect learners to have at least a fundamental knowledge in research methods, data collection, and data analysis. Sometimes it is helpful for learners to take additional courses in research methods to gain a better understanding of how all the dots connect in data collection and data analysis.

12. Embrace the dissertation process.
Embracing the dissertation process is a huge percentage of the success equation for learners going through the dissertation process. The dissertation process is managed and led by scholars who have already been through the process and are guiding future scholar-practitioners through the process. It is important for learners to embrace the fact that they are learners and need to be open to constructive criticism, multiple rewrites, and disappointments. If the dissertation process was an easy one, more people would have PhDs and less would be "all but dissertation" (ABD). To that end, it is critical for learners to follow the guidance of their dissertation chair and learn and develop as much as possible in the process. There are multiple review phases in the dissertation process, which may include reviews conducted by the chair, committee member, university research reviewer, form and style, and chief academic officer. This varies from university to university. It is important for leaners to humble themselves and make the necessary suggested changes at every phase in the process, without hesitation. The goal is to cooperate and graduate, not to create discord in the process that could preclude one from graduating.

13. *Celebrate each milestone.* Celebrate each step of the way! Every time a milestone is accomplished in the doctoral process, celebrate! When learners celebrate each step of the way, they tend to keep momentum and they remain encouraged that they can complete the program. Celebrate when the proposal is approved! Celebrate when the proposal orals are complete! Celebrate when the institutional review board application is approved! Celebrate when data collection is complete! Celebrate when data analysis is complete! Celebrate when the dissertation has been written! Celebrate when the dissertation orals have been conducted! Celebrate when the chief academic officer has signed off on the dissertation! CELEBRATE IN A BIG WAY! Earning a doctoral degree is HUGE! When I earned my doctoral degree, I purchased a brand new Mercedes CLK 320 convertible and a 24-karat gold frame for my diploma!

14. *Begin to develop your scholarly identity and brand while in the dissertation process.* Branding and scholarly identity are the foundation of becoming a true scholar-practitioner. Learners should begin to start working on these areas while in the doctoral program rather than waiting until they graduate. Branding involves developing a unique vision for one's academic and social change contribution. This should begin by joining professional organizations, presenting at conferences, publishing articles, writing books, or getting involved in community initiatives by impacting positive social change. Developing one's scholarly identity is developing a brand in the academic community and executing on that brand by contributing to existing bodies of knowledge, knowing the specific niche in which one will own and continue to build, and committing to changing communities, organizations, or some aspect of the world in some way. It's also important to connect with other scholars in the sea of scholars and consider partnering and collaborating on research projects and other initiatives. Waiting until after graduation will be too late to begin this process!

15. ***Determine your value and worth.*** Determining ones value and worth can be challenging for doctoral learners. After earning a doctoral degree, new degree holders' stock should go up, provided they have branded themselves, embraced their scholarly identity, and demonstrated they are scholar-practitioners. It's good to do homework to assess how much money scholars are making in various industries to ensure a comparable salary. It's also good to continue conducting a self-diagnostic test or self-assessment to determine if any gaps in skills and competencies need to be further developed. There is always room to grow and develop. Doctoral degree holders are always seeking new ways to rebrand or create new opportunities for enlarging their territory. As the territory enlarges, it is important for doctoral degree holders to know their value and worth, along with the expansion of roles, skills and competencies, and brands. Learners invest a lot in earning a doctoral degree and learn a lot along the way. Be knowledgeable to know your value and worth, know areas where development and growth are needed, and be competent and confident enough to go after the opportunities commensurate with the value of your stock.

16. Seek opportunities to publish or disseminate your work to the public domain. One key role and responsibility of a scholar is to become a steward of knowledge and to academia. This means that scholars are expected to contribute to existing bodies of knowledge in some way. Some opt to publish in peer-reviewed journals, others opt to write books, and others opt to present at conferences. The path a person takes in a career or profession will determine which opportunities or mediums he or she uses to disseminate the research. For example, most academics in a teaching capacity are required to publish in peer-reviewed journals and remain current in their research focus area. Some consultants may choose to write books and use them as resources for their client base. It really doesn't matter how one disseminates research or knowledge, as long as a contribution is made. Joining professional organizations and networks can be a good way to disseminate and present research. Collaborating and partnering with other scholars is another way to share knowledge with the public domain. The key is for a doctoral degree holder to use the degree to impact change in the world in some meaningful way and not just be a person with letters behind his or name who is not making a contribution!

The aforementioned best practices definitely work! I have shared these practices with all my doctoral learners at several universities and have seen tremendous improvement in retention rates and graduation rates. By using these practices, I've also seen learners begin to connect with their scholarly identity and begin to develop their brand sooner rather than later. The goal is for mentors to provide learners with the best mentoring experience possible and one way to do that is to provide best practices that produce positive outcomes!

Proven Tools and Tips From Doctors and Doctoral Candidates

5
Steven LaFalce, PhD

Information Technology

There is no substitute for hard work.
—*Thomas A. Edison*

My inspiration for earning a doctoral degree came from my natural curiosity and tendency to learn new things. I have always maintained an interest in academics, and I planned to continue my lifelong pursuit of learning through formal education. Accordingly, when I decided to enroll in a doctoral program, I realized that the journey could not be completed without developing some best practices.

Preparation

One of the best practices for orienting myself to the doctoral experience and preparing for the journey was to become familiar with the dissertation handbook for my program. The handbook described the requirements I would face and the process I would follow to complete my program. In addition to reading the handbook, I also read the dissertation rubric for my program. The dissertation rubric described the requirements I would face and the process I would follow to complete my dissertation. It is important to understand the dissertation handbook and the dissertation rubric and to clarify uncertainties as soon as possible.

One of the best practices for completing my course work was to become familiar with the course rubric. The course rubric describes the requirements to complete a course and the process the instructor will follow to evaluate the learner's work. In addition to reading the course rubric, another best practice is to develop a course work schedule based on the course rubric. Schedules can be created on paper or electronically using a device and software package. Learners should include all course assignments, due dates, and any other information needed to track assignments. It is important to understand the entire course rubric and develop a plan to ensure study time is managed effectively.

Although I created a course work schedule and planned my weekly study time, one challenge of completing the course work was managing the time needed to complete the reading assignments prior to preparing my corresponding written responses. My doctoral course work consisted of reading a considerable number of textbooks, articles, and reference materials in preparation for writing complete and insightful assignments. If I did not finish the readings according to my course work schedule, I adjusted my personal schedule to allocate more time to read and get back on task. In addition to completing the reading assignments, another challenge of completing the course work was ensuring my written assignments were relevant to my dissertation topic. I found that some of the material I learned from my course work could be applied to my dissertation. If I could not structure my responses around my dissertation topic, I included short notes about the references in a separate file for later review.

Proposal and Dissertation Processes

As I began the transition from course work to the proposal, one of the best practices for making the transition was to read the proposal rubric thoroughly. The proposal rubric describes the requirements learners will face and the process learners will follow to complete the proposal. In addition to reading the proposal rubric, another best practice is to develop a checklist based on the proposal rubric. The checklist should contain the items described in each section of the proposal and can help to ensure the proposal is complete. It is important to understand the proposal rubric and ensure the proposal addresses each item on the checklist.

Once in the proposal process, one challenge I experienced was locating and selecting applicable references for my literature review. While writing my literature review, I found an abundance of references for some sections and not many references for others. I overcame this challenge by conducting multiple keyword and combination phrase searches using several online search engines and databases. Using this technique, I located additional references for the sections that lacked references, and I evaluated each reference for its applicability for the sections that had ample references. In addition to locating and selecting applicable references, another challenge was the currentness of my references. I was required to ensure 85% of my references were published within the last 5 years of my dissertation publication date. I overcame this challenge by calculating and tracking this statistic as I added references.

While writing the chapters of my proposal and dissertation, one of the lessons I learned was to ensure grammar, spelling, and other general errors were discovered and corrected before submitting the documents to my dissertation committee chair for review. A dissertation committee chair's time is valuable and should be spent reviewing subject matter rather than correcting errors. It is important for learners or someone else to review the work and ensure the drafts are as clean as possible. Another lesson learned in the proposal and dissertation processes was to submit drafts of my proposal to my dissertation committee chair for review as quickly as I could. The time a dissertation committee chair needs to review work and provide feedback will vary and in some cases can be longer than planned. It is important to incorporate a dissertation committee chair's recommended changes quickly and return drafts in a timely manner to maintain a schedule.

Organization

An organization tool I used as a best practice for completing my proposal and dissertation was a spreadsheet of all comments and changes recommended by my dissertation committee members based on their reviews of my work. The spreadsheet contained the dissertation chapter, the date the comment was provided, the comment, my response to the comment, and the status of the required change. As entries were added to this spreadsheet, it became a historical repository of all my changes and I used it as a tool to track my progress. Another tool I suggest as a best practice for completing a proposal and dissertation is a three-ring binder of all information relevant to the dissertation topic. This binder can be organized according to dissertation chapters and used to store proposal and dissertation rubrics, notes, and reference materials. As pages are added to this binder, it becomes a convenient collection of useful information in discussions about the proposal and dissertation with dissertation committee members.

One common problem in the doctoral process that keeps learners from making progress in their program is disorganization. Students learn quickly that the doctoral process is complex and involves many steps that must be followed in sequence. Therefore, it is important to develop a system such that all documents, references, and files are organized appropriately and are accessible when needed. For example, I created a directory structure on my computer with folders for each course number and each chapter of my dissertation. All course work was stored in corresponding folders and references were organized by dissertation chapter. Creating an organized system minimized time spent looking for materials and maximized the efficient use of study time.

Another common problem in the doctoral process that keeps learners from making progress in the program is unresponsiveness. It is important for learners to develop a communications plan with the dissertation committee members that describes how and when the learner will communicate. By following the plan, learners can ensure everyone is aware of their status and any issues are addressed sooner rather than later. Dissertation committee members are an important part of the support structure and should be informed regularly.

Support Structure

Although dissertation committee members should provide mentorship throughout the doctoral process, peers who are further along in the program are a valuable resource as well. Peer mentoring in the doctoral process fosters knowledge transfer and information sharing. Mentees have much to gain from the experience of those who have completed the program recently or those who are several steps ahead. Students who are unfamiliar with a step in the process can refer to peer mentors for guidance. Peer mentors also have much to gain from the leadership opportunities and teaching skills they can acquire from peer mentoring. Peer mentors have the opportunity to teach what they have learned and to contribute to sustaining a positive learning environment.

Students also often learn quickly that they should have a cooperative support structure, such as a cohort, available for consultation. Brainstorming and innovation can be facilitated within cohort models in the doctoral process. A cohort model can expand on the peer mentorship one-on-one learning model by promoting knowledge transfer and information sharing among all members. Efficiencies in communications can be realized if all students are active participants. Also, students' accomplishments and progressions can be recognized within cohort models in the doctoral process. Setting and reaching goals as a group can promote achievement and perseverance; congratulating students for reaching milestones can be inspirational. Improvements in graduation rates can be realized if students are prepared and inspired to complete their program as well.

Degree Conferral

After countless hours spent reading, writing, communicating, participating, presenting, and not sleeping, I reached the end of the doctoral process. It was a great feeling knowing I had completed the program and that my degree was conferred. I spent some time thinking about the journey I had taken, from start to finish. I thought about the congratulatory, celebratory, and encouraging messages and assistance I received from my dissertation committee chair and cohort members for reaching each milestone and for overcoming the challenges along the way. After this retrospection, I focused on preparing for the most exciting part—graduation. It was a great feeling knowing I had accomplished my goal and that I would attend the graduation ceremony in the company of my family and friends. I enjoyed my journey through the doctoral process, and walking across the stage to be hooded was the highlight of my experience. I felt excited, grateful, and humbled at the same time. I could not have completed the program without the tireless assistance of my dissertation committee chair.

Life After Graduation

Going through such an intense research-based program, I grew as a scholar-practitioner. I have applied the research method, critical thinking, and experimental design skills I learned in the doctoral program in my career as an information technology professional. After completing my doctoral degree, I had the opportunity to design and lead several research projects at work, and I applied academic rigor to each project. Consequently, the quality of my work improved, and my value add as an effective scholar-practitioner has been well-received by my organization.

Earning a doctoral degree contributed to me knowing my value and worth in the various requests for help I received since graduating. The doctoral program introduced me to new experiences and perspectives that I have been sharing formally and informally with others in my network. For example, I have provided tutoring services and advice to doctoral students and offered assistance in writing professional and academic resumes and curricula vitae. As I have become more involved in helping others succeed, I have become more confident that the skills I learned while completing the doctoral process have enhanced my value and worth.

Accordingly, I have grown personally since becoming a doctor. The doctoral degree is recognition for completing a rigorous academic program, but the underlying principle of earning the doctoral degree is to promote the knowledge gained in the process. I have embraced not only the significance of the title but also the responsibility to effect positive social change. Although I consider myself generally a reserved person, I have become more proactive in reaching out to others and sharing what I learned in my doctoral program. In my endeavors to help others, I am reminded of the challenges I faced and the process I followed to complete my dissertation. I have since tried to approach problem solving in an objective manner using critical thinking techniques.

Scholarly Identity

Embracing my scholarly identity has meant working to establish myself in the membership of other doctoral graduates. The expertise and leadership gained during the doctoral process are personal characteristics that can help in academic endeavors after graduation. Expertise and leadership are personal characteristics necessary for a doctor to develop an individual presence in academia. The doctoral process provides many opportunities for students to build skills in developing, presenting, and defending their course work, proposal, and dissertation. These skills are applicable as scholars continue to contribute to their field of study in their academic or professional careers.

By familiarizing myself with existing literature, I began to gain expertise and establish leadership in my area of study so that I could present my work comfortably. As a doctoral student, I learned to evaluate my references for content and relevance in support of my own claims. Although my dissertation included a synthesis of content from supporting references, I developed my own representation of a solution to my research problem. Publishing my dissertation was the first step in embracing my scholarly identity, as my work represented an original contribution that filled a gap in the literature. Uniqueness, therefore, can be considered a characteristic of doctors as they embrace their scholarly identity.

Since completing my doctoral program and working as a scholar-practitioner, I have developed a tendency to structure my work as mini research projects with an academic form and style. Although not required for most of my work, it is good practice a way to maintain my research and writing skills. A challenge that I have faced in the corporate world as a result of earning a doctoral degree was exceeding the requirements of my deliverables by applying the rigor of my academic research projects. The extra attention to detail and thoroughness can be differentiators in a professional career and can help an individual work effectively as a scholar-practitioner.

A local organization's leader reached out to me for help with a business process reengineering project after learning of my recent graduation from my doctoral program. I was asked to help lead a team in guiding discussions, identifying issues, and developing action plans. I created the agenda and managed the project as a series of workshops attended by approximately 30 people. The project was successful for the organization, as the goals to address the issues and move forward were met. This has been my greatest accomplishment after earning my doctoral degree and was a great opportunity to apply my expertise and leadership outside of my professional and academic environments. I was able to employ the critical thinking skills I gained from my course work in a real-life situation. It was a great experience as a recent doctoral graduate to help a local organization solve a problem.

While developing my scholarly identity, I have been able to integrate into the sea of scholars and professional networks comprised of other doctors by joining a national honorary and professional fraternity. Membership in such organizations is beneficial in that it unites a network of professionals with common interests who can provide support to new graduates as they transition to become scholar-practitioners. I joined as a student and became affiliated with other professionals in my field as I progressed in my program. I also joined my school's alumni network to remain connected with my colleagues after graduation. This is another important way to stay current on events, presentations, and educational opportunities at my alma mater.

Final Thoughts

The most important piece of advice I would offer doctoral learners to help them be successful in the doctoral process is to find a dissertation committee chair, as soon as possible, who shares their research interests and with whom they feel comfortable. A dissertation committee chair can guide doctoral learners in making critical decisions to stay on track and maintain progress. This important relationship will continue to develop as both parties work to build the dissertation together. Although colleagues who are farther along in the program can help answer course work and dissertation questions throughout the journey, the chair can help learners accomplish their academic goal—to graduate.

The most important piece of advice I can offer doctoral learners to help them be successful after earning their doctoral degree is to stay connected to other alumni. Join the alumni network and ensure contact information is current. The alumni network can be a source of information and support while integrating into the sea of scholars. The important relationships developed throughout the program should continue as potential professional and academic opportunities arise. Recent graduates who are working busily as a new doctor should take time to cultivate the friendships they made throughout their doctoral journey. No one can complete the process alone.

6
Dereje Tessema, PhD

Federal Government

Keep Going

The dissertation process is a joint venture between a student, advisor(s), the university, and other related stakeholders such as family members, fellow students, and the domain in which the researcher is working. This community of many has defined roles and responsibilities, sets of expectations, and underlying rules that make it complex. The key stakeholder of the project, the student, begins the journey with a fervent interest in a topic and over time gains new knowledge and develops a new voice while the committee members provide inspection of, knowledge in, and experience in the research process. Family members and friends provide support, and the university leaders make sure that the playing field is level for all to take part. This relationship is not conflict immune as it goes through the stages of team formation: forming, storming, norming, and performing. The relationship also depends on the activities performed by the student. This chapter contains various resources and possibilities students can use to maintain the team dynamic and successfully complete the dissertation process.

I thought going through a PhD program while working full-time, raising children, and fulfilling other life commitments would be a nightmare and difficult to achieve. It was not easy, but now I'm on the other side of the aisle helping students in their quest to complete their MBA and PhD programs around the world. In my new role as an advisor, I use my own experiences, as well as the experiences of many of my professors and fellow students who went thought the process, to tell my students how to dust themselves off and start again when they stumble; how to slay the dragon one piece at a time; how to plan, execute, and control their research project schedule; how to take it easy in the midst of high emotions; and above all how to enjoy every moment of the process. Although this chapter may not have all the answers to the questions people ask, as I'm also still learning the process, it may give them a taste of the interesting but demanding journey. The items discussed do not appear in any order of importance.

Writing a Dissertation Is a Lonely Journey

What you knew and who you were at the start of the journey are very different from what you know and who you are at the end. Be happy that you are going through a self-indulgent journey that few people have the opportunity to experience.

Even though you have support from your advisors, family members, and friends, you are the one who walks the walk; you are the one who stays up long into the night; you are the one who writes pages and pages of a draft proposal, only to toss them out and start from scratch; and you are the one who will deal with the ups and downs of balancing your work, family, and overall social commitments. The journey begins with a determination to pursue your dream: to receive a doctoral degree and to become a scholar, professor, and contributor to the body of knowledge in your research domain. Then you go through the process to select your advisor and dissertation committee and you conduct a careful and through review of literature about your proposed destination using the experience of others' prior work. At the beginning, you may not have an idea on the importance of obtaining help from other sources. You also may not see the importance of knowing how the previous travelers managed to reach their destination, but the criticality of this process becomes clear and the fact that there is much to learn from the past. Searching the literature is time consuming, even boring, and it sometimes feels like you are in the middle of nowhere, even though you are surrounded by piles of articles, books, and web sources. The more you know, the more you realize that you don't know. At times, you feel optimistic about getting the right information; other times you feel helpless, confused, and frustrated when you end up not formulating one paragraph of ideas after spending countless hours reading; and yet other times you are drifting aimlessly or grinding on relentlessly. At 3:30 a.m. in the morning, you find yourself writing an e-mail to your advisor asking for guidance on how to get out of the loop in which you find yourself. If you are lucky, you will get guidance and be able to move on to the next section of your journey. After receiving guidance, it is up to you to make progress. If you choose not to make progress, you might as well prepare your exit strategy by designing alternative plans.

The lonely journey means that for the most part you do the job alone, with little help from others, including your advisors. At some point, your journey will come to an inevitable close. You may have mixed feelings. You may feel excited about what you have learned and about the possibility of sharing your findings with your domain. At the same time, you may feel sad that you have not accomplished all that you intended to do and left important extended items unexamined. Going through the process is an adventure worth taking. Even though nothing may seem to change on the surface, your lonely journey will have helped you to make an internal shift resulting in a more mature, confident, and determined you. Yes, it is a lonely journey, but it is worth taking.

Learn to Demystify the Dissertation Process

In one of the residencies I attended, the title of a seminar attracted my attention, Demystifying the Dissertation Process, and it was indeed a very good presentation that helped me to see the holistic picture of the dissertation process and how we should treat it. One particular slide caught my attention, "Slaying the Dragon One Piece at a Time," where the professor explained how to slay the big dissertation dragon step by step and from different directions. I thought the comparison was accurate and have since confirmed that one should take small steps from different directions to complete the process. I used this technique often by working in different chapters in parallel. Of course we have to finish one chapter to formally go on to the next but when I was stuck on Chapter 2, I would go to Chapter 3 and work on sections that were not dependent on the previous one, update my references, or work on my data collection instruments. By doing these tasks in parallel, I was able to slice away at the pie one piece at a time.

Dissertation Management Starts With Self-management

Managing a family, community, project, or simple task starts with self-management. According to Goleman (2000), the formal definition of self-management is "management of or by oneself; the taking of responsibility for one's own behavior and well-being." Self-management is also part of emotional self-awareness in the ability to recognize one's feelings. A dissertation is a project that requires a good personality. As a researcher, you will be interacting with many stakeholders, including your advisor, dissertation committee members, fellow students, organizations, and individuals you may collect data from, authors and researchers you need to ask permission from to use their copyrighted work, the university's institutional review board, and many others. You need to have good interpersonal relationship skills to work your way through the process. Treat your dissertation as a full-fledged project and follow the proper project management strategy. Time management is one of the eight modules of project management identified by the Project Management Institute (2010). Only if you plan your project properly and follow every task outlined on the schedule with consciously applied adjustments to it will you be successful. You only have 24 hours a day to do everything (work, family, school, social activities, and sleep if any time is left) and proper time management is the recipe for success. Identify tasks you will be working on for the day, week, or month; sequence them based on their priority; estimate the duration for each task; develop your own schedule; and print and post it in your office. Follow the schedule seriously, but remember you will slip now and then, and instead of bemoaning your slipup, dust yourself off, adjust the schedule realistically, and keep going.

Read Four to Six Completed Dissertations Before Writing Your Prospectus

From my experience, it is advisable to read four to six completed dissertations in your area of research before attempting to write your prospectus to understand if the research topic you have selected is addressed by other researchers, to check if you can use already developed and tested instruments, to get ideas on where to obtain literature sources for your research, and to modify and adjust your research topic. Students often struggle to develop their own research instrument without knowing there is one that meets their needs and is already available for use. This is not meant to discourage anyone who attempts to develop their own instrument but to show that it may be wise to know and consider using what is available, especially if there is one that has a record of validity and reliability tested and retested in other research projects. Going through the works of others also helps to capture information from research design, data collection, and data analysis strategies. Many research works point out potential future research areas in their conclusion section, and it is useful to see if their recommendations could be your starting point.

Whatever Doesn't Kill You Makes You Stronger

Persevering is the word I use to describe one remarkable and determined student who started the program with me. She came to the program with a different background and expectations from everyone else and was struggling to find the right advisor. An age difference, a cultural barrier in going out and asking for help, and the difficulty of finding the right professor were barriers to her acceptance by professors, even though she went to many residencies. She was finally accepted by one and spent a couple of years working with one advisor before learning that he no longer wanted to guide her. She did not give up. She continued looking for advisors for a few more quarters and paid her tuition fee without giving up. One night she called me (after I graduated) and asked me if I knew a professor who could advise her. I told her that my advisor was one of the few professors who understands students' situations and promised to ask him, even though I knew he had many students he was already mentoring. Fortunately, he was willing to take her and she started attending his class and joined the cohort. A few years passed without hearing from her and one evening I stumbled onto an e-mail trail between alumni and learned that she graduated after working on a very interesting research topic. I also learned that she was one of the active students in the cohort helping others to reach their destination. This story taught me the importance of keeping faith in oneself even when the road is bumpy.

Enough people in our circles tell us or insinuate that that we can't do it. Instead of believing what others say, listen to your inner voice, follow what it tells you, and keep going. A river will always reach its final destination because it does not resist and changes direction from blocked paths by moving through the next opening. If you look through the cracks of a closed door, you will find many open doors that will let you get to your destination. Know the path and keep going.

Enjoy the Process: The Outcome of Your Journey Is Less Important Than the Journey Itself

The journey you will be going through is significant and life changing; however, you will soon realize that the specific outcome of your journey will be less important than the process you have gone through. If you have the end in mind and work without noticing each step, you are missing the main part of the process. From your course work through developing your prospectus; from struggling to formulate Chapter 1, which is considered your guide to the rest of the dissertation, to going through a plethora of literature to identify what belongs in Chapter 2; from identifying your research method, population, and sampling techniques to selecting data collection and analysis techniques; from writing your final recommendation to describing the social implication of your study, you are embarking on a trip that you have never been on before, so enjoy every step of the way. I had a few friends who were determined to complete the process in 2 or 3 years. Some of them did, but when I talked to them a few years later, they said they regretted rushing through the program without enjoying the process. They do not remember much of when they were in the program except for the final dissertation defense and graduation. Enjoy every moment of the process, including the setbacks, challenges, frustrations, and going back and forth with your dissertation chair and committee members. Take it all with full grace, as these processes will teach you and make you wiser.

Balance Your Family, Work, and Education

Remember the goal of the dissertation process is to add to what you already have, not to substitute by losing one from your collections or achievements. The process is time consuming and demanding, especially as it requires taking time off from the activities you love to do with others. Many relationships with spouses, friends, and family members can be negatively affected as a result; however, it is your responsibility to balance family, work, and education. Try to engage them in what you do, talk to them about where you are in the process, and ask for their patience. Once in a while, take your significant others to a residency or library or have them listen in to one of your cohort discussions (or bring your spouse into the program and you will stay up together reading all night long). Some family members will welcome your effort and try to help; others may not understand the dimension and could take it differently, still others may not appreciate your preoccupation with your project at all and lose interest in your story. During this time, your advisor, committee members, and fellow students may be the only ones interested in your journey. It is your task to communicate and clear the air. Be patient.

Your Advisors Work For You: Maximize Your Opportunity

We all are looking for the ideal supervisor described by Australian professor R. Webber as someone (a) who on a personal level is not judgmental, (b) does not cut off lines on intellectual inquiry simply because they do not accord with his own preferences, (c) does not talk down to you, (d) does not turn consultation into one-way lectures, and (e) does not have mood swings and is not a control freak. You may or may not get all qualities listed from a person but remember it's your choice and your engagement style with your advisor that determine your success. Use the concept of managing the managers, where you inject the idea you want to work on, and be guided by them to the right path.

In the last few decades, there has been a paradigm shift in higher education on the relationship between PhD students and their advisors. Unlike the traditional school where a PhD student works for the professor by staying in his or her 4 x 4 room and waiting to receive instruction from the professor (often in months), the new approach allows students to be in charge of selecting their own research topic, choosing their advisor, and controlling their time. This approach has also helped professors to evolve into being servant leaders who guide students throughout the process. This is a big opportunity that allows you to maximize your unlimited access to your professors. They are there to help, and students should not wait too long to contact them, ask questions, and request guidance. The new performance-based contract between universities and professors takes account of students' feedback after a course and the instructor's course delivery method. Your feedback on their performance determines their next contract with the university. It is a two-way engagement.

Discuss Within Your Cohort: Ask Questions and Do Not Miss Regular Meetings

Every time I went to a residency, I took time to talk to students, professors, advisors, and even the conference organizers. I was often the last person to leave the cafeteria with a napkin covered with notes and information I gathered at the lunch and dinner tables. Those nuggets of tacit knowledge, information you do not find written down anywhere, could be the key pieces of information you need to complete your assignments or portions of your dissertation. What is difficult to you may be easy to others, but if you do not ask, there is no way you will get the answer. The minute you say or think "I know" is the minute you stop learning. Bite your tongue before going that route, swallow your pride, and ask. The second line of help after your advisor is your cohort or peer-mentors. These are students who are further along in the process, and their experience, disappointments, challenges, and successes will serve as input for your project.

The Dissertation Process is Similar to a Marathon

Working on your dissertation is similar to preparing for a marathon. The 26.2 mile race starts with the first mile.

During practice, one has to build strength mile by mile until reaching the 20-mile mark (the remaining 6 miles should come from the endurance on the race day). I run marathons, and to me the last 6 miles are the ones that test my patience. During one of my recent races, I was tired, my back was in pain, it was cold, and at Mile Mark 19, I decided to give up. When I was contemplating how to exit, I saw a woman cheering on a family member who was also in the race with a placard that read "There will be a day when you will say 'I can't do this' but today is not that day." Reading that message made me say to myself, "Yes, there will be a time when I will say I can't go to the bathroom let alone run this race, but until that day I should enjoy the process and keep going." That placard, even though it was not directed at me, gave me the extra energy and conviction I needed to finish the race. Similarly in the dissertation journey, the completion of each chapter is as trying and as fulfilling as running many marathons, and writing all the chapters to fit into one product is a great accomplishment that makes the completion of running multiple marathons seem easy by comparison. The message on that placard can come in handy whenever we face a challenge we think is unsurpassable. We should develop our own reminders that throwing in the towel is not an option. We need to keep going.

Make Your Dissertation a Trip From the Road Most Traveled to the Road Less Traveled

The effort made to complete the dissertation process often focuses on the road that is obvious, the road many researchers have traveled and on which they have left academic traces of their footsteps. The journey also gives the traveler the opportunity, if you pay attention, to try the road less traveled: an inner journey of soul searching, a journey to return to the root to find peace and fulfill one's destiny, a journey that begins but never ends, a journey to oneness, a journey to nowhere. Furthermore, you'll travel to the place where you can learn humility, sympathy, emotional self-awareness, and self-confidence.

Humility is one of the personality traits we learn from the process. Most of us come from an environment where we have accomplished a lot in our professional careers (thereby strengthening our ego), and we want to apply that experience to the dissertation process. It can be difficult to accept comments and critiques from classmates and professors. Many of us, including myself, have a hard time following directions from mentors and teachers. Our mind is full of pride and self-importance, and we are used to giving directions rather than receiving them (after all we came to the program to face and conquer another challenge). This is an opportunity for you to examine why you volunteered for the job.

Understand the Dissertation Process Well

In addition to your course work, residencies, and communication with your advisor, a good chunk of time is added to your schedule by the university that is totally out of your control. These tasks include getting your prospectus approved, assigning committee members, review time by the university research reviewer, scheduling your proposal exam, going through the institutional review board application and approval process, and obtaining consent from research population representatives. So when you plan your schedule, it is important to be mindful of these and include the required time in your timeline to ensure it represents a holistic view of your dissertation project and estimate your completion time properly. Find out what the latest requirements are by asking your advisor or by going through the university dissertation process material.

Be a Change Agent and Give Back What You Have: You Will Be Rewarded Triple Fold

While you are in school, do something else that will satisfy your soul. Help your or any community by giving your time and services. In my view, this is the greatest contribution one can give in life. I had the opportunity to go on a mission trip to Costa Rica with my advisor and a dozen fellow PhD students to build a house for the natives in the remote mountains. Even though it was only a week-long effort, its impact on the way I see the world was huge and strengthened my belief that it's only through giving that one can get more satisfaction. I have also learned that in order to give, one does not need to have plenty. When I saw everyone on the team sweat in the 107° F heat and humid weather digging holes for the construction, carrying wood from the virgin jungle full of deadly poisonous snakes, and eating whatever was available on banana leaves with the natives, I realized the existence of a strong bond that this program has created between students who came from all walks of life to achieve this noble goal that is by far greater than their collective imaginations. I was pleased to be part of that group and enjoyed taking time off from the pressing deadlines to do something different. These types of activities not only give us a break from our routines but also align us to the purpose of why we are here. Such activities also give us the opportunity to be closer to and know our fellow students who we otherwise only get to hear their voice or read their e-mails.

Take Time Off if Needed

Having stressed the importance of staying on track and going on in the face of challenges, I also believe it is important to recognize when it is time to take a break. If you really think you have too much on your plate and things are not moving the way you planned, it is important to discuss the situation with your advisor and take time off. This is not quitting; rather, it is being realistic and strategizing accordingly. Our ego often gets threatened if we do not accomplish what we planned to do as originally scheduled. I have a few good friends who started the program the same time as me but could not continue, partly because they already had aggressive plans in their lives and added this one without understanding the intensity of the program and the time demand that comes with it or because they underestimated the difficulty of going through a narrow path alone to reach their destination. Listen to your inner voice and follow it. If you feel you can't do it now, be honest to yourself and make the right decision. There is always tomorrow. Postponing it isn't giving up. Do not be tricked into believing what other people say about your strength or lack of it; you are the only one who knows your self-worth and the only person who can say no to you is yourself. As good commanders in a war field do, make a strategic retreat when you run out of ammunition and reorganize your resources to go back to the battlefield. This is exactly what is going on in the dissertation world. The time away from your study becomes a time of reflection, prioritization, appreciation of what you have, and an opportunity to use the knowledge from the reflection to transform yourself to a different thinking level. When you come back, your journey starts with clear focus and energy.

Putting It Together: No Matter What Happens, Keep Going

After this sometimes brutal and difficult process, you will come out with a new personality—a new you. As snakes molt, similarly you will strip away from your mind the commonly held belief that your world is as small as a stamp on an envelope and that your IQ is the only indicator of success in life to expand your understanding of success to be more related to maturity, wisdom, and emotional as well as spiritual intelligence. Joseph M. Marshall III, in his book *Keep Going*, described a conversation between a young man puzzled by the unpredictable nature of life and his grandfather, whom he asks why life sometimes had to be so difficult. The grandfather replied,

> In life there is sadness as well as joy, losing as well as winning, falling as well as standing, hunger as well as plenty, badness as well as goodness. I do not say this to make you despair, but to teach you reality. Life is a journey sometimes walked in light, sometimes in shadow. You did not ask to be born, but you are here. You have weakness as well as strength. You have both because in life there is two of everything. Within you is the will to win, as well as the willingness to lose, within you is the heart to feel compassion as well as the smallness to be arrogant. Within you is the way to face life as well as the fear to turn away from it. Life can give you strength. Strength can come from facing the storm of life, from knowing loss, feeling sadness and heartache, from falling into the depth of grief. You must stand up in the storm. You must face the wind and the cold and the darkness. When the storm blows hard you must stand firm, for it is not trying to knock you down, it is really trying to teach you to be strong. Being strong means taking one more step toward the top of the hill, no matter how weary you may be. It means letting the tears flow through the grief. It means to keep looking for the answer, though the darkness of despair is all around you. Being strong means to cling to hope for one more heartbeat, one more sunrise. Each step, no matter how difficult, is one more step closer to the top of the hill. To keep hope alive for one more heartbeat

at a time leads to the light of the next sunrise, and the promise of a new day. The weakest step toward the top of the hill, toward sunrise, toward hope, is stronger than the fiercest storm.

The title Doctor of Philosophy will come to those who keep going and work patiently. The journey will also serve as a pointer in our inner journey to become a true thinker—if we keep going.

References

Marshall, J. (2006). *Keep going: The art of perseverance.* New York, NY: Sterling.

Noella, M., & Lorraine, M. (2009). The research journey: A Lonely Planet approach. *Issues in Educational Research, 19,* 48-60.

Project Management Institute. (2013). *A guide to the project management body of knowledge (PMBOK).* Newton Square, PA, Author.

7
William Quisenberry, DBA

Professor/Consultant

Strive not to be a success, but rather to be of value.

—Albert Einstein

No One Can Take It Away From You

I had multiple inspirations to earn a doctoral degree. The first was my family, specifically my mother and father. My parents always made it a point to pursue education. Dad would say, "Get your education. Focus on your studies, and work as hard as you can. Do not waste your life hanging in the streets or chasing frivolous activities, focus on your schoolwork! Once you get that education, no one can take it away from you!" His speeches, or what my siblings and I called lectures, actually stuck with me. Even when I was not excelling in school or doing very well in other areas of my life, in the back of my mind, I always knew it was important. I did not begin to take school seriously until I was a sophomore in high school.

There was a new program under way at my school that only administrators and some teachers knew about. The program was geared toward getting more African Americans into Advanced Studies classes at my high school. I had always taken general course work and had never considered advanced classes. Within the program, teachers consulted with administrators to select African Americans who were in general studies courses but had shown some talent and ability to succeed in advanced courses. After compiling a list of names, the teachers set up a conference with the student and parents and made the proposal. The students and parents had to agree to be placed into the advanced classes.

I still remember being called into the conference with Mrs. Akins and my father. Mrs. Akins was an African American social studies and history teacher who was very popular in the Black community. She was known as a brilliant, tough teacher who really challenged all her students, but especially the African American students. Mrs. Akins was also the first lady at a popular Baptist church in town, meaning her husband was the senior pastor. I had the joy of having Mrs. Akins in middle school for multiple social studies and history courses. When I went to high school, Mrs. Akins coincidently transferred to my high school as a history teacher. Just when I thought I'd gotten away from Mrs. Akins, there she was again.

Truthfully, Mrs. Akins was a very friendly person, but she did not take any stuff. She'd worked with many inner-city kids, really knew a lot about history, had an amazing collegiate background, and loved to challenge youth with rigorous course work. Mrs. Akins not only academically challenged her students but also convinced them to grow up and be successful citizens. Mrs. Akins had an African American history class that changed my life. I took the course my senior year in high school, and it exposed me to an understanding and appreciation of the successes, fortitude, and brilliance of African Americans that I had never seen. The course did not focus as much on the plight or oppression of African Americans in the past, but instead the marvelous contributions of African American physicians, businesspersons, entrepreneurs, inventors, scientists, professors, attorneys, military officers, musicians, and much more, despite the discrimination they faced. This class helped me realize that I also had potential and should aim for greatness.

So imagine my surprise when Mrs. Akins called a conference with my father and me. I was very nervous. I kept thinking, "What in the world have I done now?" However, in the conference, Mrs. Akins presented the new initiative that was taking place at the school and mentioned that I had been selected as one of the students to move into Advanced Studies. By this time, I was a junior and living the dream. I played on the football team, I had classes with all of my friends, and school was easy for the most part. I put little effort forth and had plenty of time to hang out with my buddies all day while still passing my classes. Why in the world would I want to change that?

My father, on the other hand, saw things differently. He was overjoyed! His face lit up and he said, "This is an excellent opportunity!" I replied, "What? No it's not! I do not want to take classes with all of those preppy little rich kids! I want to stay in class with my friends!" As the meeting progressed, I quickly realized that my opinion did not matter. Mrs. Akins and my father had already come to an agreement, and I was moving into Advanced Studies. Mrs. Akins made sure that I realized this was a life-changing opportunity and how they were taking a risk by recommending me. She told me that this was a lot bigger than I was. I was not only representing the Quisenberry family, but all African Americans. I would soon find out that this was because there were almost no African

Americans taking Advanced Studies courses at my high school, which was the reason for this new initiative. If I and the other targeted African American students all took these classes and failed, it would give the administrators who did not agree with the initiative the opportunity to say, "I told you so. The number of African Americans in these courses is low because they just do not have the cognitive ability to excel at this level."

The experience ended up being a tough one; the transition into the classes was not easy. I had to study, read, and do homework for hours every night after getting in from football practice. The workload was unreal in comparison to my previous courses. We even had to read books and write reports during the summer break that were due the first day of school when fall classes started back! Who had ever heard of such madness?

I was forced to grow up, meet new people I did not normally hang around (and who did not look like me), and learn time-management skills. This was tough for a high school student; however, the experience changed my life. I was bitten by an academic bug during this experience that triggered a joy and tenacity for learning that I'd never possessed before. The experience also provided me with growing pains that would end up laying a strong foundation for the rest of my academic and professional career. As I continued to move on into college and my professional life, I noticed I was often the only African American male, or one of a few, and I was never just representing myself.

Embracing the process really helped me. When I first entered the doctoral program, the initial courses had me frustrated and I came very close to dropping out during my second class. I was not scoring very high on my written assignments due to the requirement to follow American Psychological Association (APA) style, critical thinking, and scholarly writing requirements. We had used APA in my master's program, but it primarily focused on citing and referencing. The doctoral-level classes expected thorough research, critical analysis, and strict adherence to APA style, and I had some professors who really challenged me in this area.

So I had a decision to make. I was either going to continue trying to do things my own way, which felt comfortable, or I was going to get out of my comfort zone, buckle down, and embrace the process. I chose the latter, and it really paid off. Embracing the process essentially means digging deep into the learning experience—not just seeking to get through the program, but learning! Learning how to read as a scholar reads. Learning how to write as a scholar writes. Learning how to think as a scholar thinks. I had to embrace the process of becoming a scholar, and those who attempt to avoid this crucial step of the doctoral program will either end up not making it or take much longer to finish. Squeaking by without embracing the scholarly process could make the transition out of the doctoral program and into practice or into academia much tougher. When you have a doctoral degree, there are certain skill sets that employers or clients expect you to possess. You probably will not have these skills if you do not embrace the process of becoming a scholar.

A best practice is to get a peer mentor. Your peer mentor should be either a doctoral student further along in the program than you or an individual who has already completed the journey. You can pick up valuable feedback and tips from a person who is already where you are seeking to go. A person further down the road is capable of warning you about roadblocks, traffic jams, and potholes that may be on the journey ahead.

You also need a group of peers who are currently engaging in the process with you. The doctoral journey is a unique experience, and unless you have been through it or are currently experiencing it, you cannot understand all of the dynamics involved. Not even your family, who is closest to you and who will be witnessing the torture and hard work you are going through on a daily basis, will truly be able to understand. You need a group of friends, study partners, colleagues, associates, or whatever you choose to call them to be engaged with you during the journey, so you can encourage one another and get through the process together.

When completing the course work, ensure you do not get behind. Try to find a rhythm, a delegated study time where you can read and write. Block out these hours and stick to them. Ensure friends, family, and coworkers all know this block of time is dedicated to completing school work. The same recommendation applies for completing the dissertation as well.

Try to establish relationships with your professors. Since I completed my degree in an online program, it is very easy to just take classes, do the required work, and leave it at that. However, I found that getting to know my professors on a more personable level, seeking them out at residencies or other conferences, calling them to discuss course work, research, and so forth really helped me to get more value out of the program. Remember, do not focus on just getting through but work on developing into a true scholar-practitioner. Most doctoral students are already engaged in practice or have experience with that element. The piece that requires the most work is becoming a scholar. So putting more effort and focus on this aspect can help you develop into a scholar while excelling in your course work.

The primary challenges I faced had to do with the level of writing required. I had a tough time adjusting to the scholarly writing required at the doctoral level. Professors were more rigorous in grading, and I had to learn APA, think critically at a more intense level, conduct much more research, and write much longer papers. All of this together was a tremendous challenge, and as I mentioned, I considered quitting the program during my second class.

The best way to overcome this challenge is to focus on improving as a scholar and writer. Work on reading, research, and writing every day if possible. Begin studying to understand what scholarly writing is. How do you read and write in a critical manner? How do you use online resources and databases to conduct research? You will need to learn these things. There are many resources available to doctoral learners. It is important to understand what is available and to begin leveraging those resources.

For instance, universities generally have research centers whose staff can help you learn new research skills and find cutting-edge research in specific fields, or you can be put in touch with thought leaders and experts in certain fields both inside and outside your university. Additionally, librarians can help you find specific authors or works to assist with your studies. They can also give you specific research tips for searching databases and various resource catalogs. Writing center staff can help you learn APA, improve your scholarly writing, and may provide proofreading services.

However, all these opportunities and resources will not come knocking on your door or seek you out. Instead, you must seek them out. The doctoral journey is an independent experience, and you must take initiative to get things done. Having a group (cohort) of fellow students is beneficial, as is having a great peer mentor. The resources and knowledge sharing in a group cohort can help students feel more connected and less isolated. Building relationships with professors will be beneficial, because they are more likely to embrace you as an engaged student and potentially offer recommendations regarding various resources that are available to you. Many people do not make it at the doctoral level because it is an independent, self-managed journey. It is unique compared to the bachelor's and even the master's degree. You must take ownership of your doctoral studies, take initiative, and embrace the process if you want to succeed.

I recommend that you begin thinking about your research topic and reviewing literature and previous dissertations as early as possible. Do not wait until you reach the all-but-dissertation (ABD) phase, but begin crafting a solid topic, research problem, research question, and research design early. You do not want to get to the ABD phase and find yourself going down the wrong path with a research topic that is not feasible. I will share my experience in a moment.

Additionally, begin seeking out a dissertation mentor and chair as early as you can. This relates to building relationships with professors. You may identify a professor who you think you will want to work with because of his or her authority on a certain topic, mentoring style, and so forth. You can approach the professor prior to reaching the phase of being assigned a chair and ask him or her (informally) to be your mentor when you reach that stage. If the professor accepts, you can begin informally discussing your research topic and receiving feedback. Thus, when you reach the stage when you are assigned a chair and begin writing the prospectus or proposal, you will be in a much better position and have more direction.

This was one of my best practices, I did not wait until the last minute to begin my research; instead, I took initiative and started exploring topics and methodologies, reviewing literature, and so forth. I took ownership of my dissertation research and was tenacious throughout the process. This goes back to some of my other points regarding embracing the process of being a scholar and taking initiative. You should do things because you want to, not because you have to. When you take this approach, you will always be one step ahead.

I did have a few challenges during my experience. You will need to be ready for challenges and seek to overcome the setbacks that you will face. One of the early challenges I had was that I had to change my dissertation topic. As I mentioned before, you should select a chair as soon as you can to ensure you are going down the right path. I took a lot of initiative and started looking at a potential study early, but once I was matched up with my chair and I started running it by him, he quickly recognized several holes in the project. He ultimately recommended that I consider changing the study. Although I first thought this was the end of the world, as I'd already written a 30-page prospectus, completed a lot of my literature review, and even started identifying a potential sample. However, my chair was right: the study was not very feasible for a dissertation, and it would have taken a long time to conduct the research, if I could ever get it done. So I changed my study and it ended up being one of the best decisions that I made during my doctoral journey. The topic I changed to was relevant, I had practical experience within the area, I had access to some great potential target organizations, and I enjoyed the content.

The second roadblock I faced was finding organizations that would allow me to use them as a partner and draw samples from their employees or members. I received several rejections and even had some informal agreements that fell through when it was time to finalize plans. This was another important lesson learned. Be sure to identify the organization or association that you will use to draw your sample from and collect data. You will want to obtain an informal agreement initially, but seek to get it in writing as soon as possible because individuals may tell you yes informally but do not have the authority to give you a formal approval or they back out. A high-ranking individual in the organization or association must provide formal, written agreement before you have the right to use individuals (employees, members, etc.) from the institution. You will not be able to receive approval on your Institutional Review Board application until you have obtained a written agreement with an organization. Be sure to handle this potential hurdle sooner rather than later.

I overcame these hurdles by listening to the feedback of my dissertation chair and mentor, continuing to network, staying engaged in the literature, and constantly working my way through the issues. When my chair recommended that I change my topic, I did not argue with him. I went back to the literature, started reviewing dissertations to see their recommendations for future research, and quickly found a problem and research gap that I thought I could potentially study and address. I trusted the advice and knowledge of my chair, humbled myself, and continued to move forward.

When multiple organizations refused to allow me to use them in my study and others backed out at the last minute, I did not quit, moan, or complain. Instead, I started sending out e-mails to potential organizations, working the phones, calling contacts and colleagues, and continuing to seek out potential opportunities. Once again, I met with my chair, explained the issue to him, took his advice, and moved forward. I eventually found two organizations whose leaders were willing to participate in my study and everything worked out.

The following are important lessons. Embrace the dissertation process just as you should embrace your course work. Leverage your resources and stay in communication with your chair. Listen and respond to the feedback from your chair.

This is also a great time to mention that you should ensure you get a great chair. Selecting a chair is important. You want to find someone who is well respected in the department, well liked within the university, competent in research methodology and the content area you are researching, and well connected to the practical and research community. You want a chair who is engaged and not too busy that he or she will neglect you.

You need to choose a chair who also understands how to mentor. Many professors understand their material, know how to conduct research, and may be great teachers, but being a chair is a different kind of teaching—it is a one-on-one relationship, it is mentoring. Some professors are not very good at this style of teaching. If you do not select the right chair, your process will be more difficult. If you get a poor chair, try to change your chair with the university or seek out another professor from your current university or another university who will informally mentor you through the process. Some students also choose to hire a dissertation coach or a consultant to help them if their chair is not enough. Do whatever you need to do to ensure you receive the guidance you need to succeed.

Another lesson learned is to ensure you maintain sound time management skills. The dissertation process can be very misleading. It may seem as though you have a lot of free time on your hands after you complete your course work. You can take your time, take a break, and write the dissertation at your own pace, right? Wrong! You need to engage the process aggressively so that you do not lose momentum. I have seen many doctoral students get to the ABD phase, let off the accelerator, and never get back on the freeway to completion. Just as I recommended with studying the course work, continue to read, research, or write at least 6 days per week, with maybe 1 day off to rest. Try to do something daily on your project so that you do not lose momentum.

All the university resources I mentioned before are critical to the dissertation phase. These include your university research centers, the library, and the writing center. The staff at these three areas (which are all free) will be able to point you to many other resources, techniques, and products that will help your dissertation research. Again, you will have to seek these out.

A great book I used during my doctoral journey was Dr. Marilyn Simon's (2011) *Dissertation and Scholarly Research: Recipes for Success—A Practical Guide to Start and Complete Your Dissertation, Thesis, or Formal Research Project*. This book breaks down the entire dissertation from beginning to end in a simple format. The book also discusses various research methodologies and approaches researchers can used during the research process. In terms of methodology, I recommend reading several works by John Creswell and leveraging the resources within. A few of his books that I used most were *Educational Research Planning: Conducting and*

Evaluating Quantitative and Qualitative Research (2011a) and *Research Design: Qualitative, Quantitative, and Mixed Methods Approaches* (2011b). You will also want to have the latest edition of the *Publication Manual of the American Psychological Association's* handy to ensure you adhere to APA standards.

Many issues pertaining to self-motivation, initiative, time management, and a lack of knowledge sharing all contribute to failure. No one is going to hold your hand or walk you through the doctoral program. If you are not self-motivated, you will likely struggle in the doctoral program. You have to take initiative and take ownership of your doctoral journey. Your professors and dissertation chair are there to offer feedback and recommendations, but they do not own your process, you do. If you do not take control of the journey and truly embrace it, you will struggle.

Another major roadblock at the doctoral level is many doctoral students' level of pride. By the time students reach this phase, they generally have had some major accomplishments academically, professionally, or both. As a result, they may begin thinking that the university or their professors owe them something. Students with this mentality quickly receive a rude awakening. You may be well respected a leader or manager in your workplace or in your community, but at the doctoral level, you are nothing. This may sound harsh, but it is the truth. You may have accomplished a lot in your respective circles, but you have not yet accomplished anything at the doctoral level. So swallow your pride, embrace the process, and get through the program. That level of pride can stand between you and success, because somebody in the doctoral program is going to test your ego and pride. They will question your knowledge, the quality of your work, or something else. This is all part of the process of becoming a scholar in the sea of very smart, critical thinkers. This entire process lends to you discovering and embracing your scholarly identity, and it is an absolute necessity.

A major setback many doctoral students experience is running out of gas and giving up. The doctoral journey will involve disappointments, hurt feelings, being offended, fatigue, frustration, confusion, embarrassment, anger, and so much more. The process can be a rollercoaster ride at times, but do not give up! You may have to change research topics, change chairs, take classes over, but do not give up! You may have committee members who do not like one another and take their grudge or different approaches to research or a topic out on you, leaving you in the middle, but do not give up! Your family and friends may not be able to understand why you are not spending as much time with them and may give you a hard time about this, but do not give up! Your workload on the job may be increasing, you may feel overwhelmed by the second job that you have working on your degree, but do not give up! You may be stricken with life circumstances that include illness, deaths in the family, cutbacks or layoffs at work, and much more, but do not give up! You will have to persevere over, and over, and over again. But do not give up! Tell yourself that you are not going to quit the program. Tell yourself you are going to outlast the professors, the committee members, and the administrators and finish your degree. You will eventually finish if you do not quit!

The peer mentoring model is an amazing approach that should be in all doctoral programs, especially online programs. I was blessed to have two different perspectives and experiences with the peer mentoring model, one as a mentee and one as a mentor. From a mentee perspective, my peer mentors saved me a lot of time and provided valuable feedback. You can open up to your peer mentors and ask them anything without being intimidated or feeling stupid. You may be reluctant to ask your chair questions he or she might consider silly because you do not want to look incompetent to your superior, which your chair essentially is in this process. Also, peer mentors may be more readily available so that you can save your time with your chair for more important questions and discussions. My peer mentors saved me an enormous amount of time by giving me a heads up about potential issues that lay ahead, sharing knowledge, giving advice, and providing encouragement. It is inspiring and motivating to see someone that is ahead of you in the race meet milestones, overcome hurdles, and get closer to the finish line. It helps you know that there is hope and the process can be completed.

My experience as a peer mentor was one of tremendous growth and development. I had an opportunity to improve my leadership skills as a cohort leader, to learn how to teach and mentor at the doctoral level, and to gain experience facilitating discussions and classes in an online environment. The peer mentoring program really changed my life, because I previously thought that I wanted to focus on being a consultant first and a university professor second. However, the peer mentoring experience helped me recognize that my strengths and joy were more aligned with being a professor first and a consultant second. The peer mentoring model caused me to have a paradigm shift that ultimately changed my life.

The realization of benefits within cohort models is significant for universities, students, and faculty. The university benefits by having increased student retention, engagement, and graduation rates. The university also benefits because faculty are likely to be happier because they will have a decreased workload because they will not have to respond to constant minor inquiries from students, who can instead turn to their peer mentors. This may decrease faculty turnover. Faculty members will also have more opportunities to focus on developing deeper mentoring relationships with students and serving as experts on important topics that require their attention. The students are also happier because they have a level of knowledge sharing, a support group, and the opportunity to grow as scholars along with their peers.

I still remember when the chief academic officer (CAO) approved my study, which was the final step in my doctoral program and symbolized that I was officially done. I was at work, and it had been a busy day. I had my mobile phone on vibrate because I had been in a meeting earlier that morning. I happened to glance down at my phone and noticed I had several e-mails from my University, a missed phone call from my chair, and a few text messages from my chair. I knew my abstract was out for review with the CAO, so I immediately became excited because I knew some sort of news had come back. When I opened the text, my chair had written, "Congratulations Dr. Quisenberry! It is official now; your study has received the CAO's approval!"

I got up from my desk and headed for the doorway, trying to hold in the mountain of emotions I was experiencing. I left the office building, went to the parking lot, and got into my car. I listened to my voicemails, and my chair had also left me a message congratulating me and telling me to give him a call when I received the message. I've heard people who have had near-death experiences say "your life flashes before your eyes," meaning that in your mind you begin to have a quick recap of your life. I am not sure if my experience was on a similar level, but this is essentially what my mind started to do.

I began to think about where I'd come from; some of the negative environments I had been exposed to growing up in some rougher neighborhoods; the love, wisdom, and guidance that my parents had always provided to me; mentors or people who had crossed my path when I was growing up, telling me that I could do anything that I put my mind to; horrible teachers who did not deserve to carry the title who told me I was not smart or would not be successful; excellent teachers like Mrs. Akins who said the exact opposite and challenged me; pastors and spiritual leaders who told me that all things were possible through Christ—all of these thoughts and experiences just started to rush through my head at once. All of it came to a head in tears and celebration. The tinted windows on my car prevented someone passing by in the parking lot seeing me and thinking I had succumbed to the pressures of corporate life and was having a nervous breakdown.

I called my father and gave the news to him. He was overjoyed, and I could tell he was holding back tears. He told me how proud he was of me and how proud my deceased grandparents would have been. After getting myself together, I called my chair, who congratulated me and we shared a moment of celebration on the phone. I will never forget him saying, "Now the real work begins, Doc." I actually remember and cherish this experience, at work, in my car the day my study was officially approved far more than any other. There was something special about that moment.

I have grown tremendously as a scholar-practitioner since completing the program. The doctoral experience improved my ability to think critically, to analyze variants in depth, and to be more scholarly in terms of staying abreast of current events and research within my industry and areas of interest. The program has helped me become more comfortable with who I am, while increasing my confidence. I went to Walden University, where a significant portion of the university is geared toward being a scholar-practitioner focused upon impacting positive social change. This has really stayed with me and I am always engaged in projects in my community and around the world that use my educational experience, research, and practical capabilities to improve the world in some form or fashion.

I think one of the greatest areas of growth in my life has been my level of thankfulness. Obtaining such a high achievement is a humbling experience; as you begin to get out and interact with others, you realize how important it is to have a doctoral degree. My friends, family, and community have been blown away by the accomplishment. People who have known me my entire life are amazed at how much I've grown as a person. I think seeing the bewilderment and joy in people's eyes around me helped me realize how much God has blessed me. Reaching this level of accomplishment has helped me understand that all things are possible if you believe in Christ.

When I look back over my life, I also begin to see how my steps truly were ordered and so many life circumstances that did not make sense at the time gained more perspective. The opening story I shared about being moved into advanced classes in high school is just one of many examples. It is like my entire life had been a big puzzle that God was putting together the entire time. I did not (and sometimes still do not) completely understand how the pieces fit or what type of image God is pulling together, but He knows exactly what He is doing. When you step back and look at the opportunity that has been provided to pursue a doctoral degree, knowing that only a small percentage of the world's population will ever reach that accomplishment, it is humbling and makes me extremely thankful for my life and the unique opportunity I have to affect people's lives around me.

Embracing your scholarly identity begins with embracing the process. You have to begin with wanting to learn exactly what it means to become a scholar. This involves learning who you are as a scholar and where you fit in the sea of scholars.

Embracing your scholarly identity also involves discovering the research problems, issues, topics, and areas that interest you. You have to find and engage in research that you find intriguing but that is also relevant and of interest to those around you. I embraced my scholarly identity by increasing the amount of reading that I engaged in, writing more, networking, attending conferences, and surrounding myself by thought leaders and experts. The more that you get out and engage with the scholarly community, the easier it will be for you to find your niche and participate with other scholars. All these activities have increased my ability to engage in scholarly activity and discover my unique identity in the research community.

My engagement in the scholarly community has contributed to me understanding my value and worth. My opening quote from Albert Einstein did not mention seeking success but mentioned seeking to add value. This is something that I have come to appreciate the past couple of years since completing my doctoral degree. While completing my degree and even a short time period after finishing the process, I was on a hunt for success. There was a piece of me seeking the fame, attention, notoriety, and reward associated with achieving great success. However, just as my perspective changed in many areas during and after earning a doctoral degree, my mind-set regarding success also shifted.

I realized that I had been placed in this unique opportunity not for myself but for others. I started to understand that I had received a platform that required stewardship and servitude, and I changed the focus of my attention from obtaining success and the rewards that come from success to adding value to my community, those around me, and individuals around the world. In seeking to add value and invest in people, I have found that success is the result. This is how my doctoral degree has helped me understand my value. My value is found in serving others and seeking to improve the world in some form or fashion. When the CAO first approved my study and my chair, Dr. Walter McCollum, said, "Now the real work begins, Doc." I thought he was just referring to working in a professional context. I now realize he was talking not about working toward success but about working to affect positive change or to add value.

Not everyone is not going to be cheering, jumping for joy, or looking to help you after you earn your doctoral degree. You may even run across individuals who like you until they find out that you have a doctorate. Certain individuals feel intimidated or become angry when someone has more education than they do or if they feel you are more successful than they are.

I have run across this in my career and personal life. As I primarily work in academic settings, there is often not a lot of intimidation by colleagues who have a doctoral degree. In some practical settings, non-doctoral-degree holders can be quick to label you as a theorist and out of touch with practice.

If your degree is from a nontraditional or online university, you may also receive some pushback in certain academic circles. Remain confident, embrace your scholarly identity, and seek to do things with a spirit of excellence, and you will find that this mild, often passive opposition usually offers little or no threat. Since I finished my doctoral degree when I was 29 years old, I also have had some level of pushback regarding my age. Because I typically work with nontraditional adult learners, I am often the youngest person in the room and my students are typically older than I am. Knowing who you are, being a thought leader in your respective area, and letting your body of work speak for itself will help you overcome any objections. If you do things the right way and always know your material, the respect for your position and you as a person will follow.

My greatest accomplishment has been the number of students and distinguished professionals that I have helped. I see myself as someone who is changing the world by training world changers. I cannot reach or go to all of the places my students or mentees have access to, but I can provide them with the skills, knowledge, and encouragement to go into their respective areas and have an amazing impact. So in a way, I get to live and have an impact through the many people I teach or train. This is what I feel most proud of and what keeps me excited on a daily basis. I have even had an opportunity to work with some international organizations and engage in research, teaching, and training leaders around the world, often in impoverished communities that could use educated, trained leaders. This is an amazing experience for me and made the entire doctoral experience, including the struggles, late nights, and pain, worthwhile.

By going to conferences and engaging in research and publishing opportunities, you will feel like you are on your way to becoming a true scholar-practitioner. If you go to academic, research, and professional conferences, you will have a better chance of integrating into the sea of scholars. You have to engage in these communities to become a contributor. After you have gone to some conferences to get the feel of things, you can submit papers, abstracts, and works in progress to conferences. This will give you the opportunity to present at conferences and get your name out there. After doing so, you can have your papers published in the conference proceedings and potentially published in a journal associated with the respective conference.

Another way to become engaged in the sea of scholars is to begin serving as a peer reviewer on journals. This will allow you to review manuscripts, to see how they should look, and to learn what journal editors typically look for. This will also give you the opportunity to referee at conferences, facilitate sessions, and to meet journal editors. Such opportunities will help you become more comfortable with the scholarly community and other professionals in your field.

After you start to engage in this process, you begin to develop partnerships with other scholars, which will give you the opportunity to engage in collaborative research and publishing efforts. Like much of the doctoral journey, it begins with you taking initiative and going to conferences. It is best to begin this process prior to graduating. Become comfortable with the academic conference scene during your degree program. You can also begin presenting at conferences and publishing in journals while you are still in school. The best way to initiate this process is by touching up your course work research papers and submitting them for presentation and publication. Many students mistakenly believe that you can only publish empirical research. You can and should publish your conceptual works. So begin pulling those old papers out and get in the game!

As I have continuously repeated during this reflective piece, you must embrace the process, humble yourself, take initiative, and never give up. If you can do these four things, you will make it. There has to be a solid foundation in every journey and life circumstance. For me, that rock was and continues to be Jesus Christ. All four of the pillars that I have discussed in this piece I ultimately found in Him. So while you are going through this life-changing, often challenging experience, stay rooted and grounded spiritually. Pray, take time to meditate, read and study the Bible, and stay in fellowship with other believers. These activities will contribute to your ability to embrace the journey ahead of you (embrace the process), to keep a level head while remaining open to criticism (humble yourself), fight off fear by staying engaged and moving forward (taking initiative), and continuing to persevere (never give up). If you keep God first and maintain these four pillars, I am confident that you will successfully reach this amazing milestone. It may be a difficult journey, but once you earn your doctoral degree, no one can take it away from you.

8
Daniel Hansen, Doctoral Candidate

My inspiration to earn a doctoral degree started in my childhood when I wanted to be a doctor like the ones on TV. I later discovered that my dream wasn't going to happen when I had troubles passing nursing school. I went so far as to become a certified hypnotist because the human mind fascinated me. I realized I had a knack for research when posited with a question of whether the mind was like a computer. Packed with a background in psychology, I went to DeVry University to learn about computer science to compare the two. I ended up developing my own hypothesis and model for the mind but never did anything with it. That will be a good topic for my next book.

I found a niche in computers, especially database design and basic programming, and I landed a job designing and programming multimedia touchscreen kiosks placed in hotel lobbies to provide dining and entertainment venues in the area, printed directions, and coupons. While designing the kiosks, I found that I was good at information management and earned my bachelor's in computer information systems in 2000. I went back for my master's degree in network and communication management with an emphasis in e-commerce in 2006. The focus of my master's and my ability to do multimedia and computerized kiosk development garnered a speaking opportunity in Thailand.

The inspiration for earning my doctoral degree occurred in 2007 when I had an opportunity to consult on an information system for the Thai government. This opportunity included a free trip to Thailand and provided an opportunity to share my knowledge with students, PhD professors, and government officials. Armed with my newly acquired master's degree and over 25 years of experience in computer programming and designing kiosk systems, I gave presentations at King Mongkut's University of Technology Thonburi on network protocols, kiosk design, teleconferencing, and the future of wireless technology, and it was amazing to learn that I had something to offer. I was even asked to go back and teach there. The only obstacle I had was not having a PhD, which is when I enrolled at Walden University.

My first best practice was finding a balance between my work, family, and course work. I often got up 2 hours before work, worked during lunch, and worked when my family was asleep, which meant I worked through the night to get posts and assignments ready and posted on time. I worked hard to be a week ahead on projects and assignments. I never let my course work interfere with my job and vice versa. That balance has been difficult to maintain as family and work conditions have changed. I committed to the journey knowing that sacrifices had to be made, and I made sure that my family knew what that entailed.

Another best practice I implemented was finding my mastermind alliance or group support system. I made friends at residencies and I formed a support group. I also found colleagues who have been through the PhD process and formed bonds with them. I found a way to collaborate with my peers and other scholar-practitioners through social media like LinkedIn and Twitter. It was through associations with these like-minded people that we were able to share in and learn from our experiences. Most important, I had to get my family behind me to become a part of this support system, even though they didn't understand what I was talking about.

Then I had to learn to ignore people who asked what I am going to do with my PhD or why bother. The most difficult part of this journey has been putting on blinders to all those who said I couldn't do it. I had teachers who suggested I not go to college because I couldn't cut it in academia due to my test scores. I did it anyway, and when I finish my dissertation, I plan to give autographed copies to those naysayers.

Most important, I had to get organized. This has been hard for me because I am not a neat freak but I always find what I am looking for. However, I should have started cataloging information much earlier in life. I think a course in coding would have been very helpful even in other areas of my life. One thing I did early on that helped tremendously was journaling. Journaling was the best way I found to organize my information and thoughts for my dissertation and other class projects.

The first thing I discovered was that I had to work in groups. While working on my masters' degree, I created a system for selecting group members for projects. I watched when and how students posted in discussions. I didn't always pick the ones who posted the first day but pretty close. I also noted the quality and depth of their posts for signs of dedication and a deep understanding of the topic discussed. I took on the role of group leader from the beginning and relinquished leadership when someone was more qualified.

I also found that 15 minutes a day made a difference in the quality of my work and how well I absorbed what was being taught. I could spend 15 minutes looking over notes or making notes, reading an article, or journaling ideas on the topic I was working on. Fifteen minutes often turned into hours, but the act of picking up and moving made a difference. I found that 15 minutes moved me to action and that I did not need to have a set time to do it. Not having a set time was important because I had to steal minutes wherever I could find them. It might have been first thing in the morning or waking up in the middle of the night because something popped into my head. The consistency came in the minimum number of minutes, and using more minutes was even better.

Someone had to handle mundane tasks for me. This ended up being my wife, son, and older brother, who took on sorting mail and gave me a kick in the butt to write or finish my projects or homework. The support they gave me kept me going when I didn't think I had it in me. Regardless, I still needed a reward system.

I created a reward system for completing projects or for reaching the end of a quarter. I made an appointment with the chiropractor to straighten out my back after being hunched over my keyboard. I also turned off my phone, TV, and Internet so I could enjoy some time away from technology. This was important because I started getting headaches while writing, so spending a day away from technology felt great. Then I spent a little time finding a creative outlet.

Despite all the course work, I found time for other passions in my life. I found creating a podcast not only filled a need to be creative but also an avenue or platform for my scholarly work. I learned a new skill in podcasting and the Web content management software WordPress. I started dabbling in it because people always asked what I would do after I finish my PhD. I decided that writing and speaking were passions I wanted to pursue before I began my PhD, so why not afterward.

I didn't have any major challenges during the course work; instead they started cropping up while working on the dissertation proposal. I had just finished my master's degree online through DeVry University, so I was used to online classes and had no difficulty getting through them. I had good balance between my job, schoolwork, and family. Therefore, I didn't have to make any adjustments. As I stated earlier, all my greatest challenges came during the self-directed part of the PhD program, and I thought I had good practices going into the proposal/dissertation process.

I saved all my course work and catalogued it for future ideas or inspiration for my dissertation. I had done all my course work and projects with my dissertation in mind; even though my topic changed, the foundation for it was based on my earlier works. I had to work around a strange work schedule, and I created a system that worked for me. I found time in the day to do work by taking 15 minutes here and there, working through lunch, and pulling some all-nighters when needed.

Most important, I found a way to create a support team within an online class. I made a note of the instructors who influenced me the most and built a relationship when it came to picking a mentor. Then I looked at the discussion threads to see which students were interested in creating a support group and we planned to meet at residencies. Next, I selected who I thought were high achievers who wanted to succeed and created interactions to build study or project groups as the core while including those who were as lost as I was. Through Skype and other media, we collaborated or just talk about ordinary things and built our own peer mentoring system.

Challenges and Setbacks Experienced in the Proposal/Dissertation Process

Challenges

Just when I entered the proposal phase of the dissertation, I lost my job due to lay-offs. I figured I would go on unemployment, look for a job, and work on my dissertation at night, just like I did during my course work. However, because I was enrolled in school, unemployment didn't pay any benefits, and once that was straightened out with the help of a judge, unemployment claimed that I hit my maximum benefits of $10,000 when they had only paid me $413. The situation was frustrating and stressful, my job search was not getting any results, and depression started kicking in when I felt that I wasn't wanted. This resulted in a period of self-doubt and procrastination because I have a tendency to overthink the writing process. All my problems arose because I allowed life to take advantage of me to the point that depression affected me, and I entered periods of inactivity, which lead me to become unorganized.

Staying in school with little or no income really hit me hard. Because my life was disorganized, I was not getting anything done. I had no structure laid out during my course work. I shut down at one point because I couldn't see the light at the end of the tunnel. I found myself scrambling to get things done. I had a feeling that no one cared if I existed, especially at Walden, because the school got my money every quarter. I found my feelings were false because of a program my mentor created.

Adjustments

One adjustment provided by my mentor was a peer mentoring and cohort program that provided a sense of connectedness and belonging. This support system helped me get through all my knowledge area modules and the dissertation process. We had weekly calls that provided accountability and we talked about our progress, which ended my procrastination. When procrastination appears, all I have to do is text, e-mail, or call one of my peers or my mentor to regroup and keep moving. Then my finances started to work themselves out.

Living on what little income I could scrape together and student loan monies, my family is surviving. I am grateful that it is only my wife and keeping a roof over our heads that I have to worry about; my son is grown and has a job, which I found very discouraging. I have stress about going on Medicaid because I have never had to rely on the government for anything and I stubbornly surrender. I even began selling healthy coffee, which hasn't paid off yet, even though I've made some money at it.

I overcame the grieving process over the loss of my job by improving my technology skills, creating a podcast, and rejoining Toastmasters to network and to improve my public speaking skills. When I couldn't write scholarly enough, I would write something else like fiction or a screenplay. I forced myself to get up every morning by 6 a.m. to work out and to get to work on writing by 8 a.m. This created a new self-directed work ethic, and I worked on my proposal, blog, and podcast; sold coffee; and looked for work. I even created a perfect week by charting activities I had to do and stuck to it.

I had to incorporate technology and organize my workspace for better workflow. I had to rely heavily on technology because I didn't have the physical space to spread out. I kept two dissertation journals: one in a paper notebook and one in a program called Evernote, which I installed on my cell phone, laptop, and desktop to access from any computer with an Internet connection. Another technology that I used was Dropbox, which allowed me to access my dissertation, presentations, articles collected to read, and any other files I needed access to no matter where I was. This became a huge advantage for me because I never knew where I could get to work, whether it was a library, at home, in my car, at a coffee shop, or at school.

To overcome a lack of connectedness, I reached out to some local PhD students in my area, and we met a couple of times a month. We also would support each other through text messages, e-mails, and phone calls. I volunteered to be a peer mentor and lead cohort calls for our PhD online class. I also made sure that I connected with my mentor, peer mentor, and other students regularly. With their encouragement and support, I was able to get back on task.

Another way I dealt with issues of connectedness was to start a podcast to connect to an audience that wasn't there through a virtual cohort. Since I started leading the cohort group and became a peer mentor, I no longer do my podcast, but I want to start it up again or start a new one because I liked it. Just talking about the dissertation process to my microphone helped me get back on task by keeping it in the forefront of my mind. I'm in the process of reinventing the podcast to transcend and include my research, the journey, and beyond.

Having a plan to accomplish the dissertation was a huge help to get back on task. My dissertation chair and mentor helped me design a plan that would help me finish. I taped this plan to the wall. I did go through times when I didn't stick to it because I let life get in my way. A call or e-mail to my mentor, working with my cohort group, and looking at the plan always put me back on track. Being a slow writer didn't help.

Because I am not a fast writer, but I am very hard on myself, sticking to the plan was difficult, and I had to learn to get out of my own way. One way I did this was to take a 30-day mental challenge that forced me to read dissertations, write anything, including a blog, and work on personal development. I found it necessary to get back on track by reevaluating why I was getting my PhD and how I wanted to get to the finish line.

Looking for work kept me from staying on task not only because of the time it takes to find a job but also because I felt depressed when I felt that no one wanted me or my skills. To overcome depression, I borrowed money to get through not receiving money from unemployment. I started a small home-based business that is slowly starting to pay off. Finally, I decided to treat my dissertation like a job by setting my alarm to get up, go to the gym, get dressed, and go to work by 8 a.m. every day. This simple exercise got me working when I didn't feel like it.

The three greatest lessons I learned were not to overthink the process, to get well organized, and to reach out to others in the same situation for support. When I overthought the process, I fell into writer's block, which caused me to fall behind. By sticking to the rubric and the dissertation checklist, I was able to work more efficiently. Getting organized was important too.

Organization was key to staying on task, and getting organized was the most important lesson I learned. I was working on many computers in different locations, working between digital and nondigital information, and did not have a permanent place to stay organized. I learned to use technology to my advantage by using Dropbox for storage,

Evernote for journaling my information, and Excel for tracking my articles. I also found that being scattered caused me to overthink the process because I was lost in so much information.

I learned not to overthink the process or life itself. By getting out of my own way mentally, I was able to have more clarity of thought and vision for my proposal. By sticking to the dissertation rubric and the dissertation checklist, I was able to write more efficiently and effectively. I also learned not to reinvent the wheel, which meant following the plan, not rewriting it, and embracing it.

I highly recommend using Skype to connect with mentors, peers, or cohort team members for accountability, brainstorming, and interactions (connectedness) and recording the conversation when needed. This will be helpful for doing phone interviews for my study after my proposal is approved. To take notes from any computer or mobile device, I suggest Evernote. I like Dropbox for accessibility to work on various technologies while keeping all my work current. I recommend Microsoft Excel for tracking journals and citations for the dissertation or other research.

I recommend three books. The first one is a must-have in your library. *Dissertation and Scholarly Research: Recipes for Success* (Simon & Goes, 2013) laid the foundation for my dissertation process and contains step-by-step instructions on the structure of writing your dissertation. I refer to this book frequently and have it handy on the shelf where I write. The next book takes a different approach.

The second book I recommend focuses more on the writing process. *Writing Your Dissertation in Fifteen Minutes a Day* (Bolker, 1998) is more about sticking to writing and actually finishing your dissertation. Bolker (1998) suggested breaking up the task of writing into 15-minute intervals and provided tips on how to get through writer's block while building stamina to write. This book was given to me by my family, which demonstrated their supported for my PhD journey. The last book complemented the other two books.

The last book I recommend is *The Dissertation Journey: A Practical and Comprehensive Guide to Planning, Writing, and Defending Your Dissertation* (Roberts, 2010). This book has been helpful for getting through the proposal phase and has great tips on defending your dissertation. I particularly liked how the book complemented the other two by including a step-by-step approach to the dissertation process and adding tips for the actual writing process. None of these books prepared me for barriers that prevented me from making progress.

Several experiences kept me from making progress in the doctoral process. The first was a feeling of not being connected to other students, my mentor, or my institution. I somehow slipped through the cracks, and the mentoring I received for the course part of my program was nonexistent. When I was about to complete my courses, another student asked who my mentor was, and I just shrugged my shoulders because I didn't know. This was discouraging because when I finally selected a mentor, my mentor was shocked that I had no idea of what was going on. It took several weeks to become acclimated to the mentoring process, which led to other issues.

Another problem I experienced was overthinking the process. I had a fear of being perfect and thought very hard on a problem to the point of distraction. I was trying so hard to be perfect that getting distracted came easily and led to procrastination. As with creative writing and screenwriting, I had to learn that it was okay to make mistakes. That's what editors are for. I had to get out of my own way by allowing myself to make mistakes and keep moving. I still deal with this problem, and I am getting better.

Finally, not being connected brought my progress to a halt. My mentor created a peer and cohort system that skyrocketed my progress and then ended those sessions for various reasons. I felt lost and alone, as though no one cared whether I existed or not, which made me shut down. Accountability and fellowship made sharing my progress and pitfalls more manageable. I had to get creative to get over that by creating a podcast and blogging; no one listened or followed, but I felt connected to a virtual support group.

Peer mentoring was great for accountability. The peer mentor program was invaluable to me because I could connect with a student having some of the same issues I was experiencing. This buddy system made me feel connected, as though someone cared enough to listen and be there for me. I was also grateful that I had the opportunity as a peer mentor to help by sharing other students' trials and tribulations and making a difference in their experience.

The cohort model brought a new dimension to peer mentoring by having a group of peers support each other. The cohort model created a system for feedback and support, a sense of connectedness with other students, and a community of like-mined people with the same goal: graduating. The cohort members shared their best practices for getting through various stages of the dissertation, as well as sharing the responsibility of leadership. We created a community of scholar-practitioners with a goal of cooperative learning.

References

Bolker, J. (2010). *Writing your dissertation in fifteen minutes a day: A guide to starting, revising, and finishing your doctoral thesis.* New York, NY: Henry Holt.

Roberts, C. (2010). *The dissertation journey: A practical and comprehensive guide to planning, writing, and defending your dissertation* (2nd ed.). Thousand Oaks, CA: Corwin Press.

Simon, M. K., & Goes, J. (2013). *Dissertation and scholarly research: Recipes for success.* Cottage Grove, OR: Dissertation Success.

9
Tom Butkiewicz, PhD

Adjunct Professor and Operations Manager

Saint Francis of Assisi wrote, "Start by doing what's necessary; then what's possible; and suddenly you are doing the impossible."
—*Catholic Encyclopedia, 1909, p. 221*

The quote by Saint Francis of Assisi is my favorite because creating the future is a challenging task, but it can become clear when I think of the diverse possibilities when a doctoral learner goes beyond what is possible for change. Doctoral learners have unprecedented opportunities to create their future by establishing a new brand, scholarly identity, value, and worth to affect social change positively (Chiang, 2011). Pursuing a PhD embodies a major life change for doctoral students because it is a particularly demanding and challenging process.

Students start their doctoral program anticipating their success, but only those who are willing to pay the price and do what is required are able to finish. My mother had passed away before I embarked on a journey toward a doctoral degree. She is an inspiration beaming from heaven and her belief in me keeps me motivated to reach my lifelong dream of earning a PhD. Creating intrinsic motivation from the heart is essential to completing this doctoral journey. The real gauge of success is the ratio between what we might have been and what we have become (Stubb, Pyhältö, & Lonka, 2012). My second inspiration to earn a PhD is the process of discovery to challenge my intellectual limits by conducting research, teaching, and consulting. The outcome is multifaceted, with a focus on making a positive impact on social change. Approaching the dissertation journey with inspiration, motivation, and a can-do attitude equips students with the skills needed to earn a doctoral degree.

Orienting yourself to the doctoral experience and preparing for the journey necessitates several best practices. My doctoral learner best practices include commitment, perseverance, endurance, a positive mental attitude, and courage. Doing what is necessary to achieve a goal requires commitment (Brew, Boud, & Sang Un, 2011). I made a promise to myself, and my mother, to persevere in the doctoral journey, despite the obstacles along the way. Doctoral learners must proceed resolutely despite obstacles, criticism, and fears and must overcome disappointment. Relentless hours of work are essential over a long period. High achievement is dependent on the desire and perseverance to withstand the extra effort needed to become a PhD. Thus, doctoral learners must recognize the potential difficulties when trying to balance their big-picture goals with the stresses of working full-time and family obligations. Having a positive mental attitude is paramount for success in life. Therefore, it is important to avoid deficit-based thinking and negative self-talk to achieve the high level of performance required of doctoral learners. Facing fears and anxieties takes courage in preparing for a doctoral journey. I found that being honest about self-doubt and worry involves courage. Sharing fears and anxieties with family members goes a long way toward bringing out the courage that sustains the most fearful.

Learning the fundamentals of research was my primary motivation for successfully completing course work in a doctoral program. The learning process can be challenging at the beginning of each course because it is difficult to predict how long it will take to understand certain lessons (Lahenius & Martinsuo, 2010). Maximizing my productivity for completing all course work involved effective time management. Getting and staying organized are important skills for doctoral learners. The first best practice for completing the course work was to have a systematic plan for organizing assignment deadlines. The next step was to identify the time of day and location that was most conducive for reading and writing productively. Focusing on the outcome enabled me to complete each assignment and submit it by the deadline. The course assignments in a doctoral program require time to be strategically scheduled while balancing work and family responsibilities. The positive result was a culminating experience that prepared me to take the next step in the doctoral journey.

Writer's block was my biggest challenge for completing course work. I often found myself longing to be doing other activities instead of being in front of the computer. Everything else in my life seemed to take control as an escape from writing to avoid being discouraged, depressed, or frustrated. My emotions were predictable, knowing that my course work writing must be at the doctoral level. I had to identify the obstacles that stifled my writing. Immediate action was needed because negative feelings are immobilizing, drain energy, and keep doctoral learners from completing their course work. Riding my bike and taking my dogs for a walk were necessary adjustments for getting back on task. Most adult learners will agree that it is easier to revise than to create because writing is a complex process (Gazzola, DeStefano, Audet, & Theriault, 2011). The increased effort put into completing course work resulted in greater pride and accomplishments. The achievements during the doctoral journey that are worthy of acknowledgment and reward should be celebrated as they occur. Having dinner out with family and friends was an efficient way to commemorate course work successes. The celebrations made the difficult times more bearable.

Making the transition from course work to the proposal/dissertation process required knowing what I wanted and why I wanted it and a willingness to make sacrifices and overcome obstacles. Doctoral programs require a tremendous amount of hard work and have high demands and expectations from doctoral learners (Tweedie, Clark, Johnson, & Kay, 2013). Best practices for making the adventure-filled transition encompass a change in personal brand that consisted of being distinct, authentic, and deliverable for social change. My personal approach to branding required the highest level of honesty coupled with demonstrable knowledge transfer to others. The outcome is for individuals to know who I am, what I do, and why I do it. People would make the connection to my personal brand as being passionate, honest, and driven. My personal brand has an emotional connection because it transformed my life and will contribute to the lives of others as a scholar-practitioner. I found the proposal/dissertation process filled with valuable learning and discoveries about myself, others, and my field of interest.

The challenges and setbacks experienced in the proposal/dissertation process were the result of a lack of appropriate support from faculty chairs and committee members. Not receiving proper feedback at the concept paper phase caused significant delays without making progress in the doctoral program. Doctoral learners need to be aware of their strengths to build on them, and similarly they need to acknowledge opportunities for development to address them and therefore become more successful (Can & Walker, 2011; Hopwood, 2010). Long-term success is affected by how doctoral learners respond to their challenges and setbacks. The other challenge was the financial impact because of the tuition required for additional courses to continue in the doctoral program even though no progress was made for 2 years. The result was an excessive time and financial hardship for my family and me. The negative impact also delayed the transition from a corporate business manager to a scholar-practitioner in my career.

Effective faculty chairs are scholars who have achieved their doctoral degree. Faculty chairs possess the wisdom of experience, know the terrain, and can assess the abilities and limitations of doctoral students. Effective faculty chairs also offer encouragement and share what must be done to earn a PhD (Bullock & Ritter, 2011; Simon & Goes, 2013). Overcoming the challenges and setbacks to get back on task required entry into the Ombudsman's Program. Dr. Walter McCollum agreed to be my faculty chair in June 2013. The personal burden of not making any progress in my doctoral program for 2 years seemed to be eliminated after meeting with Dr. McCollum. I knew entering into the Ombudsman's Program was a blessing after receiving my new faculty chair's letter of introduction. The blessing was reaffirmed after speaking with Dr. McCollum. The discussion between Dr. McCollum and me set the stage for a nurturing relationship that was clearly dependent on meeting high standards. I have made considerable progress in the dissertation process under the leadership of Dr. McCollum, and he has shepherded me through roadblocks and acknowledged excellent work. Providing weekly updates was my duty as a doctoral learner, as producing a high-quality dissertation reflects not only my scholarship but also that of both Dr. McCollum as my faculty chair and Northcentral University.

Organization and planning are the greatest lessons learned in the proposal/dissertation process. Working hard was not enough because working smart was paramount. Most doctoral learners would agree that working smart means organizing a place conducive to writing (Bullock & Ritter, 2011; Chiang, 2011). Working smart also requires developing a time schedule consistently adhered to even when there was a lack of inspiration. Knowing the peaks and ebbs of my energy patterns was also a fundamental routine for getting through the challenging proposal/dissertation process. Dr. McCollum, my faculty chair, introduced me to the powerful concept of *organizing from the inside out* as a way to work smart (Morgenstern, 1998). Mastering strategies for removing obstacles to become organized allowed me to focus on who I am and what is crucial on the path toward graduation. Effective organization forced me to see the big picture, not just a piece of the frame, so that the planned system was finished.

The learners' portal available at Northcentral University has a plethora of books, technology, and resources as tools for completing the course work, proposal, and dissertation. For instance, the dissertation center includes dissertations from doctoral learners who completed the process and graduated. A best practice for learning the dissertation landscape is to become familiar with dissertations in your field of study. Understanding the format and style of approved dissertations offers doctoral learners insight into the academic level of scholarship. No previous writing experiences prepare doctoral learners for such a challenging and rigorous task. *Dissertation & Scholarly Research: Recipes for Success* (Simon & Goes, 2013) is widely accepted by academic scholars and doctoral learners as a valuable resource for finishing a dissertation. *Organizing From the Inside Out* by Morgenstern (1998) is another great resource for doctoral learners striving for their pinnacle of academic achievement. Dr. McCollum encouraged me to use the aforementioned books for diverse best practices that furthered my understanding of the fundamentals of research and to remove obstacles holding me back in the dissertation process. Using tools as best practices for completing the course work, proposal, and dissertation was critical for developing my scholarly identity. Having a detectable image requires being in a place that parallels academic superiority. An effective faculty chair guides doctoral learners so they see the total picture on their journey.

The general problem in the doctoral process that keeps learners from making progress in the program is the thought of writing a dissertation as a daunting task. Many doctoral learners are tempted to keep reading to avoid writing (Holley & Caldwell, 2012; Simon & Goes, 2013; Stubb et al., 2012). Breaking down the task of writing the dissertation one chapter at a time helped me to overcome my trepidations. I thought of each chapter within the dissertation as a unique paper.

Structuring paragraphs were a common writing problem until Dr. McCollum introduced the MEAL plan (main point, evidence, analysis, and a link sentence). Getting ideas on paper gets doctoral learners moving in the right direction, but perfectionists usually cringe about having to make revisions (Gazzola et al., 2011; Simon & Goes, 2013; Tweedie et al., 2013). I doubt that any doctoral learner, regardless of giftedness, can write an acceptable first draft of a concept paper, proposal, or manuscript. Accepting the fact that doctoral learners will be writing several drafts may help them alleviate some pressure in the dissertation process.

Peer mentoring provides both emotional and academic support in the doctoral process. Conducting research and writing a dissertation can bring about a sense of isolation for doctoral learners (Holley & Caldwell, 2012). Some doctoral learners may drop out of their program because they feel no one understands or cares about supporting them. Connecting with other doctoral learners is a valuable asset via peer mentoring for opportunities to support, empathize, and coach. For instance, peer mentoring often includes providing an ear to listen or even helping to lift the spirits of another doctoral learner. The faculty chair is always the appropriate person to consult with regarding the dissertation and university policies. Peer mentoring also can involve offering doctoral learners valuable insight from other doctoral learners who are further along in the dissertation journey, including those who have already graduated.

Doctoral learners need others who are affirming and supportive to achieve each milestone for a doctoral degree. Faculty chairs who create a viable cohort model in the dissertation process offer benefits to doctoral learners by helping them to develop personal goals, expectations, and working procedures through the dissertation process (Holley & Caldwell, 2012; Tweedie et al., 2013). Dr.

McCollum developed a playbook for each member in the cohort to establish time periods and completion dates for each dissertation activity. Another benefit within the cohort model is acknowledging dissertation successes when each milestone is achieved, which can fuel motivation in others in the cohort. The cohort model's strength is apparent when attending each other's oral defense for support while taking feedback notes. I anticipate cohort members become lifelong friends as scholar-practitioners who celebrate each other's successes, both personally and professionally, beyond the pinnacle dissertation journey.

References

Brew, A., Boud, D., & Sang Un, N. (2011). Influences on the formation of academics: The role of the doctorate and structured development opportunities. *Studies in Continuing Education, 33*, 51-66. doi:10.1080/0158037X.2010.515575

Bullock, S., & Ritter, J. K. (2011). Exploring the transition into academia through collaborative self-study. *Studying Teacher Education: Journal of Self-Study of Teacher Education Practices, 7*, 171-181. doi:10.1080/17425964.2011.591173

Can, G., & Walker, A. (2011). A model for doctoral students' perceptions and attitudes toward written feedback for academic writing. *Research in Higher Education, 52*, 508-536. doi:10.1007/s11162-010-9204-1

Chiang, K. (2011). The experience of doctoral studies in the UK and France: Differences in epistemology, research objects and training. *European Journal of Education, 46*, 257-270. doi:10.1111/j.1465-3435.2011.01480.x

Gazzola, N., DeStefano, J., Audet, C., & Theriault, A. (2011). Professional identity among counseling psychology doctoral students: A qualitative investigation. *Counseling Psychology Quarterly, 24*(4), 257-275. doi:10.1080/09515070.2011.630572

Holley, K., & Caldwell, M. (2012). The challenges of designing and implementing a doctoral student mentoring program. *Innovative Higher Education, 37*, 243-253. doi:10.1007/ s10755-011-9203-y

Hopwood, N. (2010). Doctoral experience and learning from a sociocultural perspective. *Studies in Higher Education, 35*, 829-843. doi:10.1080/03075070903348412

Lahenius, K. K., & Martinsuo, M. M. (2010). Personal study planning in doctoral education in industrial engineering. *European Journal of Engineering Education, 35*, 607-618. doi:10.1080/03043797.2010.500719

Morgenstern, J. (1998). *Organizing from the inside out.* New York, NY: Holt.

Saints. (1909). *Catholic encyclopedia.* New York, NY: Robert Appleton.

Simon, M. K., & Goes, J. (2013). *Dissertation & scholarly research: Recipes for success.* Lexington, KY: Dissertation Success.

Stubb, J., Pyhältö, K., & Lonka, K. (2012). The experienced meaning of working with a PhD thesis. *Scandinavian Journal of Educational Research, 56,* 439-456. doi:10.1080/00313831.2011.599422

Tweedie, M., Clark, S., Johnson, R. C., & Kay, D. (2013). The 'dissertation marathon' in doctoral distance education. *Distance Education, 34,* 379-390. doi:10.1080/1587919.2013.835778

10
William Dzekashu, PhD

Argosy University, Faculty

To be absolutely certain about something, one must know everything or nothing about it.
—*Olin Miller*

My doctoral experience was mixed with emotions of fear, uncertainty, sometimes lack of confidence, and a strong commitment to my faith. I was raised as a Roman Catholic and have African roots. This background forms my personality. To traverse the thorny doctoral path, I relied on support from several sources for inspiration. Because of its complexity, I elevated the doctoral path to a spiritual journey in my mind and accordingly it required team efforts (Nelson, 2009). I needed family support, academic advising, and spiritual guidance. My relationship with my mentor was successful. He encouraged me to look beyond what was obvious. I looked back and recalled advice received from elders around me in my youth and went to church on Sundays to fulfill my religious and spiritual obligations. The doctoral process was an interesting page of my life.

While I pursued my master of business administration, one of my professors—the associate dean of the business school found my work to be advanced and encouraged me to pursue a doctoral degree upon completion of the graduate program. This sounded rather flattering to me as a second-generation immigrant to the United States, and this built in me a drive that quickly turned to a dream. However, the resources to pursue such a venture were limited. As I was an international student who depended on my parents' financial support of my academic pursuits, this was not going to be possible because other siblings also needed to be educated. After I obtained a modest paying job, I determined that I could turn that dream to a reality. My goal was to attain the highest degree achieved within my family circles or to surpass it. This goal was certainly realized when I became the first holder of a research doctoral degree in my family.

Teenagers and adolescents generally do not possess the maturity to make certain decisions about their lives and future and hence rely on their parents and school instructors for directions and advice. This contrasts with adult learners, whose decision to seek advanced academic pursuits is mostly borne of the need to succeed. Success in this context is not limited to financial empowerment, career improvement, and prestige, but includes an intrinsic need to be able to affect lives, contribute to social change, and add to the existing body of knowledge. Ego development theory, as expounded by Loevinger (1976), describes the steps in behavioral maturity as individuals who develop from manipulative, self-protective behaviors to an integrated understanding of the self in relation to the environment. This is a higher level of consciousness when individuals are expected to be responsible for their own actions and decisions. If the ego is a holistic construct representing the fundamental structural unity of personality (Loevinger, 1976), then mature persons make decisions as a total of their whole or their ego. According to Shirkani (2003) some leaders excel technically but fail when it comes to interpersonal skills due to inflated ego.

The Dissertation as a Culmination of Doctoral Studies

A dissertation confirms a candidate's ability to research a major intellectual problem and arrive at a conclusion independently and the ability to construct an original contribution to a field of knowledge (Council of

Graduate Schools, 1991). The dissertation is an invaluable evaluative tool that encourages students to become active and self-directed in their learning (Barratt, 2004). Although many students who failed to complete the dissertation process have used the all-but-dissertation designation, McAloon (2004) described it as a "special status—an incomplete, deficient state of 'perpetual becoming,' not of 'being,' a condition unconsciously used to torment the self and others, characterized by unrealized promise and a dogged inability or unwillingness to complete this final academic hurdle" (p. 229); such failure is usually due to lack of guidance. Many doctoral students deem the dissertation as a task that is larger than life, which is one of many reasons that researchers have identified as a barrier to dissertation completion (Flynn, Chasek, Harper, Murphy, & Jorgensen, 2012).

The Doctoral Study and the Mentor

The history of doctoral learning confirms the role of dissertation advisers as being critical to the completion of research projects and the preparation of students for the role of instructor (Katz, 1997). Over time, the nomenclature of this role has mutated from project assistant, dissertation advisor, or chair to mentor. Whatever the appellation, such is the key player who guides and supports the academic pursuits of another to ensure completion. Many studies in the area of counselor education have explored how mentoring future researchers (Briggs & Pehrsson, 2008) and doctoral student experiences (Hoskins & Goldberg, 2005; Protivnak & Foss, 2009) contribute to this discussion. In a complex world, decisions about the pursuit of advanced degrees are made very seldom by individuals but mostly through recommendations of instructors.

To avoid feeling a sense of isolation as I progressed in both my doctoral studies and my dissertation (Katz, 1997), I sought the support of a mentor turned dissertation chair and research collaborator. This mentor helped me build a network of mentee collaborators—a great resource I still connect with. Using the resources provided by the school is not always enough; hence, the mentor assigned to me by the institution set up cohort mentorship programs within his structure of mentees to complement this support. Mentoring is the most appealing method of knowledge transfer because people learn shared experiences from experts who act as coaches and provide assistance in career development (Dzekashu, 2009). This mentorship structure is considered the management system for doctoral students who are completing course work, preparing for research, developing a prospectus and proposal, and defending the dissertation (Katz, 1997). System in this context should be viewed as an "attempt to bring a methodology that can unify the sciences" (McCollum, 2004, p. 22).

Several studies have identified dissertation advising as crucial for effectiveness, timeliness, and completion (Council of Graduate Schools, 2010; Protivnak & Foss, 2009). The role of a mentor is to be a leader, a counselor, and an adviser to doctoral students. In order to be effective, the adviser must have the ability to solve complete social and technical problems (Mumford, Zaccaro, Harding, Jacobs, & Fleishman, 2000).

In order to maintain a balance between work life and studies, I had to work weeks ahead on assignments and also prepared for lessons ahead of time. This was not an easy task. My wife was also pursuing a doctoral program, and we had a baby just before the end of my second quarter. The burden (financial and otherwise) of child care was unbearable, but there was only one option: staying the course. My circumstances were my real challenge. To stay the course of completing my studies, and to manage all the emotions of fear of failure and uncertainty, I relied on faith (my spirituality) and lessons from my cultural background.

However, recommending faith without action would be bad advice to give to doctoral students.

Charting out a course completion outline called a Program of Study (POS) and a Personal Development Plan (PDP) was a very engaging exercise that helped me stay focused. The PDP, though aimed at charting a career path and which I am still following today as a career roadmap, was also important in helping me stay engaged in both my course work and my dissertation process. The POS is a more appropriate item of discussion in the context of conducting a doctoral-level study.

The POS outlined all the different courses required for program completion, including residency requirements, research projects, planned term of enrollment, assigned credits, and grades earned (see figure above). The POS was my checklist, and I used color codes to denote required courses, courses to be taken the next term, courses currently enrolled in, and courses successfully completed. This document helped me measure my progress and doubled as a checklist.

Challenges and Recommendations to Overcome:

The national doctoral attrition rate has stayed between 50% and 80% for several years (Council of Graduate Schools, 2010; DiPierro, 2007). The inability to complete the process is the result of several challenges in the doctoral process, including a lack of good program advisers. Flynn et al. (2012) described the impact of the environment on the ability of doctoral students to stay motivated throughout the dissertation process. Academic pursuits require a certain level of comfort to ensure success. The dissertation process, which begins with the development of the prospectus and proposal, must adhere to certain ethical requirements. Even though I was able to complete my course work in record time, I faced several challenges. Descriptions of a few challenges follow, along with recommendations for overcoming them.

To complete my course work, I found that it was important to have my assigned course textbooks ahead of time. Having the books several weeks prior to the start of the class gave me the opportunity to jump-start the reading of the course material from which I was able to gain an idea of the course content. I used several materials that guided me through the proposal and dissertation, including books that described the dissertation process in detail. One notable book recommended to me by my mentor and committee chair was *Dissertation and Scholarly Research: Recipes for Success—A Practical Guide to Start and Complete Your Dissertation, Thesis, or Formal Research Project* by Marilyn K. Simon. This handbook is loaded with details on how to plan and execute a research project. To save time, I used Endnote referencing and citation software with add-on capability to Microsoft Office Word. This software helped me save articles that had been read or reviewed and were used as references cited in my works. Other resources used included the county public library, university digital libraries, and other local libraries.

My university provided great support to learners by way of academic advising on program requirements, course requirements, and online support. As a new student in the virtual environment, I found it difficult to find information that could lead to successful completion of the program. Academic advisors, faculty mentors, and technology support staff were generally available to facilitate or help me navigate through the program. These support points helped to reduce my concerns through communication. During residency sessions, active participation in conferences and symposia helped me adjust to the course work and task completion requirements. I attended my first residency during the second quarter of my program, which was one of the most valuable decisions I made during my doctoral studies. I was advised to think about my dissertation topic and to tailor most of my essay projects toward that topic as a way of gaining writing synergies. This strategy worked well for me, as it helped me build the literature review of my dissertation in record time.

    The time that I lost when I was unable to obtain a letter of cooperation from the prospective company I selected to participant in my research was used valuably in designing my research process and execution. I had quickly learned that the quality of the research depended greatly on the design and on ethical considerations. It was important that I stayed in contact with my committee to ensure the number of reviews and return comments remained small. Thinking positively is usually the first step to achieving your goals, and it might help to know that most researchers have faced and overcome difficulties such as the one you are currently facing. The challenges encountered can be overcome if your mentor can guide you through the process and the content of the program. Mentors usually have knowledge of both the content and the context in terms of processes and tasks required for program completion. Some of the challenges I experienced during my study included my course work and my dissertation. Recommendations on how to tackle them to ensure successful completion of the course work and dissertation include the following:

1. The fact that the pursuit was virtual rather than in a traditional classroom setting (except for residency requirements, where the symposia and conferences were face-to-face) posed some challenges for me. After the first two classes, I became comfortable with the online platform, which although asynchronous, required discipline in terms of engagement and time management. To overcome the strict milestones, I worked 2 to 3 weeks ahead of my classes.

2. My failure to secure a letter of cooperation from an organization where I intended to conduct my study was a major hurdle. The challenge led to the loss of valuable time, which in turn resulted in financial losses too. With the setback in obtaining a letter of cooperation, I was able to turn to my roots in Africa to seek an organization that fit my research objectives. The organization's management was thrilled to work with me in a mutual agreement in which I obtained a letter of cooperation and

they received an assessment of their workforce, tasks, processes, and technology.

3. It took me several terms to recognize that the fate of my success was more in my hands than within the control of the institution. Inasmuch as the culmination of the dissertation is a reflection of the quality of learning at the institution, it is the doctoral student's responsibility to recognize early on that he or she is in charge of the outcome of the study. To be successful, students need to be proactive rather than reactive.

4. Sometimes my dissertation appeared to suffer from scope creep as a result of my inability to stay focused. Conventional wisdom holds that the best dissertation is a done dissertation. To complete their dissertation, students are encouraged to narrow topics into manageable (interesting, relevant, defensible, and feasible) projects.

5. After I started the doctoral program, it appeared to be highly exposing and I felt a lack of self-confidence. Sometimes this concern was serious and led to anxieties that I felt could affect my ability to perform. Students can sometimes overcome such anxieties by

assessing their skill sets, recognizing incremental competencies, and seeking positive feedback for actions.

6. Time management is a critical part of any study; when it becomes an issue, you should spend some time planning, dedicating an appropriate length of time to tasks, and reviewing progress.

7. The doctoral studies environment can sometimes feel lonely. Overcoming this conundrum can be achieved by taking advantage of opportunities to build support networks. Ensure that you use all the key contacts appropriately and find out if the university offers mentoring programs. If this is not offered, reach out to senior researchers to seek some help and advice.

Feeling of Satisfaction and the New Anxiety

I was in a meeting at work when I received two e-mails on my Blackberry—one from my dissertation committee chair and the other from another committee member. The e-mails contained the dissertation approval from the institution and congratulatory messages to me for completing the dissertation process. For the first time, I was addressed as Dr. Dzekashu; it sure felt good. My dissertation had just been approved, but that was not all; I had to complete an exit survey, decide if I wanted my work published by ProQuest, request bound copies printed for me, and take a survey about whether I was interested in pursuing a postdoctoral fellowship. Sure, it had been a long road, but the dissertation committee and chair (mentor) had made it seem short and easy with their constant support along the way. It was very important for me that I be hooded by my mentor, who was there from the very beginning of the process. I have since published an article in the *International Journal of Applied Management and Technology (IJAMT)* and am working on completing my first book.

After completing your doctoral studies, you will find that you face new anxieties and challenges. The knowledge acquired during the study—content and process—should help you manage the new set of challenges. Some of the challenges may include finding your dream job in industry or academia, maintaining the writing skills acquired during the doctoral process (challenge with publishing), remaining relevant with the body of knowledge you have acquired, and garnering the confidence required to forge ahead. These all represent new sources of anxiety.

Conclusion

It continues to be a mystery that the more a person knows, the more that person finds that he or she doesn't know. This is an interesting paradox of knowledge. This nature of knowledge reveals humility in individuals and the continuous need for collaboration as a way of growing knowledge. I continue to maintain a close network with some of my cohorts and my mentor, who has continued to be a mentor in my life, even after graduation. Thanks to this relationship, I have been on dissertation committees as both a subject matter expert and a chair. This role and instruction continues to shape my identity as a scholar-practitioner. In this role, I am able to bring industry experience to the classroom and take theory back to the work environment. One of my greatest challenges since graduation has been my inability to assume a leadership role that would allow me to make a full impact on the organization's process improvements. The most important piece of advice I would like to leave doctoral learners with is to use every resource available, create synergies in all course work projects to shorten the dissertation process, and seek letters of cooperation early in the process. I would like to close my chapter by revealing that my academic mentor and life coach is none other than Dr. Walter McCollum!

References

Barratt, A. M. (2004). The dissertation: What sort of animal is it and how might it be better trained? *British Journal of Theological Education, 14*, 208-228.

Briggs, C. A., & Pehrsson, D. E. (2008). Research mentorship in counselor education. *Counselor Education & Supervision, 48,* 101-113.

Council of Graduate Schools. (1991). *Role and nature of doctoral dissertation.* Retrieved from ERIC database. (ED331422)

Council of Graduate Schools. (2010). Ph.D. completion project: Policies and practices to promote student success. Retrieved from http://phdcompletion.org/information/book4.asp

DiPierro, M. (2007). Excellence in doctoral education: Defining best practices. *College Student Journal, 41,* 368-375.

Dzekashu, W. (2011). *Integration of quality management into the tacit knowledge capture process* (Doctoral dissertation). Available from ProQuest Dissertations and Theses database. (UMI No. 3355037)

Flynn, S. V., Chasek, C. L., Harper, I. F., Murphy, K. M., & Jorgensen, M. F. (2012). A qualitative inquiry of the counseling dissertation process. *Counselor Education & Supervision, 51,* 242-255.

Hoskins, C. M., & Goldberg, A. D. (2005). Doctoral student persistence in counselor education programs: Student-program match. *Counselor Education and Supervision, 44,* 175-188.

Katz, E. L. (1997). Key players in the dissertation process. *New Directions for Higher Education, 99,* 5.

McAloon, R. F. (2004). Publish or perish: Writing blocks in dissertation writers—the ABD impasse. *Modern Psychoanalysis, 29,* 229-250.

McCollum, W. R. (2004). *Process improvement in quality management systems: A case study analyzing Carnegie Mellon's capability maturity model (CMM).* New Bern, NC: Trafford.

Mumford, M. D., Zaccaro, S. J., Jacobs, T. O., & Fleishman, E. A. (2000). Leadership skills for a changing world: Solving complex social problems. *Leadership Quarterly, 11,* 11-35.

Protivnak, J. J., & Foss, L. L. (2009). An exploration of themes that influence the counselor education doctoral student experience. *Counselor Education and Supervision, 48,* 239-256.

Nelson, A. E. (2009). Spiritual intelligence: Discover your SQ. Deepen your faith. *Publishers Weekly, 45,* 42-42.

Rockstuhl, T., Seiler, S., Ang, S., Van Dyne, L., & Annen, H. (2011). Beyond general intelligence (EQ): The role of cultural intelligence (CQ) on cross-border leadership effectiveness in a globalized world. *Journal of Social Issues, 4*, 825-840.

Shirkani, J. (2013). Ego vs. EQ: How top leaders beat 8 ego traps with emotional intelligence. *T+D, 12,* 67.

11
Markus Shelton, PhD

Cyber-security Engineer/Entrepreneur

For everyone to whom much is given, of him shall much be required.
—Luke 12:48

Ever since I began undergraduate college application process, my dream was to obtain the terminal degree in my field. Early in my life, my parents, Mr. James C. and Dr. Esther D. Shelton, instilled in me the intrinsic value of education. Both of my parents were educators. My mother earned a PhD from the University of Pennsylvania and taught students ranging from middle school to college, while my dad taught at the high school level. My parents raised me to understand that the pursuit of knowledge is a lifelong endeavor. Their high expectations and unwavering support helped encourage me to set high goals for myself. My parents' confidence in me provided me with the confidence that I needed to know that I was capable of reaching my goal of obtaining a PhD

When a good friend of mine, Dr. Anthony Waul, graduated with a PhD in 2007, I began to realize that obtaining a PhD was an attainable goal for me. Anthony and I were former classmates, and we graduated from University of Maryland at College Park's electrical engineering program together in 1997. Anthony was willing to share his experiences about matriculating through a PhD program. When Anthony explained the obstacles that he encountered during his PhD program and how he overcame them, he began to demystify the PhD process.

I knew that a PhD could help me improve my critical thinking, public speaking, writing, and research skills. A PhD would open up doors for me to teach courses at the university level. Also, a PhD could help differentiate me from other candidates as I serve as a scholar-practitioner and independent contractor in the field of cyber security. Finally, a PhD in applied management and decision science could help me develop the management skills that I needed to expand my cyber security practice. For all these reasons, I was inspired to earn a PhD degree.

I believe that one of the best practices for orienting yourself to the doctoral experience and preparing for the journey of earning a PhD is to make a major effort to improve your public speaking skills. One of the requirements of most doctoral programs is an oral defense of your proposal and dissertation. The more comfortable you are with presenting to your dissertation committee, the better chance you will have with being successful during your oral proposal and dissertation defenses. One approach for improving your presenting skills is to join public speaking associations like Toastmasters International. I joined Toastmasters, and it helped me become a more comfortable presenter.

You should begin to develop strong working relationships with the professors at your school. Doctoral learners should consider asking professors that they have a good working relationship with to join their dissertation committee. It is important to ensure that the professors you select to serve on your dissertation committee work well with one another. During the dissertation phase, you will need to apply many of the key principles you learn in the course work phase. For example, key ideas from statistics and key principles of quantitative and qualitative research will manifest themselves again during the dissertation phase.

Strong time management skills are critical to a students' success in a doctoral program. Many doctoral learners will matriculate through the program while simultaneously having career and family obligations. To improve your time management skills, understand when you are most productive. Some people are most effective in the morning, while others are most productive with their studies in the evenings. Dedicate your most productive hours to your studies. At the start of each week, block out time for your studies. Commit to making progress each day, even if you are only taking minor steps.

When you begin the dissertation process, reach out to your family and friends. Explain to them your desire to obtain a PhD. Let your support system know that obtaining a PhD is an extremely challenging endeavor that will require your total commitment. Make it clear that you may not be as accessible and responsive during the doctoral journey. It is important that you have the support of your family and friends when completing the PhD process.

During the course work phase of the program, develop a routine for when you perform the required reading and writing. Work on your assignments on a daily basis and participate as much as possible. After you have made your best attempt at figuring out the material, do not be reluctant to reach out to your professors with any questions. Participate in both individual and group study sessions.

During the course work phase of the doctoral program, I had difficulty finding time to complete the assignments and to perform the required reading because of my demanding family and work commitments. In some cases, my job required me to work long hours and travel frequently. To overcome this challenge, I woke up earlier than normal and dedicated the first 2 hours of each day to my studies. Additionally, I dedicated most weekends to my studies. I also formed a study group and did not hesitate to ask my professors questions when I needed further clarification on a specific topic.

When I transitioned from the course work phase to the dissertation phase of the process, I knew that there would be significant changes in what was required from me to be successful. The course work phase of the PhD process is more structured, while the dissertation phase relies on independent study. During the dissertation phase of the program, I had to set individual goals for myself at the start of each quarter. To reach the goals that I had set for myself each quarter, I divided the quarterly goals into monthly and weekly goals.

Thankfully, I was a member of Dr. Walter McCollum's cohort group during the dissertation phase. As a member of Dr. McCollum's cohort group, I listened intently to the cohort lead and those cohort members who were further along in the program than I was. I compiled a list of statisticians and editors other members of the cohort group had used and recommended. I interviewed those statisticians and editors and selected a statistician and editor I felt I would work best with.

In the proposal and dissertation phase of the program, my work responsibilities consumed the majority of my time. Early in the dissertation process, the contract that I was working on ended and I had to relocate. In addition to moving, the new contract opportunity that I identified required me to obtain additional industry certifications in cyber security. Because of the move and the requirement to obtain industry certifications, I could dedicate even less time to my educational goal. Even during the quarter that I had the least amount of time to dedicate to my studies, I kept my eye on my goal and continued to attend all the cohort meetings. Despite the fact that I could not reach the goals that I had set for myself that quarter, I still made every effort to make as much progress as I could.

I strongly recommend that doctoral learners entering the dissertation phase of the PhD process read Dr. Marilyn Simon's book *Dissertation and Scholarly Research: Recipes for Success*. I also recommend that PhD students investigate using the services of a professional editor. Students performing quantitative studies could also benefit from using a professional statistician. In many cases, students executing a qualitative study could benefit from transcription services. If offered, I would highly recommend attending a dissertation intensive residency.

I have witnessed several common problems that prevent doctoral learners from being able to make progress in their PhD program. First, some doctoral students expect that their completed dissertation will be a masterpiece. This can lead to students feeling extreme pressure to produce a work of art and can slow down their progress. It is important for doctoral students to realize that they have their entire career to dedicate to publishing articles on subjects that are close to their hearts. The purpose of the dissertation is to prove that you understand the research process and that you are capable of executing a research study.

In many cases, doctoral learners do not dedicate enough time to their studies. Another common problem that prevents doctoral learners from reaching their goals is that they do not have a good working relationship with their committee members. In other cases, doctoral learners do not take the advice of their dissertation chair. Sometimes a student's fear of making mistakes slows their progress. Many students encounter setbacks because they make significant structure changes to their study in the middle of their research. For example, students may change their methodology from a quantitative study to a qualitative study. In other cases, students may seek to develop their own instrument as opposed to using an existing instrument to measure a phenomenon under study. These types of changes made during the middle of the research effort will likely extend the time required to matriculate through the program.

I am a strong advocate of peer mentoring. I had the opportunity to be a member, co-leader, and leader of a cohort group for doctoral learners. I learned a lot from the leaders of my early cohort groups. As members of the cohort completed major milestones and got closer to graduation, it gave me inspiration to work hard to complete my goal. I listened to the obstacles that my peers further along in the program were experiencing and learned how they overcame those obstacles. When I encountered those obstacles firsthand, I was better suited to overcome them. When I finally had the opportunity to serve as the cohort leader, I felt honored to be able to share the knowledge that I had gained about the dissertation process from the cohort group with the new members of the cohort group. When I had the opportunity to lead the cohort group, I patterned myself after cohort leaders before me for whom I had a great deal of respect. The key to an effective peer mentoring group is a balanced give and take among the cohort members.

Many students' pursue a PhD to help them open up doors to teaching at the college level. Many of these students never have the opportunity to teach at the college level prior to graduating with a PhD. Leading the cohort group and having the opportunity to teach and mentor PhD students gave me the opportunity to begin to develop my teaching and mentoring skills and to have them evaluated and critiqued by Dr. McCollum.

Many students who are not in cohort groups do not remain in continuous communication with their dissertation chair. In many cases, students feel that they might be becoming a burden to their dissertation chair. In other cases, students fear that they may ask their dissertation chair a question that will reveal the fact that they are not progressing at the expected rate. As a result, the students avoid communicating with their dissertation chair. The cohort group is effective because it provides another support system for doctoral learners. In the cohort group, students can communicate with their peers in an open forum. The cohort group helps students feel a sense of community and keeps students feeling connected. For all these reasons, a cohort group is especially beneficial for students in an online program.

The cohort group was also an effective medium to allow current students to communicate with recent graduates of the program. Dr. McCollum arranged for recent graduates of the PhD program to serve as guest lecturers during cohort meetings. The recent graduates would often provide lessons learned from their transition to academia. These stories inspired me and were invaluable to my success. School leaders would be remiss if they did not investigate implementing cohort models.

I felt elated when my doctoral degree was conferred. When I was notified that I had met all the degree requirements, I realized that I had reached a major personal goal that I had set for myself. When I was notified that I had graduated from the PhD program, the joy felt like the culmination of 5 years of hard work and dedication. Knowing that I would be able to walk across the stage and have Dr. McCollum hood me made the challenging work that I encountered in the program, and the grueling process that I endured, all worth it.

When I walked across the stage to be hooded, I felt honored. I was relieved that I did not let my dissertation chair, Dr. McCollum, down. Dr. McCollum graciously agreed to allow me to participate in his cohort group, served as my dissertation chair, and invested in me as he guided my scholarly pursuits. During the interview process that Dr. McCollum required before joining his cohort group, I assured him that I would not squander the opportunity to join the cohort. When I realized that I had reached my goal, I was relieved to know that I had made the most of the opportunity. I also felt that I made my friends and family proud of me. Walking across the stage on graduation day in January 2014 so Dr. McCollum could hood me was exciting and memorable.

I have grown as a scholar-practitioner after going through such an intense research-based program. I learned more about research and the field of cyber security while matriculating through the program. In addition, I learned about the writing and the oral presentation process. I improved as a critical thinker and met invaluable contacts. Lastly, I set new goals as a result of this process. I now recognize that the journey has just begun as I enter the sea of scholars.

I have grown tremendously since becoming a doctor. I have realized that I am recognized as an expert in my field. I take that responsibility of being an expert seriously, and I feel obligated to obtain even more knowledge. As a result, I am in the process of obtaining additional certifications in the field of cyber security. I also feel more committed to positively impacting social change. As a result of obtaining a PhD, I have gained confidence and grown as a scholar-practitioner and a person.

Embracing my scholarly identity means recognizing my worth and being committed to positively impacting social change. In order to positively impact social change, I make an effort to help others achieve their goals. Embracing your scholarly identify means creating a brand as a scholar and practitioner. Embracing your scholarly identity also means that you must hold yourself to the highest ethical standards. Finally, embracing your scholarly identify means that you dedicate yourself to making contributions to the academic community.

Now that I have obtained the terminal degree in my field, I realize that I have contributed to the academic community. My greatest accomplishment after earning a doctoral degree has been taking on a managerial, client-facing security lead role. In fact, the day after my degree was conferred, I accepted the position. As a security lead, I moved away from a typical hands-on engineering or operational role and transitioned into a client-facing managerial role. In my current role, I keep the client's senior-level executives abreast regarding the state of security and help reduce risks in the environment. As a security lead, I benefit from the critical thinking, management, and presentation skills I developed in the PhD program.

After obtaining my PhD about 6 months ago and attending graduation only a few months ago, I am still in the process of integrating into the sea of scholars. I am actively applying for online teaching opportunities at the college level. I also plan to increase my involvement with professional organizations in my field, including the Institute of Electrical and Electronics Engineers (IEEE) and the National Society of Black Engineers (NSBE). I look forward to having the opportunity to come back to Dr. McCollum's cohort group and share my experiences about the dissertation process. I also look forward to presenting at conferences, writing books, and publishing articles. I have come to realize that after you complete a PhD, the journey just begins.

The most important piece of advice that I would offer to doctoral learners to help them be successful in both the doctoral process and after earning the doctoral degree is to follow your heart and dreams. It is critical that you understand what is important to you. Once you identify what is important to you, prioritize your goals accordingly. Next, develop a plan for achieving your goals. While executing your plan, don't let anything prevent you from putting in the work required for you to achieve your goals. If you are not successful at first, keep your eye on the prize, continue to execute your plan, and do not give up on your goal.

12
Gladwyn Sandiford, PhD

CEO/President, Joy and Gladness Children's Center

Life is a gift, and it offers us the privilege, opportunity, and responsibility to give something back by becoming more.
—Anthony Robbins

Many times as children, we play the part of a professional character. My imaginary friend was me playing the part of a medical doctor, a teacher, and sometimes a nurse. I just had the feeling that I would be a doctor one day. However, I thought that I would be a medical doctor. I did everything I could to prepare for medical school while working at a full-time job and taking care of my two sons. When the opportunity presented itself for me to go to medical school, I faced the decision of going to school full-time to achieve the goals of becoming a doctor or working on a nine-to-five job that gave me more time to spend with my two sons. My priority was being available to mentor my sons. I knew I could not accept going to school all day and working in the lab at nights, because I had to think about taking care of and financially supporting my sons. I opted for the closest thing I could do in the medical field, which was registered record administration.

As a registered record administrator, I would be able to work at my full-time job while attending classes in the evening, therefore making enough to maintain the family financially. I worked for a while in the hospital as a registered record administrator, supervising the medical record department by covering both the evening and the midnight shifts. The title of registered record administrator was later changed to health information management. I acquired a management position at the hospital while conducting my clinical residency there. However, I continued to feel as though something was missing and that I should continue with my education. Dr. Skeete, a good friend and a great surgeon who knew my potential, motivated me and inspired me to continuing my studies. He listed a number of medical professions he thought were right for me and recommended the best medical schools, but it was not until I focused on what I wanted to do that I found the energy to enroll in the doctoral program.

Challenges started for me approximately 6 months into the program. My mother became sick and I would travel every month to Barbados to see her. This went on for a while until she finally went home to glory. As soon as I picked my momentum up again, my brother became ill for a time, and he also died. I experienced many other challenges along the way; some I was able to share while others I could not. I literally had a conversation with myself, asking what was the point of pushing to get a doctoral degree. I had a secured government job and felt I was comfortable but deep within me I knew I had to complete what I had started. I knew my mom would have wanted that.

Spiritual inspiration and positive thinking were my daily practices of preparation for the doctoral experience and journey. I had to spiritually see myself in that place where I was able to manage a business, work a full-time job, continue working in many ministries of the church, be there for my family, and still work on doctoral studies. Starting a process is usually hard, especially if it is something new. My focus was not only how I started, but also how I channeled my attention on the finished product. I always kept my eyes on that light at the end of the tunnel. At times, it looked blurred, but I kept my focus. I knew that many before me had started the process and were content that they were all-but-dissertation (ABD) qualified. Those letters, although confusing to me, were also an inspiration to me. I could not see myself going three quarters of the way and then giving up. I also got strength when those I believed in or looked to for support told me that the work was tough but it was okay if I dropped out if I realized it was too much to handle. This was bad advice, but it made me more determines to complete my program.

I encouraged myself by talking to myself in songs and through the scriptures. I knew failure was not an option for me. I thought of and created a strategy for completing my course work. I could not give up going to church, because that was my refilling station. I did not want to give up working in the various ministries, but was able to do less work by delegating assignments to other members. I sacrificed some social activities and slept less, but allowed a little time for family. I kept a list of things to do as well as things I read or that other classmates said had helped them, which were their best practices. Working on these things and crossing them off my list felt as though I had obtained a great achievement. At times, I knew what I had to do, but I had to generate a plan on how to get it done. An alternate plan was good because the original plan didn't always worked effectively, and neither did the same plan work each day of the week, so I was my toughest critic.

Self-discipline can be very effective, but a plan must be in place. My main challenge in completing the course work was time. Initially during the course work, I had a feeling of being all alone or deserted. There was little interaction outside of the classroom unless we worked in groups, and there were many other personal setbacks with family sickness issues. Not knowing of anyone in my vicinity whom I could call on made it tough and lonely, but going to residencies, meeting other classmates, and exchanging contact and other information made the process much easier. I was also given written permission to exceed the amount of course credits to be taken during the quarter if I was sure I could handle the load. I did take extra credits for a few quarters after planning for and setting aside the time to complete my work.

The transition from course work to proposal writing was another challenge. To me, working on course work was synonymous with being a follower. There is a mandate for what has to be done and the time it should be done. It is easier to divert from the plan that is written, yet be able to complete the project by the due date or face consequences.

Working on the proposal/dissertation was more like taking on a leadership position. I had to establish my destination, plan how to get there and which tools to use, and then try to get there. I could see why people settled with being ABD, but knew that was not part of my genetic make-up. I had to complete my program. Many students are not fortunate enough to have a chair interested in their daily well-being and who established a cohort group as a recipe for their success, but I was fortunate to have that type of supervision in my mentor, Dr. Walter McCollum.

I first met Dr. McCollum by being assigned to his forum. I was struggling, but didn't want to ask anyone for help. I wanted to keep my struggles private. How silly was that? How could someone help me if they didn't know that I needed help? Dr. McCollum firmly let me know that if I wanted to stay in his cohort I had to get it together. I had to group with those who understood the process, and reach out to him so that he could help me. It was what I now call "tough love." I cried that night. I have said that Dr. McCollum is the first man who made me cry. I thought, how could he understand all the challenges and struggles I was going through without me telling him or confiding in him? Dr. McCollum sensed that I was experiencing something, but didn't know what. He told me he was going to a residency in Minneapolis, and that if I was going, I should look for him there. I went to the residency, met Dr. McCollum, and at first sight, we loved and embraced each other. He set me up to work with others who were progressing well. After joining and working with other students in Dr. McCollum's cohort group, I started to make progress. I still had other setbacks, and family sicknesses and deaths, but working with my chair, Dr. McCollum, and his appointed peer mentors, helped me make a smooth transition from my course work to my proposal and then my dissertation.

Proposal/dissertation writing is much different from writing done for course work. There is a formula that has to be followed. The guideline my school used was American Psychological Association (APA) style, which covers headings, punctuation, spacing, indentation, references, in-text citations, and many others writing elements. My setbacks were learning and following APA guidelines and making myself familiar with the expectations of my committee members. After learning what their requirements were, researching other work that they had approved, and reading books that they suggested, I was able to move on with my writing.

The greatest lesson learned in the proposal/dissertation process was that I was not trying to prove a theory. Someone had done a similar study before, so I would be able to find articles to use as references. Using other people's work without referencing the source is plagiarism, which can carry serious consequences. By talking to others in the cohort about the progress they had made and my expectations, in addition to being accountable to and for someone in the group, helped in making the dissertation journey so much easier. Connecting with my chair was most important, as he had taken that journey before and had led many others down the path to success. I knew that if I trusted him and followed his guidance, I too would become a success story.

Students can use many tools to complete the dissertation process. I strongly recommend using the APA's *Publication Manual* for writing and *Dissertation and Scholarly Research: Recipes for Success* by Marilyn K. Simon, which is a step-by-step guide to completing your dissertation. The recipes are outlined in her book, and are accompanied by a compact disc and a website. Creswell has many books on qualitative and quantitative research that outline the research process in a simple form. Students should also use the guidelines from their school as well as research dissertations that their committee members have already approved to get a sense of what their committee expects of them.

When students are not accountable for their work or their actions, disaster can result. Students may be stuck on some part of their work, but because they don't know who to reach out to, or they don't have a relationship with their chair or committee members, they just do nothing. Students cannot progress in their work by doing nothing and expecting positive results. Students confide in their committee members and student cohort leaders and can go into withdrawal when they feel confidentiality is breached. Students often get frustrated about the process, but it is normal to be frustrated because success usually follows frustration (Robbins, 1991). When individuals make a mistake, or the results are different from what they had expected, they often see the outcome as a failure. However, if they look at these outcomes as opportunities to do something better the second (or third or even fourth) time, they will see that what they called a failure was just success in progress.

Students learn differently, and they all come from different backgrounds and teachings. Students and teachers have different ideas about scholarly writing. Therefore, students need to learn their committee's expectations in addition to the styles or methods they learned in other programs or institutions. Just as students learn the positive from other students, they also learn the negative. Students often hear the dissertation process is difficult, and they come into the program already defeated, thinking they will have a difficult time. When students rush and take the course work without laying the foundation for the proposal/dissertation process, they may get stuck at the proposal stage because they do not understand the course work that should have prepared them for the proposal process. Students who grasp the content but not the process set themselves up for challenges or negative outcomes.

Peer mentoring in the doctoral process should be a requirement. Students can learn from peers who are passing on information that they experienced. Peer mentoring kept me in a positive mode and reminded me that I was not on the journey alone and that other colleagues were journeying with me. Family and friends who have not experienced the doctoral process may not be aware or understand that doctoral work can cause a person to go into seclusion for periods of time. Aligning oneself in a peer mentoring group brings cohesiveness, and students can talk and share with each other or with their mentor. Being able to send an e-mail or make a call to a colleague will help release some stress. The solution often presents itself after sharing thoughts with a colleague.

Cohort models work because there is greater support for the students. There is strength in numbers, and students learn from each other. Understanding from a peer's point of view can help clarify some questions for students. Cohort models allow students to take on the role of peer mentors, giving them the experience of both teaching and learning. Cohort models also allow students to become proficient in presenting before a group, which could help in preparation for their dissertation oral defense.

My doctoral degree was conferred in November 2013. When I received the e-mail confirming that I was finished and my degree was conferred, I screamed, jumped, and praised the Lord, because I knew then that the years of hard work, long nights, and seclusion from my friends and family had finally come to an end. I felt as though a weight had been lifted, and I was finally able to breathe. I was also in disbelief. I kept asking myself if I had really finished or if I was dreaming. I completed everything I was asked to complete and submitted. I bought my regalia, booked my room and flight, and traveled to Orlando, Florida, for the ceremony. I kept asking my friends if it was true that I had finished. I told them that I would believe it when I walked across the stage and Dr. McCollum hooded me. No matter how many mistakes I had made along the way, or how many negative outcomes I experienced, I knew I was ahead of those who stopped trying or who didn't make the effort to start. I had told myself that success was like a recipe, and if I followed it, I would have positive results. One of my pep talks was repeating a phrase I had heard that reminded me that if I found a successful person and followed his or her directions, I could also be successful. I knew I had listened to my chair, Dr. McCollum. I was doing everything he said to do. I knew he was a success story; therefore, I had no reason not to believe that I too could be a success. He had prepared me for that moment and had imparted something into my life for me to remember the rest of my life.

As I walked toward the stage, I wanted only to see my chair. Seeing him took away all fear, and I was nervously excited. Involuntarily, my hands went up and I started to praise God, I knew it was official when my name was called. It reminded me that after my hard work here on Earth is all done, I again expect to hear my name called. At that time, my chair will not be Dr. McCollum hooding me, but my chair will be my Lord and savior Jesus Christ, who will be crowning me. I expect to hear, *Well done, good and faithful servant.*

Since going through the intense research-based program, I have received offers to teach academically but have been unable to accept any new positions. I have grown in self-confidence, my public speaking has improved, and I have conducted a number of workshops to encourage and promote education. In addition to being CEO of one organization, I am now chairwoman of a United States–Caribbean initiative corporation. I am a model for students who came from a home with a single parent, a model of a single mother, a person who believes she can accomplish anything she sets her mind to do, knowing that "I can do all things through Christ which strengthens me" (Philippians 4:13, Kings James Version). My mother was not a mentor academically for me, but she was a spiritual mentor and taught me to believe in myself. She taught me that I was doing it not only for me but for those around me and those who would hear my story. I didn't understand what she meant at the time, but it has since been revealed to me. I have become the person my mother taught me to be. I am now encouraging friends and others who I meet about the value of an education and a life spent trusting God to see me through. No one can take your education away from you.

Since becoming a doctor, my goal has been to continue embracing my scholarly identity by making it possible for someone or some community to also acquire an education. My work is not complete, but I must continue to affect positive social change working with both parents and children in helping them in their achievement of and learning the benefits of acquiring an education. I had previously started the Joy and Gladness Cultural Center where I taught parents who were high school dropouts and gave them an opportunity to get their general equivalency diploma (GED), which is equivalent to a high school diploma. I taught the classes until I began my dissertation process, and I am now in the process of restarting these programs. I have traveled to Barbados and spoke about using technology for education delivery. My goal is to work with the Haitian government to implement technology in the schools blended with face-to-face instruction.

Working toward a doctoral degree caused me to examine my value and worth. I worked in government, where employees are paid and promoted based on the number of years on the job or by taking a multiple-choice exam rather than their educational qualification. I had the highest qualifications in my department, which in government meant nothing compared to longevity. With a doctoral degree and working with the same department, I would continue to receive the same pay and be supervised by someone who had longevity and a high school diploma. I left the position to complete my dissertation and work for myself. I am still learning my worth since earning my doctorate, but I am enjoying being self-employed.

As a self-employed person, I have not experienced any challenges in the corporate world, but I receive recognition wherever I go. I receive respect when introducing myself or being introduced as a doctor. I am asked to speak in places or functions that I had never previously attended. In churches, I am addressed and introduced as doctor and receive great respect. At a few functions, some individuals have told me that they have been encouraged by my achievement to go back to school.

One of my greatest joys after earning my doctoral degree was being told that part of my name was being added to the name of a corporation, which changed from

Winnane Inc. to WinnGlad LLC. I was also asked to be the chair of that organization. In recognition of the work I did in achieving my doctorate, my family organized a graduation dinner for me. It was awesome and brought together people who had known me most of my life, both internationally and locally. I was happy my two grandsons were there to see and hear how determination and believing in oneself could help a person achieve his or her goals. After the celebration, my 8-year-old grandson Arron told me that he had an assignment from school to write about someone who made a change in the community, and he wanted to write about me. He wanted to know about some of the places where I went to work with the children shown on the PowerPoint presentation at the family celebration. He also wanted to know about the foster children that I took care of and why they had to live with me. He took his book report to school and talked about me in class. I was extremely proud, not because the project was about me but because a child believed the things I am doing have a positive impact on the community.

I have been able to integrate into the sea of scholars and professional networks comprised of other doctors and to exchange information on various opportunities and progress made after I received my degree. Because of other commitments, my communication is not as frequent as when we were working in the cohort, but the network of colleagues has grown tremendously. I have been able to integrate more with, and spend more time with, pastors of churches, many of whom also hold doctoral degrees.

The doctoral journey can be very lonely. It is a tough road to travel, so my advice to others in the doctoral process and postdoctoral process is to encourage yourself in the Lord. There may be a road map set out before you. Take it and use it to your advantage. It is not a one-way street, nor do you have to take the shortest and fastest route. Sometimes what should be the fastest route has delays because life happens. It is better to follow a route that has been tried and tested and got people to their destination, even if you stay in the slower lane. During your doctoral process, do as much work as you can during a semester, especially if you are using school loans. Remember, those loans have to be repaid, so you want to get through the process as quickly as you can. While pushing through your classes, leave room to relax, especially during your breaks.

You will never be able to relive the days that have gone by, so make the most of every day. Plan to take your vacation and attend a residency at the same time, if possible, and choose places you have really wanted to go when planning your residencies. Plan to make each day the best day you ever lived. Having a positive attitude determines your altitude. Don't wait for something to happen for you, go ahead and make something happen. Spend time in prayer—prayer works.

Postdoctoral students should spend time to celebrate their success with family and friends. Make it a memorable occasion. Reward yourself and market yourself well. Once again, you can choose a mentor or role model who is going somewhere that you would love to go and reach out to that person. Remember, success is like a recipe: follow the directions and you can be successful. "But the God of all grace, who hath called us unto his eternal glory by Christ Jesus, after that you have suffered a while, make you perfect, establish, strengthen, settle you" (1 Peter 5:10, King James Version).

Reference

Robbins, A. (1991) *Awaken the giant within: How to take immediate control of your mental, emotional, physical, and financial destiny.* New York, NY: Free Press.

13
Lewis Saunders, PhD

Federal Government

The inspirations that led me to earn a doctoral degree include listening in earnest to my father and mother concerning personal responsibilities; selecting role models to emulate; using key individuals within my community as role models, especially those who could make stimulating speeches, show their expertise in mathematics, and present a certain style of dress in public places; selecting those in my work environment who possessed the knowledge required to perform tasks; and being cognizant of opportunities that might be available to me.

My father was always in a hurry and worked day and night. He worked during the day for a large landowner, and during the night, especially during spring and summer months, he cleared, plowed, and planted our 23-acre farm that he inherited from his father and mother. Therefore, he was only able to spend a small amount of time with my brothers or me. My father was stern. He meant what he said and said what he meant. He did not emphasize education, but he neither encouraged nor discouraged any of us to continue school. My mother, who had a sixth-grade education, loved to write and attempted many times to publish a few short stories without success. Even though none was published, my mother kept trying, believed in the magazine, and idolized those who wrote for the magazine. The magazine was *Truth Stories,* and those who wrote for this magazine were illustrious writers; nevertheless, she believed she was just as good.

I grew up in the rural south of Virginia near the birthplaces of two U.S. Presidents: George Washington and James Monroe. Other historical figures also had roots there, including Robert E. Lee, who committed treason against the U.S. government, even though he had the benefit of an excellent education at the United States Military Academy, West Point. I often wondered what I could do to contribute in a positive way to our society. My mother did not have a clear answer to my question, but she always ended these conversation by stating, "Continue to go to school and learn as much as you can."

My high school agricultural teachers taught me the need to conserve and to believe in hard work that could yield a successful harvest from the land. In my classes on agriculture, I was introduced to Robert's Rules of Order and the correct way to conduct meetings. These rules remain with me today. The teachers required us to learn parliamentary procedures, and I became deeply interested in the subject and participated in a contest to determine the correct answers to Robert's Rules of Order. As I sat on the stage representing my high school (A. T. Johnson) at Virginia State College (now Virginia State University), Petersburg, I was thwarted by not correctly answering one question posed by Dr. Reed, a professor at Virginia State. The answer to the question stayed with me for many years, and from that brief encounter, I decided to earn a PhD just like Dr. Reed.

I tried to learn everything I could, especially mathematics and public speaking, and I was encouraged by my high school principal (Mr. Leroy Richardson), who could count as fast as any calculator. My introduction to high school algebra deepened my thirst to learn geometry, trigonometry, calculus, and other mathematics and eventually led me to choose physics as a major, but no one in my small high school could or would teach any mathematics higher than high school algebra.

I graduated from Adams State University, Alamosa, Colorado, with a degree in physics. The U.S. Office of Personnel Management rated me as a physicist and I was off to find a job. I applied for a physicist position at Ft. Belvoir, Virginia, which was very close to where I sit today. I was denied the position because I could not develop the four Maxwell's equations from Ohm's law using differential equations and advanced calculus. I applied and received a position as a physicist at Dahlgren Naval Weapon Laboratory, Dahlgren, Virginia, where I tracked satellites within the atmosphere. I left that position and began working at the U.S. Department of Commerce, Bureau of Standards. I loved to work in experimental physics and my highest grades in school had been in experimental physics, but I was given a termination notice due to cutbacks and I landed a job as an associate engineer with RCA in Springfield, Virginia. This job lasted for 4 years, and then I returned to the government as an operations researcher/management analyst. Today, I work in the same position, and to move forward in my career, I had to earn a PhD.

I found that there are three primary steps in preparing for the doctoral journey. The first step was an idea that implanted itself in my mind even before I turned

16 years old: I understood that I would be responsible for my own future and that there was a path to receive a college education no matter what the sacrifice or cost. My dream was to attend Virginia State College to study agriculture because I believed abundant food could grow from small seeds to feed many people; this belief eventually developed into my philosophy today, which is from a small investment (i.e., a contribution to a positive social change), abundant growth in positive changes can be realized.

The second step involved obtaining funds to make the journey to college, as funds were not available within my family. However, this did not dissuade me from hoping and trying. By the time I was 17 years old, based on the law of Virginia, I had to leave high school and attend college. There were no funds available, and the only alternative was to pick tobacco in Connecticut. I knew that picking tobacco would not provide enough funds for the first year of college so I entered the Air Force. Without the G.I. bill, I worked extra jobs at night and studied as much as I could. After 4 years and 6 months in the Air Force, I entered civilian life and attended Hampton Institute where I majored in physics; however, after 2 years, the funds disappeared and again I worked and saved to complete my college education. After working for approximately 1.5 years, I had enough funds and an academic scholarship to enter Adams State College (now Adams State University) of Colorado and graduated with a degree in physics and a minor in mathematics; thus, as explained earlier, my journey to employment began.

The third step involved seeking a job in my chosen career. This was difficult because the field of physics was populated by those who had earned at least a master's degree in physics; however, after several interviews, and one interview in particular at the Army Base, Ft. Belvoir, Virginia, I was asked to develop the Maxwell equations. There were four Maxwell equations and the equations had to be developed from Ohm's laws using calculus and differential equations. I had taken these courses, along with advanced calculus and numerical analysis, but I was not fully grounded in the theories and manipulations required. I was not offered the job but was offered a job at a naval base located in Dahlgren, Virginia. This job required tracking the information from satellites' footprints developed from debris and actual satellites from the United States and other countries. It was a fun job that required knowledge of physics, astronomy, and the computer language FORTRAN. Nevertheless, because of the work location in the southern part of the United States where I had grown up, I decided that I should move further north where there were more opportunities for advancement within my chosen field of study.

When I decided to earn a PhD, I followed four steps in completing the course work: (1) finding a place to work, (2) gathering the right material, (3) selecting the computer, and (4) time management. First, a student must devote attention to completing a task associated with any assignment. To concentrate on an assignment, I set aside a room, which I call the library, where I completed most of my assignments. When the library begins to overflow with papers, I have work areas in the basement and even in the family room where I can concentrate.

Gathering the right material is a decision that must be made before the work begins. Using computers at home and while commuting on the train is a valuable time saver. My choice to keep a computer with me at all times greatly assisted in completing assignments and writing articles for publication. This habit will help you manage your time as a scholar-practitioner.

The first procedure I used for completing my course work was to ensure I understood the course assignment.

The requirements were not always clear and often required more than one reading. I usually skimmed the required information and then read for understanding. The second procedure I used was to ask questions as I reread the assignments. I kept the following posted in my library:

Asking the Right Questions:

What are the issues and the conclusion?
What are the reasons?
Which word or phrases are ambiguous?
What are the value conflicts and assumptions?
What are the value conflicts and assumptions?
Are there any fallacies in the reasoning?
How good is the evidence?
Are there rival causes?
Are the statistics deceptive?
What significant information is omitted?
What reasonable conclusions are possible?

Source: Brown and Keeley (2014, p. 13)

The best practices for making the transition from course work to the proposal/dissertation process is to understand what the transition involves. It is important to understand that course work is over and the process of becoming a scholar begins. I have found that becoming a scholar requires not only critical thinking but also being creative in a way that will make an independent positive contribution to society. Some of the best practices I used in making this critical transition were as follows:

The first best practice is to critically analyze statements made in writing and in conversations; it is important to become a critical thinker when reading, writing, or speaking. One of the best ways to practice critical thinking is by asking the right questions at the right time. Brown and Keeley (2004) noted to be successful in resolving problems in speaking or writing, factual knowledge must be reviewed, including historical references. Readers will be looking for your conclusion in your writing; therefore, I started with the adage "bottom line up front"; this could also provide a means to improve the logic of your writing.

The second best practice is selecting a chair and committee members. The individuals who agreed to be my chair and committee members were well known in the academic community and were involved in the kind of research that my dissertation would require: information technology involving cell phones. Both my chair and my committee members had served on other dissertation committees. I was interested in many areas of science, but the use of cell phones and the relationship between cell phones and identity theft was my greatest interest. After searching many databases and using the funnel approach, I understood that researching and writing a dissertation required exploring a subject area that had not been researched by others in order to establish a correlation between two major entities that might depend on each other and that the process involved publishing the research after completion.

Publishing the research involved obtaining the approvals of a chairperson and committee members, but the first step was to obtain approval for the prospectus. The challenges and setbacks I experienced were (1) understanding how to move forward in the doctoral process, (2) learning where to find the information needed to complete the PhD journey, and (3) knowing the questions to ask at each residence.

After taking the courses and reaching a point where the end was in sight, I progressed to preparing my oral presentation for my proposal and I realized I did not know the meaning of an elevator speech. An elevator speech in doctoral programs is a 60-second speech encompassing the key components of a doctoral student's research. After presenting my proposal orals, there was a discussion between my committee members and my chair, and my chair instructed me to join the graduate cohort group. This was the best instruction I have ever received. After becoming a member of this group, I never missed a meeting and I learned something new in each meeting. By attending each meeting and listening to the advice of each member, I overcame all the roadblocks and enjoyed every moment.

The greatest lessons learned involved being ready at all times to present an elevator speech, to let others know about my goals and aspirations, and to be ready to present my dissertation proposal or dissertation to community groups and members at my church or even to members of the Toastmasters club.

My suggestions for best practices when completing the course work and proposal/dissertation are as follows:

1. Join the nearest Toastmasters International club.
2. Keep your classwork with you at all times.
3. Have more than one computer available.
4. Keep in constant contact with your chair or mentor.

5. Join Dr. Walter McCollum's graduate cohort group.

Participating in the activities offered by Toastmasters clubs will teach a person how to present his or her scholarly work. Huff (1999) noted a presentation is nothing but a verbal account of your work presented to an audience. New scholars can use the clubs as a way of presenting their scholarly work to a wider audience.

Keep your assignments or what you are writing with you at all times, because there are times (often referred to as downtime, i.e., on trains, buses, and even at restaurants) when you might be able to review and make adjustments (i.e., corrections) to your scholarly work. Keep more than one computer available with files backed up and located in different locations. Private companies can provide backup to files for a reasonable cost. As a student, you should keep in constant contact with your chair or mentor, thus providing the transparency in order to make a smoother transition from student to scholar. Most important, become a member of Dr. McCollum's graduate cohort group because within this group of students and scholars, you will find help and guidance that cannot be gained from any other support group.

The following are some problems I experienced in the doctoral process that prevented me from making the progress that I should have made:

1. Not understanding the requirements to complete the journey, i.e., the time limit.
2. Not understanding how to use the computer in a distance learning environment.
3. Not having all members of my family involved in each decision.
4. Not knowing what can happen during a vacation; thus, not having adequate clear connectivity in performing the course work.
5. Procrastination.

Peer monitoring is an excellent idea and should be assigned to each new student. Peer monitoring should continue in order to ensure that those who have graduated will rebrand themselves so they will be assisted in transitioning in the workforce and continuing to develop as scholars.

Cohort models must be implemented in the doctoral process. Without the cohort model, I would not have completed my doctoral journey. The cohort model taught me leadership and instilled within others the desire to support others.

Graduation is July 12, 2014, and I will walk across the stage to be hooded. I can only speculate on how I will feel. I can truly say, without hesitation, that I will be immeasurably thankful that the process is over and I am excited to continue working toward the publication of my book on cell phone use and identity theft, as well as articles developed from my course work.

I have grown beyond measure as a scholar-practitioner since completing the doctoral process; for example, I wrote, practiced, and presented a speech (without notes) at my Toastmasters club on March 27, 2014. I had to develop this speech within a few hours and I believe those who were present enjoyed the presentation as I stood before the room of approximately 40 people and delivered the speech with sincerity and confidence thanks to the host of my graduate cohort in my PhD program: Dr. McCollum.

I have grown personally since becoming a doctor by reaching out to other members of the graduate cohort group, and I have become more confident in presenting speeches and selecting books that will assist me in publishing my articles and writing books. I attend church functions and am reaching out to other PhDs who work for the National Science Foundation for advice in rebranding.

I am the first in my family to have the opportunity to attend college and to reach this highest level in education, and this experience has meant more to me than words could never explain; therefore, contacting other PhDs is the key to completing my rebranding. Additionally, I have joined the Speaker Bureau of Toastmasters International because I enjoy speaking before groups. Earning a doctoral degree has shown me that I am valuable to society and I must prove my worth to society repeatedly.

One of the challenges I am facing is not being recognized as a scholar-practitioner. I am aware that many people will not address me as doctor; however, with my upcoming publications, and over time, I believe this will change. I believe scholar-practitioners must publish.

My greatest accomplishment to date has been standing before an audience and presenting a speech without any notes. I attributed my success to the newly acquired confidence that I have gained by completing all the requirements for my PhD.

I have contacted the National Science Foundation and the points of contact have provided me the information necessary to conduct further study related to my dissertation, which is titled, *The Relationship Between Cell Phone Use and Identity Theft*. Additionally, I am a member of the Society of Public Administration, Maryland Chapter, and I will use this forum for speaking. I will attend conferences and join the Blacks in Government organization. I am sure my research will contribute to existing bodies of knowledge. I believe the cell phone is arguably the most consequential global technological development of the last 25 years. The cell phone has changed people's behavior and relationships in myriad ways. As with any tool, a cell phone can be used for good and for ill. Minimizing its potential for harm is a responsibility shared by government, business, and private citizens. I hope the results of my study will contribute to the responsible and productive use of cell phones and impact positive social change across various industries.

A resource that I'd like to share is a book by Ann Sigismund Huff titled, *Writing for Scholarly Publication*.

Huff (1999) noted if you are to share your ideas, you must fully participate in the scholarship of your chosen field; therefore, you must write. Scholars must pay attention to writing, which is also a way of participating in scholarship.

References

Brown, M. N., & Keeley, S. M. (2004). *Asking the right question: A guide to critical thinking* (7th ed.). Upper Saddle River, NJ: Pearson Education.

Huff, A. S. (1999). *Writing for scholarly publication.* Thousand Oaks, CA: Sage.

14
Scott Evans Willette, PhD

Senior Operations Analyst, Department of Defense

Today the network of relationships linking the human race to itself and to the rest of the biosphere is so complex that all aspects affect all others to an extraordinary degree. Someone should be studying the whole system, however crudely that has to be done, because no gluing together of partial studies of a complex nonlinear system can give a good idea of the behavior of the whole.
—Gell-Mann, 1997

Many personal and professional influences in my life inspired me to earn a doctoral degree. These included my own desire to continue my education, the support of my family and supervisors, and the example set by one of my mentors. I finished my undergraduate degree after 8 years as an enlisted U.S. Marine. As a marine, I had come to appreciate the value of a college degree and graduated as part of an enlisted-to-officer program. Just a few years after becoming an officer, I took the opportunity to apply for and attend graduate school within another marine program. Upon arriving at my next duty station, I found that my supervisor had followed a similar path and was now pursuing his doctorate. Throughout my first 3 years in that position, I had several discussions with him about his decision, as well as about the additional resources available to support me if I chose to enroll in a doctoral program. Nevertheless, other forces had a stronger influence over my decisions.

My wife has always been my strongest supporter when it comes to academics. She has encouraged me to apply for every program and degree that I have attained. After returning from a yearlong assignment away from my family, we began to talk about my career and possible retirement from the Marine Corps. At the time, I was attending a multiple-objective decision analysis class as part of my professional development. The instructor, who also happened to be one of my mentors, was explaining how the decision process could be used to help make personal and professional decisions. As an example, he shared how he had multiple objectives that included spending quality time with his family, achieving a certain standard of living in retirement, and attaining recognition as an expert in his field of expertise. Every major decision could be evaluated against the final model to determine its overall value to his objectives.

On a professional level, I found myself identifying strongly with the instructor's objective of becoming an acknowledged expert in his field. He showed how several decision points had been reached regarding his education and how they had fared in the model. Earning a doctoral degree had scored very high, with additional positive impacts on his career advancement and retirement quality of life. That was the final push I needed to begin researching doctoral programs in my field. Without my positive academic experiences as a marine, the resources that were available to help me on my doctoral journey, the support of my wife, and the examples provided by my supervisor and mentor, I do not think I would have ever started the process.

For me, the key to becoming oriented to the doctoral experience was having a strong foundation of learning and self-discipline. It was important to have the mind-set that the journey would be a marathon rather than a sprint. I read about the university's programs and discussed the processes with friends who were pursuing, or had completed, their own doctorates. They were able to prepare me for the amount of work required. In addition, having recently completed a master's degree helped prepare me and my family for the evenings spent reading and writing. I made certain we all understood the time commitments before I committed to a program. After I was confident that I could complete the work, and that the work–school–family balance could be managed, I knew I was ready to begin.

Completion of course work depends entirely on the method of instruction and the timelines involved. My early course work was entirely self-paced learning. My curriculum was broken up into knowledge area modules that required a significant amount of self-discipline. The modules were a series of three large research papers on a related topic. The key to completing the modules was to set realistic weekly goals for completing readings or writing sections of the research papers. While a learning agreement would be created with a faculty mentor to define the scope of the papers, timelines were not part of the contract. Because progress was subjectively assessed, self-discipline and progress against the weekly and monthly goals became the only way for measuring near-term success.

Later in my journey, I switched to primarily course-based work. The early practice of setting goals and timelines became even more important. The mode of instruction for most of these courses involved extensive weekly readings followed by individual and group writing assignments as well as required postings on online discussion forums. The most effective technique I found was to complete the readings before the following week began. It was tough at first to get ahead a week in the readings, but once I was, there was much less pressure to finish the assignments on time. In addition, looking ahead to major assignments and getting started on them early helped me avoid too many late nights.

The biggest challenges to completing the knowledge area modules were assimilating new theories and learning how to synthesize current research. The first module always involved investigating theories for potential application to a problem. Sometimes, identifying the right family of theories was difficult. Since the modules were essentially both self-paced and self-taught, becoming oriented could be a difficult. Because I had chosen a technical area of concentration within my field, I also found it difficult to teach myself some of the more difficult methodologies. Eventually, I had to opt for a less technical path to my dissertation.

Although this posed an obstacle, I feel it was the aspect that prepared me best for the dissertation process. The key to ensuring I had the right set of theories became interacting early and often with my faculty mentors. Their broad knowledge of the theories in my subject area helped to identify those that might be useful in the research papers. Through the process of researching, discussing, and selecting different theories, I broadened my own scholarly repertoire.

The second module consisted of an annotated bibliography with a literature review. This was my introduction to synthesized literature reviews, and I was at a loss regarding how to organize them. Early on, I found that research software packages such as EndNote were great tools for gathering and organizing large amounts of research materials. For my first three knowledge area modules, I relied extensively on EndNote for collecting the research articles and books and assigning them to various parts of the research papers. However, after being away from the tool while concentrating on course work and course papers that did not require that level of organization,

I found that I was not able to transition back to EndNote when I began my dissertation.

For those in a course-based model, especially one focused on weekly assignments, making the transition to the proposal/dissertation process can be daunting. I credit my previous experience with the knowledge area modules with preparing me for the shift from a deadline and assignment mind-set back to a research and discovery mind-set. Although the course work provided a more structured exposure to the current theories and applications in my field than the knowledge area modules, the lack of focus on synthesis of these concepts could delay students' transitions to their proposals and dissertations.

The common thread throughout the modules, course work, and dissertation was my topic. My university emphasizes the benefit of being a scholar-professional, interweaving our careers or our passions with our academic journey. Having a subject area early allowed me to approach the problem from multiple directions, depending on the focus of the class or module. This had the added benefit of building a strong foundation of scholarly articles and books that I could draw upon when I began my proposal.

The two biggest challenges I had when writing my dissertation were organization of the literature review and gaining access to my sample. After completing the course work, I found that I had amassed an extensive library of journal articles and books on my subject area. Unfortunately, I had not been cataloging and organizing them as I went along. In addition, I had stopped using EndNote, and what was in EndNote had not been keyword coded to topics germane to my dissertation. Instead of spending time fixing my database, I opted for a new strategy that I have come to love. Using old-fashioned 5- by 7-inch index cards, I captured all the data that would normally be found in an annotated bibliography for every reference that I thought could apply to my dissertation. After reading enough articles on the likely theoretical foundation for my research, I began coding the cards and filing them according to their primary topic. For example, Richardson (2008) wrote primarily about taking a certain approach to empirically examining my theory. The index card for that reference was filed under theoretical approaches. However, Richardson also discussed other aspects of the theory in that article, so I created cross-reference cards that pointed back to the primary location and placed them according to their topics. When it came time to write a section or refer to a specific topic, it was easy to pull out the right references and refer to the articles that I had filed separately and alphabetically by author.

The other setback I encountered was the result of having an ambitious plan to recruit participants from eight different organizations across the four U.S. military services. The problem included an incomplete understanding of the processes for getting approval from each service to conduct human research and the timelines and difficulty in obtaining agreement from individual organizations. While perseverance and tenacity were needed to get the limited number of approvals and cooperation letters that formed the basis of my study, what I really learned was flexibility. Instead of four services and eight organizations, I ended up with only two services and three organizations. I had to be able to adjust my scope and expectations between my proposal and data collection. This included having to update my research questions to reflect the narrower scope. Without this flexibility, it would have been difficult to overcome these obstacles.

I learned you have to do four key things to be successful in the dissertation process: you have to read, you have to have an organization strategy that works for you,

you have to write, and you have to form a committee that works best for you. Reading starts while you are still completing your course work. As I began to explore theoretical constructs related to my topic, I took the time to read many of the seminal works by the original authors. Anyone who has read a current research article will have noticed that the researchers invariably claim a foundation in one or multiple theories. It is important to be conversant enough in those theories to be able to determine if the researchers are accurately describing the theorists' intentions. It is not a good idea to wait until you are conducting the literature review to build a strong foundation in your theory. Start early and read often!

However, unless you have an eidetic memory, you must have an organization strategy. If you have not had to organize large volumes of research articles before, then I recommend trying different strategies until you find the one that works for you. You should start this process early, so that you are comfortable with your strategy by the time you begin the dissertation. Whatever method or tool you choose, make sure you have a way of efficiently recalling pertinent articles and related media (books, names of websites, etc.) that relate to your chosen topic.

I mentioned before that the doctoral journey is a marathon, not a sprint. I may have understated the process, as the dissertation itself is a marathon that might take anywhere from 9 months to several years of your life. To be prepared to write what might be your first publishable research, you have to know how to write publishable research. Writing, like most things, takes practice. I was fortunate to have completed a thesis-based master's degree. I also benefited greatly from the writing experience gained during the knowledge area module portion of my journey. While professional editors are great for checking form and style, they generally cannot make you a better writer. Only practice and good critiques of your work will improve your writing ability. If your university has a writing center, and you know that your writing could use some polishing, I highly recommend engaging the writing center staff early in your journey.

Finally, I cannot overemphasize the importance of forming the right committee. This does not mean finding the two or three faculty members with whom you get along the best. Nor does it mean finding committee members known for not providing a critical review of your work. It is more important that your committee members are experts in your content and methodology. Committee members are not a barrier to finishing the dissertation; they are enablers. They should be engaged early and often when you have methodological or content concerns because they provide a wealth of knowledge in your field. To that end, it is important that they work well with each other. I found that finding my committee chair first, and then asking my chair whom he would recommend to be on my committee worked out great. Your chair knows which other faculty he or she works well with and who could fill either the content or the methodology gap.

The two most important tools to have are an organization process and a copy of the *Publication Manual of the American Psychological Association* (6th ed.; American Psychological Association [APA], 2009). I liked the EndNote reference management software for managing my library and creating bibliographies in APA style. I made the mistake of not using fully the keyword and custom library capabilities to organize my references. If properly used and managed, EndNote could be a very powerful tool for doctoral candidates. However, there are other software-based and old-fashioned card-catalog tools for organizing research, and I would encourage students to find a tool that works for them as early as possible. The second tool is the APA style guide. Doctoral students that are required to use

APA should read this book form cover to cover. While it makes a great desktop reference for formatting, the first four chapters were invaluable in setting me on the path of scholarly writing.

I understand the stress that the doctoral journey can put on the family–work–school balancing act. My own journey took 6 years. During that time, I retired from my first career, took a 6-month leave of absence, changed jobs twice, and changed my doctoral specialization. What I noticed during this time is that the things that kept me going and helped me to finish my journey appeared to be obstacles that prevented many of my peers from moving forward. In addition to the absolute necessity of a strong support network and advanced writing skills previously mentioned, these obstacles also include poor planning and execution skills. Many of the students I have met during academic residencies and through online discussions have appeared wholly unprepared for the demands of the doctoral process because of problems associated with these obstacles.

Time management in a PhD program is a combination of detailed near-term planning, researching, and writing, combined with taking a longer view of the process. For a time, I worked in a high-stress job in a military command and control agency. The job required its personnel to absorb a tremendous amount of planning information in a short period, followed by fast-paced execution of the plan. The work entailed absorbing a lot of current information and making immediate decisions based on the situation and the plan for the near future. As an instructor, I often told my students that they had to have a Type A personality while preparing for the day, and a Type B personality (see Billing & Steverson, 2011) while implementing the plan. Just like these command and control officers, doctoral students have to be organized and be able to manage their time carefully. They must ensure they fully understood everything they need to know before sitting down to write. However, when writing a section, they must have the overall plan in mind so that they can maintain a common perspective throughout the writing process. It seems that much of the frustration experienced by doctoral students is centered on having to rewrite sections and entire chapters because the larger plan was forgotten during the process.

I have been a big proponent of peer mentoring in both my professional and academic careers. While mentoring in the traditional model of having someone with great experience guide your personal and professional growth is invaluable, I have found that peer mentors can be just as important. Peer mentors are an excellent source of recent lessons learned and become a major part of a student's support network. Mentors often have the most current knowledge about the processes and challenges that a student is experiencing. Further, this knowledge is sometimes unavailable through the university resource centers because either the policy is too recent, or the lesson learned provides a deeper understanding of the process. Peer mentors are also often more available, or more appropriate to use, than faculty mentors. Finally, because of the lived experiences that the peers share, they can be a catalyst for encouraging academic progress.

At first, I was a little leery of the cohort model. My early doctoral experience had been based on the individual-based learning of the knowledge area modules. Even during the course work phase, I intentionally kept group interaction to the minimum required to complete an assignment. However, that all changed when I entered my doctoral cohort. The cohort model provided immediate access to peer mentors who had also made that final step to begin their dissertations. The dissertation-focused cohort was an excellent forum for passing information vital to successful completion of the journey. Each member was encouraging and always willing to provide advice to candidates behind them in the process.

Earning a doctoral degree can be a smooth road if students develop a system that works for them. Some of the key components that students should ensure are that part of their system includes family support, a student network, a favorable relationship with faculty (both chair and committee members), time management, and organization skills. The icing on the cake for doctoral program completion is being connected and engaged in a cohort model with other students to share knowledge, lessons learned, and best practices.

References

Billing, T. K., & Steverson, P. (2013). Moderating role of type-a personality on stress-outcome relationships. *Management Decision, 51,* 1893-1904. doi:10.1108/MD-01-2013-0018

Gell-Mann, M. (1997). *The primer project: International society for the systems sciences (ISSS) seminar.* Retrieved from http://www.newciv.org/ISSS_Primer/seminar.html

Richardson, K. (2008). Managing complex organizations: Complexity thinking and the science and art of management. *Emergence: Complexity & Organization, 10*(2), 13-26. Retrieved from http://emergentpublications.com/ECO

15
Phillip R. Neely, PhD

Educator

Blessed are the peacemakers, for they will be called children of God.

—Matthew 5:9

I was born and raised in Atlanta, Georgia, by my grandmother, Willie Lue Ellis. My mother passed away when I was 3 years old, and my father was in Georgia State prison. Family members told me I would not graduate high school and would end up in prison like my father. My grandmother left school after the fifth grade to work. She always stressed education and pushed me to graduate high school and to continue onto college.

My goal was to become chief of police and teach college courses in criminal justice. The abstract nature of management and the concrete precepts of management and leadership provided me with the knowledge and helped me reach my full potential intellectually, academically, and professionally with an advanced education. Public service is a noble profession, and my PhD in public policy and administration with a specialization in public management and leadership has provided me with invaluable skills for dealing with a diverse community in the 21st century.

My doctoral journey required attending a university that offered flexible working conditions and that allowed me to continue my daily activities and receive a quality education at the same time. Walden University taught me a better understanding of leadership principles and the discipline needed to achieve my advanced degree while managing a family and working full-time. As a scholar-practitioner who effects social change, I conducted extensive research that provided me the ability to transform from an inexperienced college graduate to a respected professional. My research helped me grow into a more confident and independent individual who developed the ability to set goals and to focus on the path to achieving them.

The doctoral experience prepared me to make the most of future educational experiences and provided the opportunity to develop my most cherished personal characteristics. As an experienced leader, manager, scholar, and professional, I have a lot to contribute to effect social change. My analytical, critical thinking, and interpersonal skills have helped me to become more competent as a leader and manager in the fields of public administration, public policy, and criminal justice.

When conducting research, I have found it both helpful and necessary to access articles and journals reviewed by peers or experts on the topic. As a scholar-practitioner, I want to make the most of the academic achievements that are available, presentations, conferences, and consulting. I had the opportunity to read and refer to some of the best scholarly materials available while completing my postgraduate work at Walden University. Walden University Library provides students access to peer-reviewed articles in journals through the EBSCOhost database.

Setting expectations was a vital part of my best practices for completing the course work for my PhD. Planning, establishing goals, and setting expectations were vital to meeting deadlines and remaining focused, which allowed me to look ahead and use critical thinking while reflecting on past research. Setting expectations allowed me to see the unfolding changes in scholarly research and prepared me for draft revisions by mapping out my plans for oncoming challenges. By planning and setting attainable goals, I was able to manage my time and make efficient use of the resources available.

Being prepared was a way to stay ahead. I used time management strategies and planning to stay ahead and be successful throughout the dissertation process. Effective knowledge of technology was a key to successful online learning.

Time management helped me in the online learning environment and allowed me to plan, manage my time, and make efficient use of the equipment available. I developed an action plan that guided me through each part of the dissertation process, which took 2 years. By being proactive, I was able to use the plan to direct my time and schedule my workload to be productive. Time management allowed me to manage my time for research, rewrites, and addressing questions posed by my dissertation chair. The action plan is a unique plan used to stay ahead, be productive, and map out the path to the final defense. From tips provided by classmates and mentors, I set short-, medium-, and long-term goals that were valuable in helping me to complete my dissertation and my academic career at Walden University.

Writing was a challenge for me, including proper use of grammar and punctuation, spelling, organizational skills, and initiating writing. In the past, I had struggled with transferring the ideas in my mind into a written document. I had also struggled with proper paraphrasing, summarizing, and using in-text citations. My struggles often caused me to lose concentration and forget ideas while writing. I would write short, simple essays even though I could verbalize more in-depth ideas. Caring faculty guided me to the writing center and provided useful websites that helped me overcome this issue.

I used tutors and study aides to help me, and I was able to find confidence in my writing. It was important to be able to write at the graduate level. I developed a good working knowledge of American Psychological Association style to cite and identify quoted material properly. I was able to direct questions about formatting and related matters to the writing center. Learning to use the resources Walden University offered was key to improving the quality of my writing. The writing and dissertation centers had a number of important documents. I strongly recommend "Things You Should Know About Writing a Dissertation" in the dissertation resources. I learned to accept constructive criticism throughout the course of my dissertation process, knowing that I would be asked to make changes to draft papers I submitted. I took time after each draft to read it carefully and then make the appropriate changes. It is important that all aspects of the dissertation meet university standards and follow the required rubric. I was encouraged to read, think, and then free write. I was also advised to read what I wrote and then rewrite it for accuracy. When I faced problems, became confused, or experienced tunnel vision, my mentor suggested I take breaks. I experienced these issues throughout the dissertation process, but my mentors provided moral support, ideas, and encouragement to stay on course.

Good listening skills and effective critical thinking helped me to choose the right thinking process and ensured I used the proper techniques when evaluating the comments on paper for revisions. As a critical thinker, I had to free my mind to wander and make unbiased decisions in critical situations. Critical thinking allowed me to base my decisions on rational thoughts that expressed my experience and allowed me to demonstrate a high quality of knowledge in my writing when responding to comments for draft revisions. As a scholarly thinker, I think clearly and with an open mind.

Joyce Haines, David Milan, and Walter McCollum provided the quality assistance needed to make a smooth transition into the doctoral journey. Dr. Haines provided the instructions needed to be successful throughout the dissertation process. Dr. Milan provided the success strategies needed for online learning. Dr. Milan continued to provide positive feedback on drafts of each chapter and helped me to understand the overview of the Walden University doctoral program.

Dr. McCollum provided the essential skills for managing the entire process. He provided me with the timelines needed keep me on track and focused. He also encouraged me to think creatively by presenting an online course forum. Drs. Haines, Milan, and McCollum provided me with the success strategies I needed to succeed in my doctoral process.

Writing my proposal showed me the importance of research and provided the roadmap needed for successful completion. I needed to have peer-reviewed articles and journals to conduct research on my topic. As a scholar-practitioner, I like to make the most of speaking engagements and research opportunities to remain current and up to date. The scholarly articles and journals allowed me to read and refer to some of the best material available during my postgraduate work at Walden University.

After the prospectus was approved, I faced many challenges. I experienced a lack of communication, no direction or guidance, and little engagement from my committee chair. These barriers slowed my progress and led to feelings of frustration and isolation without a point of reference with which to interact. Consistent communication and interaction were important to addressing the obstacles. I believe academic growth occurs when there is shared interest, mutual communication, and positive interaction with committee members and mentors, as well as a strong support group. As a result, I developed a community that was vital to my success as a student.

I met Dr. McCollum at a Walden University residency in Liverpool, England. Dr. McCollum was engaging, was positive, and seemed to care for all his mentees. Upon returning to the United States, I kept in touch and asked Dr. McCollum to become my mentor. Dr. McCollum accepted me with a warm "Welcome, Mentee!" and stated he would be honored to be my mentor during the dissertation process.

To accomplish the mission, Dr. McCollum provided a list of several key items that would be necessary for me to be successful during the dissertation process. I was advised to seek constant and timely feedback from my dissertation chair to help meet the timeline and complete the project. I also needed to ensure I met academic rigor by providing an understanding of what was expected and by making the corrections needed.

Dr. McCollum was always accessible to discuss any questions or concerns I had about academic research. I could call him or meet with him to address areas of concern and to review any comments on a dissertation draft. Dr. McCollum helped me to meet deadlines and encouraged me to review drafts carefully before I resubmitted them.

By using the essential skills I developed during the dissertation process, I was finally able to clear my mind and relax. As I walked across the stage to be hooded, I thought about my grandmother, who inspired me to be all that I could be, which led to attaining my doctoral degree. Now that I have graduated, I am able to see that the process was designed to stimulate my mind and give alternative solutions for everyday problems of work and continued research. The doctoral journey gave me the ability to think creatively while solving problems and to continue with daily work assignments and handle family life while struggling with ongoing research material for upcoming draft revisions.

I developed excellent decision-making skills during my academic journey, which allowed me to understand the reason I sought a doctorate degree. I constantly seek ways to impact society as I expect the unexpected. I have impacted society by publishing a peer-reviewed article in a journal, presenting at professional conferences, and making presentations at higher education institutions.

I retired from law enforcement after 21 years. I worked as a correctional officer in a juvenile/adult facility and as a police officer. I have had the experience of working in all areas of law enforcement. Serving the community and having the ability to effect social change was a key factor in my decision to pursue a doctoral degree. My goal is to think creatively by trying to find a way to understand the ongoing problems in society and by providing solutions through scholarly research. Looking back on my doctoral journey, I was able to see that the trials I went through made me stronger, matured me, and helped change my way of thinking to have my mind work in a positive manner and to think outside the box. The lessons I learned provided me a better understanding of the concepts of research and helped me to apply them to real-life situations.

Obtaining my doctoral degree showed me that education provides a key piece of personal development that opens doors of opportunity for my future success. Education provides the building blocks for the decisions and choices that people make when seeking to reach their full potential. It is my responsibility as an educator to lead students toward the success they visualize. It is up to educators to help students develop the attitude, knowledge, and skills needed to become positive contributors to the world. Many learners find education fascinating, but the methods of teaching the topic seem intimidating and complex.

My own experiences provided me with the understanding of how inclusion can play a key role in student development. Institutional leaders need to take into account the diverse economic and cultural backgrounds and the unique learning styles that students bring to the classroom. Students are continuing to bring different abilities that require an educational opportunity that will meet their needs. I am a continuous learner, and I am always seeking to improve my teaching skills. Learners will seek to reach their full potential when they are provided with something they are interested in. My goal is to understand the entire student, which represents a 360-degree view. I want to ensure the learners are included in the process. Collaborative activities are central to engaging students and capturing their attention and interest. I enjoy interacting with faculty and students and am inspired by the innovation and creativity that develops from those relationships. I hope to leave my students with a positive impression of education that encourages them to become continuous learners. Education should be an environment that fosters support, inclusion, and safety where students excel.

Success in a doctoral program comes from choosing the right instruction. Walden University has been progressive as a cornerstone in diversity. The shared community from various cultural, racial, and socioeconomic backgrounds has been parallel to none as the history spans many years of tradition. The leaders of many universities and colleges ignore the need for personal nurturing, as well as their students' educational aspirations. To magnify my success, there must be a continued effort focused on my mind, body, and spiritual health to enhance personal development.

Because of my life experiences, I am a walking testimony of the mission and values of Walden University. I am a living example of what was not supposed to be. Like most people, I have been challenged and tested by life's ups and downs. My grandmother raised me because my mother died when I was 3 years old and my father was in prison. I could not foresee the commitment I had to make to myself. I seemed destined to become just another statistic. Thankfully, I became an exception to the rule after becoming the first in my family to obtain a doctoral degree. I am proud of my accomplishments, and I continue along the path of greatness. I want to inspire others with my personal growth. Everyone has a story, but often it is never told. I aspire to motivate others to be the main character in their personal stories.

As an instructor of adult learners, I am able to relate to potential students and explain the value of a college education as opposed to the numerous excuses of life associated with limited finances, a lack of time, family obligations, and work. Through responsible stewardship, I can help students realize that I am here to help them with their educational goals. Having been raised by an uneducated grandmother, I can dispel the negative belief that people are limited by their situations. Walden University staff members have a moral responsibility to treat those they serve with dignity and respect. Regardless of whether they have received unfavorable treatment, staff members' goal should be to avoid engaging in injurious behavior as they are molding minds and personalities.

In my own life, I have the ability to relate to various people, and I recognize the importance of engaging in various types of dialogue to exchange pertinent information. My goal has always been to treat people with the highest degree of courtesy and respect at all times. The poor temperament of support staff can damage or even destroy the reputation of a good university. Maintaining the highest level of integrity through honesty in the written and spoken word can elevate the university to new heights. To remain within the parameters of excellence, I pledge to uphold the high standards and the reputation to be an asset to everyone I encounter.

16
Madhu Rao, Doctoral Candidate

Educator and Student, Master of Divinity

Tell the truth once and you won't have to think twice.
—Author Unknown

In 2004 after the premature death of my father, himself a PhD, I decided to embark on a learning journey to complete my doctorate. In the United States, the attainment of the doctorate is considered the pinnacle of education, as only 1% of the U.S. population has earned this degree (U.S. Census Bureau, 2011). My inspiration to earn a PhD was related to honoring the achievements of my father and other doctoral graduates. A few other reasons contributed to this decision. One of these includes the revelation of a question that was so intriguing and pervasive that it formed the basis of my doctoral research study. Another includes having the letters "PhD" after my name to signify the accomplishment of a personal endeavor that many of my friends and family know is important to me. Professionally, the development of new skills and knowledge as part of the doctoral journey process and the opportunity to rebrand myself as a scholar-practitioner is extremely inspiring to me. Lastly, the potential new employment opportunities that may derive from this achievement also serve as an inspiration to complete my doctorate.

Apart from consulting the doctoral resources available from my school, which include guidebooks and templates, I reviewed some of the best practice discussions in the education portal as well. One of these described bridging the academic–social divide, which includes greater social integration by fostering sharing knowledge and skills with others (Spaulding & Szapkiw, 2012). The ability to create a sense of community with others in an academic setting is of great interest to me. Building on this, an additional best practice includes participation with other doctoral students in an online cohort to share our best practices and lessons learned. Participation in this cohort validates the feeling of community and connotes an esprit de corps knowing the entire group is likely encountering many of the same feelings as I am at any given moment.

My educational course work included several core curricula and elective courses. The ability to work independently, at my own pace, and choose from a variety of courses is important to me and many other doctoral students (Church, 2009). Factors enabling the successful completion of my course work included the following best practices: (a) technology, (b) time, and (c) networking. In terms of technology, use of a personal computer calendar program is helpful to schedule time for research, reading, and reflection, as these are three discrete activities and require dedicated time for their completion. Additionally, the use of an online storage vault such as Dropbox to store educational materials enables their retrieval at any Internet website, which is a huge time savings when traveling.

Regarding the time component, a best practice to achieving a high level of productivity includes a consistent method of organization from course to course. This includes developing a common file nomenclature to find these files, or material within them, quickly. One resource is software such as Agent Ransack. This program performs a keyword search of all files on a computer and generates a list of all documents containing the keyword. Use of this resource reflects a best practice that saves time and shows the progression and interest of a specific topic in prior courses and potentially the work of other researchers encountered in prior courses.

The third best practice is professional networking through sites such as LinkedIn, which helps to identify a vast group of researchers sharing similar professional and academic interests. The ability to contact members of this group is valuable to doctoral students for current and future research opportunities. Membership in professional and personal societies is also a best practice to pursue. Many societies offer a built-in pool of research candidates for a survey, participation in meetings and speaking opportunities, and professional mentoring opportunities to give back to the community.

The doctoral research journey includes the following components: core curricula course work, comprehensive exams, dissertation proposal completion, data collection, manuscript completion, and defense. Challenges to my dissertation proposal completion included behaviors such as procrastination and perfectionism, which are commonly described in the literature as barriers for many doctoral learners (Liechty, Liao, & Schull, 2009). The result is a lower threshold to frustration, difficulty making decisions, and greater self-criticism. As a result, the ability to complete research is delayed due to a feeling of paralysis. Methods I used to redirect such thoughts included greater self-awareness, increased focus on opportunities to increase self-efficacy, use of technology to develop and manage milestones (e.g., using a Microsoft Excel file to track progress), communication of milestones to family and friends to instill accountability, and assignment to a new chair whose background provided a supportive, advocacy-oriented environment. These change-oriented processes helped foster a sense of urgency and desire to complete the dissertation proposal.

Additional opportunities to get back on track include increasing resilience and persistence. Resilience refers to a positive interaction between a student and previous stressors in the environment (Spaulding & Szapkiw, 2012). Persistence is fostered when students are able to view their potential contributions in a broader sociocultural, change-oriented context. Persistence may also be enabled by the future-oriented vision that upon graduation, a student may be invited to participate in scholarly activities with former faculty.

In comparison to doctoral prerequisite courses, some of which involved group discussion, much of the doctoral course work is conducted independently. My primary contact in this course sequence is my faculty chairperson, and communications with my chairperson is an important enabler of the quality of the educational experience for myself and other students (Lechuga, 2011). My assessment of the positive transition from course work to the proposal/dissertation process is largely related to two concepts: (a) the ability to research a topic of interest to me and (b) the ability to work at my own pace without regard to teaching or publication requirements typically associated with doctoral students at many schools. The best practices to aid doctoral students in this transition include easy-to-use statistical analysis programs, word processing, and access to global online libraries. These are the technical best practices. The personal best practices include honoring the wisdom of your faculty chair, his or her faculty colleagues, and any students in a peer group. This insight helps facilitate the transformation of student to scholar-practitioner and connotes that successful doctoral completion is within reach and an opportunity to join the faculty ranks is nearby.

Successful and timely completion by doctoral students is important for all the key stakeholders involved: students, faculty, universities, and external groups (family, funding agencies, society). Reports of doctoral attrition rates vary from 10-20% to 85%, with many citing a 50% rate (Jiranek, 2010; Spaulding & Szapkiw, 2012).

Regardless of the current rate in the academic community, students are likely to focus on the rate that matters to them the most: their anticipated date of completion. The reasons affecting degree noncompletion are many and may include family needs, employment, financial, interpersonal, academic, and personal.

My personal barriers include behaviors such as procrastination, perfectionism, and negative self-efficacy. These barriers are commonly reported by other doctoral students (Liechty et al., 2009). Their impacts included a delay in estimated doctoral proposal completion time from 1 to 3 years and two requests for an extension. Progress toward proposal completion accelerated once the self-limiting beliefs were addressed, new faculty chair relationships were developed and deepened, and I joined a new cohort of students also completing the doctoral journey.

Completing the doctoral journey is a task that involves the student, the faculty chair, and university research facilities. The interrelationship is depicted in the figure below (Jiranek, 2010). The first step to regain my momentum was the development of a contract with my new faculty chair that clearly highlighted the mutual expectations, timelines, and deliverables of both parties. The second step involved a critical self-examination and awareness process that included researching the leading barrier to task completion: a reduced sense of self-efficacy.

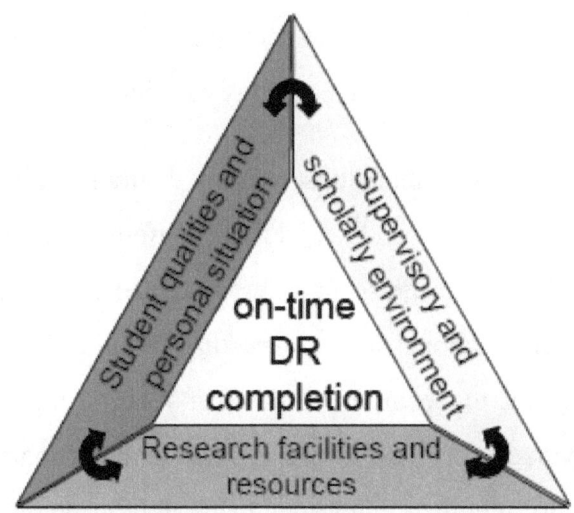

Figure 1: The Dissertation Research (DR) Completion Triangle showing the three broad groups of factors which contribute to timely completion by higher degree research students. The arrows are indicative of the inter-relationship of these factors.

Dissertation Research Completion

Research and coaching insights toward understanding Bandura's (1997) theory of self-efficacy with my faculty chair enabled my progress. Weekly updates provided an opportunity to discuss any issues and provide visibility toward timeline completion. Some recidivism has occurred, but the ability to rebound quickly, maintain a positive attitude, and sustain focus resulted in a fully approved dissertation proposal in a few months and the potential to graduate soon thereafter. This is in contrast to my previous multiyear delay to achieve the same result.

Communications with my chairs included providing written updates and scheduling conference calls as needed to discuss progress and lessons learned. In time, these communications led to trusting relationships with the potential to become peer-to-peer relationships that would eventually provide to present and publish together. Many faculty members view mentoring and academic support as integral to their work. One lesson learned included making the shift from student to scholar-practitioner. As above, this shift is supported by a deepening of the relationship between student and faculty chair (Spaulding & Szapkiw, 2012). Additionally, another lesson learned is that faculty chair and student relationships are critical to the overall success of students completing their doctoral program, the number of doctoral students graduated by the faculty chair, and the university's overall doctoral success rate. Faculty chairs who excel at coaching and graduating their students are in high demand.

Another lesson learned relates to the importance of brand development. Brand characteristics associated with faculty chairs include their areas of expertise, publications, mentorship, and, teaching expertise (Close, Moulard, & Monroe, 2011). Accordingly, employers can appreciate the future value they may gain from hiring a student with these brand attributes imparted by their faculty chair.

Doctoral students have access to a vast number of resources when compared to those preceding them a few decades ago. Given that many students are used to relying on Internet search engines for insight, an opportunity exists for students to demonstrate mastery over the tenets of research methodology to conduct independent research (Liechty et al., 2009). Students have usually been exposed to the deliverables of research, but the dissertation is likely to be their largest research project to date. A resource to aid such completion is *Dissertation and Scholarly Research: Recipes for Success*, by Marilyn K. Simon, PhD and Jim Goes, PhD (2013). An additional resource of interest is *Methods in Behavioral Research* by Paul Cozby (2012).

Apart from the above research methodology textbooks, an opportunity exists to increase the overall preparation of doctoral students for the research process. Acquisition of writing and research skills are commonly mentioned as important components of doctoral preparation (Wao & Onwuegbuzie, 2011). An important best practice is the importance of synthesizing research concepts through scholarly research writing. As time to doctoral completion is negatively affected by deficiencies in writing skills, highlighting the economic impact of increased time to completion may help motivate doctoral learners to increase their preparation in this area (Wao & Onwuegbuzie, 2011). One approach to achieve this goal is the early introduction of hands-on research writing activities. The use of a writing lab may help achieve this objective.

The doctoral journey may be represented by core curricula course work, comprehensive exams, and dissertation proposal completion, with each phase requiring an increased level of self-efficacy as evidenced by the ability to synthesize and summarize a variety of educational resources. The following potential barriers may impede the progression of doctoral students: lack of clear personal and professional motivations for pursuing a PhD, lack of an academic match between the student and the university, lack of a social-personal match between the student and faculty chair, lack of a social support network to guide students through each stage, lack of goals and strategies to achieve these, and loss of financial support such as employment, scholarships, grants, or research stipends (Spaulding & Szapkiw, 2012). These barriers may directly affect the overall doctoral completion rate, but they are not insurmountable, as evidenced by the number of academically successful students, chairs, and educational institutions in the United States. Students who are successful and graduate have demonstrated the ability to persist through the multiyear process, embrace change, maintain flexibility, and remain open to a variety of inputs in their academic journey.

The quality of relationships between the student and the faculty chair and among students allows for the rich sharing of life experiences that can help provide context and insight to the doctoral process. The quality of these relationships predicts doctoral student satisfaction (Nwenyi & Baghurst, 2013). Doctoral student satisfaction is also achieved through peer mentoring that enables students to work together and learn from each other. Recognizing this, academic curriculum developers are including group activities, discussions, and presentations in the course programming. These tactics are not restricted to in-person settings; their presence and use also harmonize well in an online academic environment. Students' experiences are also shaped by their interactions with the components of a college environment: culture, policies, and people (Nwenyi & Baghurst, 2013). Creating a supportive environment through peer-to-peer mentoring appears to be a precursor to increasing student satisfaction. Conversely, when students fail to become integrated into personal relationships, they are more likely to withdraw. Peer mentoring offers the opportunity to develop a relationship and to learn from someone who recently encountered a similar situation, developed best practices, and can share lessons learned.

The opportunity to learn from others, including academics, lay personnel, and peers, is a benefit to doctoral students. The opportunity to participate in a student cohort learning model has led to the development of a positive relationship between student engagement and completion of their academic studies (Liechty et al., 2009). In such a model, students report their progress with each other through regular meetings, which has the effect of increasing the accountability and visibility of their progress. Members report increased productivity and satisfaction with their progress by joining the cohort.

Evaluations of cohort learning programs indicate that this support structure is helpful in the early phases of the dissertation, as participants experienced a reduction in feelings of isolation (Liechty et al., 2009). Best practices associated with cohort development include setting expectations regarding the objective of the cohort (e.g., individual doctoral completion), defining the cohort experience, establishing principles to ensure respect for the cohort community, ensuring collaboration rather than competition, and ensuring cohort accountability (Holmes, Birds, Seay, Smith, & Wilson, 2010). Members of a cohort who participated in workshops on research methodology and writing presented a summary of these best practices to their cohorts. This activity had the effect of creating a knowledge base for members to access and use in their studies as they joined a cohort.

References

Church, S. (2009). Facing realty: What are doctoral students' chances for success? *Journal of Industrial Psychology, 36*, 307-316.

Close, A., Moulard, J., & Monroe, K. (2011). Establishing human brands: Determinants of placement success for first faculty positions in marketing. *Journal of the Academy of Marketing Science, 39*, 922-941. doi:10.1007/s11747-010-0221-6

Holmes, B., Birds, K., Seay, A., Smith, D., & Wilson, K. (2010). Cohort learning for graduate students at the dissertation stage. *Journal of College Teaching & Learning, 7*, 5-11.

Jiranek, V. (2010). Potential predictors of timely completion among dissertation research students at an Australian Faculty of Sciences. *International Journal of Doctoral Studies, 5*, 2-13.

Lechuga, V. (2011). Faculty-graduate mentoring relationships: Mentors' perceived roles and responsibilities. *Higher Education, 62*, 757-771. doi:10.1007/s.10734-011-9416-0

Liechty, J., Liao, M., & Schull, C. (2009). Facilitating dissertation completion and success among doctoral students in social work. *Journal of Social Work Education, 3*, 481-497.

Nwenyi, S., & Baghurst, T. (2013). Demographic and attitudinal factors influencing doctoral student satisfaction. *Canadian Social Science, 9*(6), 47-56. doi:10.3968/j.css.1923669720130906.3040

Spaulding, L., & Szapkiw, A. (2012). Hearing their voices: Factors doctoral candidates attribute to their persistence. *International Journal of Doctoral Studies, 7*, 199-219.

U.S. Census Bureau. (2011). Current Population Survey, Annual Social and Economic Supplement. Retrieved from https://www.census.gov/newsroom/cspan/educ/educ_attain_slides.pdf

Wao, H., & Onwuegbuzie, A. (2011). A mixed research: Investigation of factors relating to time to the doctorate in education. *International Journal of Doctoral Studies, 6,* 115-134.

17

B. Bernard Ferguson, PhD

Former U.S. Postal Inspector

The only thing we know about the future is that it will be different.
—*Peter Drucker*

I have always been a lifelong learner, so after I completed my master's degree, pursuing a PhD was an easy decision. In addition, after spending over 21 years as a federal law enforcement agent and approaching retirement, I decided that what would bring me the most joy during the next phase of my life would be to transition from putting law breakers behind bars to academia, where I believe I can best use the experience I have gained from my profession and through earning my doctoral degree to provide others with some insight to keep them from becoming a criminal statistic. I have always believed that based on my time in law enforcement, others would be interested in hearing my story and the PhD title behind my name demonstrates that I had the discipline to further my educational growth, and I believe others will now listen more intently to what I have to say and believe that what I am saying is evidence-based rather than pure speculation. This provides me with a tremendous platform to reach others, which aligns with my objective of effecting social change.

Realizing the doctoral journey would require a significant time commitment, one of the first things I did prior to committing to the process was to communicate my academic goals to my family and explain that pursuing my doctoral studies would result in me having to prioritize my academic endeavors. Still, I made a point to carve out precious time to spend with family and friends to the extent possible throughout my doctoral journey. Another best practice I used in accomplishing my goal of becoming scholar-practitioner was to communicate consistently with my committee chair and ensure I immediately responded to requests for action to ensure I was not the cause of delays associated with completing my studies on time. I realized early in the process that my committee chair worked in accordance with the responsiveness demonstrated by the student. As such, I made it a point to answer inquiries I received from my committee chair as soon as possible to move the process along. This practice kept me moving along rapidly without undue delays, and I noticed that working in such a manner facilitated a positive working relationship between my dissertation committee and me.

Never falling behind in my studies helped me keep on top of my course work throughout my time at Walden University. I rightfully anticipated that issues would arise throughout the process that would potentially interfere with my ability to remain current in my course work. I found that because I made it a point to work ahead of schedule, anytime issues would arise, I was still able to complete my course work on time without falling behind. I also found it beneficial to set aside time for attending to my course work. By scheduling my day to include moving forward in my academic endeavors, working toward the completion of my degree became routine and something I looked forward to rather than a task. During my doctoral journey, I also learned that I am truly a morning person when it comes to writing. Because of this, I made it a point to schedule the majority of my writing to occur in the early morning rather than at the end of the day after encountering issues such as traffic jams and typical work-related problems.

The greatest challenge I encountered during my academic pursuits was keeping what I was doing from my employer. I learned early on that not everyone supported what I was doing, and rather than create a situation where my personal endeavors would be questioned in terms of detracting from my ability to perform my job, I felt it was best to keep this part of my life to myself. Other challenges involved balancing between my course work and ensuring I did not neglect my family. In striking such a balance, I made it a point to spend quality time with my family whenever possible. I discovered that by ensuring I placed a priority on my family and took time away from academics occasionally to spend time with them, I maintained their support through the process. When my family insisted I spend time with them rather than do schoolwork, I tried to be understanding and set aside my academic projects with a personal commitment that I would make up the work later.

I found the transition from course work to the proposal/dissertation process relatively easy due to knowing my dissertation topic early on and working toward that end throughout my doctoral journey. I feel that having an idea of my area of study greatly assisted me by ensuring the research articles I focused on throughout my doctoral journey would ultimately contribute to my proposal/dissertation. I also found it useful to network with PhD students who had already completed their doctoral studies and could provide me with insight as to what I could expect as I continued in the program. I feel that having an idea of what would be required of me in the future helped me in preparing not only mentally but also in my course work by ensuring what I was working on would be useful. For example, when I first started in my doctoral studies, I selected topics that appealed to me and spent a significant amount of time conducting research on that topic for my weekly assignment. When speaking with a former Walden student about what I was doing, that person suggested that I "make everything count" and ensure to the greatest extent possible that I could use my research toward writing my proposal. That bit of advice helped me hone in on a research topic, which ultimately guided me in the selection of the topics for my weekly assignments where I now ensured anything I wrote about somehow related to the area I had selected as my dissertation topic. Although some of the references I used for my weekly assignments were outdated by the time I completed my dissertation, the knowledge I had learned along the way related to my research topic still aided me when it came to writing my proposal and dissertation, regardless of whether I used a particular reference. I also found that for some reference materials that were outdated by the time I was ready to submit my proposal, I was able to find an updated version of the same material, as I discovered that researchers want to remain current in their work, so they often revise and update their material and reprint it.

The greatest potential challenge I experienced while pursuing my academic endeavors involved the loss of my mother. Prior to her passing, I spent as much time as possible with her, which served as a needed distraction from what both she and I were going through but also resulted in having to work extra hard just to keep up with my studies during this difficult time. I also experienced a couple of delays in getting through the Institutional Review Board and chief academic officer's review process that are probably fairly routine in nature but reaffirmed to me the importance of working ahead of schedule to ensure such delays do not result in missing a deadline and being ineligible to graduate as scheduled. What I found most important with making revisions was to do whatever was asked of me. That appeared to be the most efficient way of obtaining approval to move to the next step. I also found it important to know the difference between suggested and mandated changes when revising my dissertation. Making such a distinction and working through my committee chair ensured I did not lose any momentum due to delays associated with revising my document.

I used this potential setback as motivation for completing my degree. Because it was my mother who initially inspired me to work hard in school, completing my degree was in essence a tribute to her and her desire for me to achieve success in my academic endeavors. The loss of my mother served as a motivating force to work even harder to complete my doctoral studies. In handling the unanticipated delays associated with making revisions to my document requested by the Institutional Review Board and chief academic officer, rather than become frustrated and argue over the requested changes, I viewed the requests as a rite of passage and made whatever revision was requested with the belief that once I satisfy the requests, I would be granted permission to transition to the next step. I therefore developed a mind-set that to move along in the process, it was incumbent upon me to satisfy the wishes of those requesting that I make the revisions.

The greatest lessons learned for me were to take the necessary time to be as accurate as possible when submitting documents because the turnaround time between submission and review of documents had the potential of unnecessarily delaying the completion time of my proposal/ dissertation. I also found it critically important to pay close attention to the requested revisions received from all those reviewing my documents. There were a couple of instances during the process where I either misread or misunderstood something. This taught me to ask questions if I was not absolutely clear what was being asked of me. I also found it useful to review the dissertations of former students of my dissertation chair and university research reviewer to get a feel of the writing style students used who were successful in getting through the process. This aided me in better understanding both the intent of the requested revisions as well as how my document should be formatted.

I found that submitting my proposal to the Walden University Writing Center to get feedback on my document aided me in my later document submissions. I also learned that submitting to the same reviewer simplified things by that individual becoming accustomed with my work and therefore better able to follow my thought process. The information found on the Walden website was extremely useful, such as examples of dissertations and copies of student oral presentations that were available for a specified time for others to review. Everything a student needs to complete the doctoral process is available somewhere within the Walden online resources.

A recurring problem I observed during my time in the cohort was cohort members not keeping to the established timeline for completing the dissertation process. I also observed that when some of the members made their weekly progress reports, they had not actually made any progress. Based on the reports of cohort members who have fallen behind, a myriad of problems have been reported, including changing jobs during the doctoral process, where because they have switched jobs, their academic work takes a backseat to work while they go through the learning curve associated with their new position. Other problems associated with cohort members losing momentum had to do with some individuals feeling they had all the time in the world to complete their studies and effectively making themselves vulnerable to missing established milestones when they faced unanticipated situations requiring their attention be placed in areas other than academics.

As it is in a work environment, having the right peer is important any time instructions are given to another by a person at the same level. That is, unless peers have demonstrated that they are worthy of being listened to, the peers have very little influence on those they have been positioned to direct. Within a cohort environment, one of the most important attributes of a peer mentor is to possess the necessary skills to keep the cohort functioning effectively by communicating instructions passed along by the dissertation chair and facilitating an environment where cohort members can update others on their individual progress. The atmosphere within the cohort should be one in which the members openly share their successes and failures so that others can learn from those experiences. A cohort environment does not work when the selected cohort leader misuses that position and, rather than simply facilitating communication, talks down to other group members. To ensure the cohort leader will be effective, it is important that the person selected is someone who remains current in their course work and has demonstrated the ability to achieve the stated milestones by the due dates. It is equally important that the cohort leader has excellent communication skills and is able to keep the cohort teleconference on track by not allowing members to stray too far off course from what is important to the cohort.

Working within a cohort while pursuing a doctoral degree is an effective process, particularly for students who have a difficult time working on their own and who have not established a network. A cohort environment connects students throughout the doctoral process, which is particularly important with distance learning where students experience no direct contact with others outside of the time spent at academic residencies. The outside speakers, including cohort graduates, bring tremendous insight to the cohort process by sharing knowledge with others coming behind them. I benefited from the experiences of more experienced cohort members and by hearing about their successes and challenges. For example, I learned about how references needed to be within a 5-year timeframe at the time of review, and although references might be current at the time the information is used, if delays are experienced along the way, some of those references could end up being outside the 5-year window at the time the student's proposal is reviewed. Upon learning about this, I made it a point to use references that were 2-3 years old to ensure they would still be current when I completed my dissertation. I also benefited from learning from more experienced cohort members what to expect during the oral defense process. The cohort is not a replacement for commitment on the part of the student, who must do his or her part to acquire knowledge from more experienced cohort members and then complete the work in accordance with the dissertation chair's feedback.

Completing a doctoral degree is a process that can't be circumvented. Students need to become familiar with the university's processes, faculty requirements, and tools and resources available to support doctoral program completion. When students choose not to follow the process and embrace it, they will add more time to their program and incur additional costs. When students work in partnership with their faculty mentor and follow the dissertation process, they will be successful in reaching their academic goals . . . earning a PhD!

18
Gary Lee Lucy, Sr., PhD

1st Class Stationary Engineer/1st Class Refrigeration Operator

Life's greatest revenge is success!

—Unknown

Perseverance Is the Key

My doctoral degree journey began at birth. My parents instilled a thirst for education in my three brothers, my sister, and I by placing major emphasis on education at an early age. My father graduated from high school, entered the military, and after completing his duty, worked for 30 years at General Motors before retiring. My mother graduated from Alabama State with a bachelor's degree and received her master's degree from Wayne State University in Detroit, Michigan. She taught first grade for 27 years at the Detroit Public Schools before retiring. They always told us that we should take advantage of every opportunity and go further than they did in education. That statement stuck with me throughout my life.

I graduated from Cass Technical High School in Detroit in 1976 and attended Lawrence Institute of Technology (LIT) for 4 years, but did not complete my degree. While at LIT, I began working as a traffic engineering technician and did that until I was laid off in 1986. I got married in 1985, with the first of my three children born that same year. In 1986, I applied for a 4-year apprenticeship program for stationary engineering with the International Union of Operating Engineers (IUOE), passed all of the tests and requirements, and was accepted into the program. I was assigned to work at the Detroit Public Schools and became a member of the IUOE. I completed the stationary engineer apprenticeship in 1990 and obtained my First Class Stationary Engineer (boiler operator) and First Class Refrigeration Operator licenses. Although I worked alongside many people with doctoral degrees (both EdDs and PhDs), I never envisioned that one day I would be joining that exclusive club.

I retired from Detroit Public Schools after more than 24 years of service. I became more involved in labor union activities in 1991. In 1995, I won an election to become an auditor for IUOE Local 547, and in 1998, I became vice president of IUOE Local 547. I was a labor union official for over 12 years. During this time in my life, I had an opportunity to go back to school to pursue a bachelor's degree at the National Labor College (NLC), in Silver Spring, Maryland. The NLC was the only accredited college in America founded to educate labor union members. I was able to transfer credits from LIT and the apprenticeship program and as a result was able to graduate from NLC in 2000 with a bachelor's degree in union leadership and administration. It was one of the proudest moments in my life. My family, my mother, and many of my dear friends drove all the way from Detroit to attend my graduation ceremony in Silver Spring.

The University of Baltimore had a relationship with NLC graduates and offered a master's in public administration. Being accepted to this program was a major step for me because I would no longer be in class with labor union members only; rather, program included students from diverse backgrounds. I entered the program in spring 2000 and completed my master's in spring 2002. While at the University of Baltimore during a residency, I had a chance to speak to my professors about applying to a PhD program after completing my master's degree. They were very encouraging and told me that I should do research on the various schools that offered online degrees because of my workplace and family commitments. After researching many online doctoral programs, I decided to enroll at Walden University to complete a PhD with a concentration in business administration.

Before embarking on this PhD quest, I tried to familiarize myself with the many components necessary to complete this journey in an efficient and productive manner. I tried to envision many different timelines and scenarios that could arise and cause disruptions along this journey. Guess what I eventually discovered? You cannot prepare for everything—life happens. That is why I have titled this paper, "Perseverance is the Key." I will never judge a person when they have been knocked off their feet due to unforeseen circumstances. Instead, I will admire them for their resurgence after defeat. Life has a way of making its own plans, and we have to be prepared to make the necessary adjustments and continue to strive to achieve excellence.

After reading over the first course's syllabus, I realized that doing the course work during the quarter would be important. I realized that I had to place more emphasis on quizzes, midterms, and homework assignments, thereby minimizing the impact and importance of the final exam. This proved to be genius. Although there were some very tough classes, I completed all of the course work with a 4.0 GPA.

The doctoral journey has many challenges besides the course work. Balancing time between family obligations, workplace obligations, and course work was a major challenge. Adjustments had to be made on all three levels—priorities had to be created and tough decisions made. There were many instances when I had to work 12- and 16-hour shifts at work, when there were no relief personnel available to cover vacancies. A PhD candidate must be able to balance family events such as weddings, funerals, vacations, sporting events, recitals, concerts, etc. during this arduous journey. You will have to turn down invitations and say no to some events.

Going through a divorce can be a very difficult and disruptive process in anyone's life, especially if there are children (at any age) involved. Going through a divorce while in a PhD program is exponentially harder. The divorce almost derailed my PhD quest; it affected me mentally, physically, and financially. I hesitated to tell my dissertation chair about the divorce proceedings, which turned out to be a mistake. When I told Dr. Walter McCollum what I was going through, he gave me words of wisdom that sustain me even now. His encouragement turned my entire focus 180 degrees and put me back on the right track. He believed in me when I did not believe in myself. I gained enough confidence in myself that I shared my story with my cohort members and they too were very supportive. What a revelation—by releasing my painful story, I became free. I know that I am not the only person who has gone through a divorce during their PhD journey, but I want to tell this part of my story because there may be students who believe a divorce can end their PhD journey. They need to know that it is possible to get through this process and persevere.

Going through divorce was not easy, but nothing in life that is worthwhile is easy. If it was, then everyone would be successful. Perseverance is the key to life. Surrounding yourself with positive people is important, and bonding with other students to share knowledge and experience is the key to success in a PhD program.

The course work is usually completed in a structured environment; class work is usually scripted, with the same assignments given to every student. Writing a dissertation requires self-motivation and thinking individually. The transition can be challenging for most students, because writing a dissertation is unlike any other document that you will ever attempt to write. A best practice for making the transition from course work to writing a dissertation is to select a topic about which you are somewhat knowledgeable. Because the transition involves conducting advanced research and features theorists and methodologies pertaining to the subject matter, the topic must be one that you want to investigate.

The proposal/dissertation process requires the selection of a dissertation committee, and selecting the right committee is crucial. Not selecting the right members for your dissertation committee can cost you dearly. During my PhD journey, I have had to change dissertation chairs twice, and one committee member had to be replaced. These actions set me back at least 3 years. If a member of your dissertation committee is continually missing deadlines or not responding to your e-mails or phone calls in a timely fashion, replace him or her as soon as possible.

The lessons to learn are many, but the greatest lesson learned is that before you begin your PhD journey, you should have a very good idea about what you are going to focus on in your dissertation and how you will collect data for the study. I have heard from many students at residencies that most students change dissertation topics or titles at least three times before they complete their PhD journey. This indecision can add weeks, months, or years to your PhD journey.

A tool that I have found to be important for PhD students is Walden's dissertation rubric. If a student follows Walden's dissertation rubric, he or she cannot be denied success in this program. One of the best supplemental tools for students to use is *Dissertation and Scholarly Research: Recipes for Success* by Dr. Marilyn Simon. The book is comprehensive and provides step-by-step directions for students to complete their PhD journey. Another book that all PhD students should own and use is the *Publication Manual of the American Psychological Association* (6th ed.). Owning this book is not enough; all students should use it from their first papers through their dissertation. Walden's online library is another excellent tool. Brick and mortar libraries are also an essential component for completing the dissertation. Every doctoral learner should have a library card.

One of the most common problems that I have experienced is lack of communication—in particular, not staying in touch with my dissertation chairperson. Students do not have to hold 15-minute conversations weekly with the chair but should check in weekly with a quick phone call or e-mail with a brief update or status of where you are in the process and how you are doing. This process can keep the lines of communication open and bridge any gaps between you and your dissertation chair.

Another problem is lack of commitment. If you embark upon this PhD journey, you must establish priorities and make decisions accordingly. To complete the program, a student must set aside between 15 and 25 hours per week toward the program—there are no successful shortcuts to this process.

I believe that peer mentoring has been one of the most rewarding aspects of the doctoral process. The camaraderie developed by our peer cohort group has been invaluable in achieving success in the program. The knowledge and experience exchanged among cohort members has helped us to succeed.

The benefit of cohort models is that students benefit when they hear what other students have experienced or are experiencing during their PhD journey. Students can receive helpful advice from instructors and from committee members, but hearing it from peers in the same situation, or maybe a little further ahead, serves as confirmation. The cohort model should not be the best kept secret at Walden—it should replicated across all of the colleges within the university structure.

19
Richard T. Brown, Jr., PhD

Professor, Consultant, Writer

If you can dream it, then you can achieve it. You will get all you want in life if you help enough other people get what they want.
—Zig Ziglar

I have always been intrigued with learning. Even at an early age, I knew that I liked school. Learning something new each day is a satisfying experience. In the seventh grade, I decided I wanted to be a microsurgeon. My mother was a nurse practitioner and my influence in the medical profession. After years of school and military training in the U.S. Air Force, I separated after working as a medical technician. I got a job in a doctor's office, and I continued to make plans for medical school, but I soon realized that my passion for medicine was no longer there. Instead, I decided to work on my Plan B, which was a career in the information technology (IT) field. I had the opportunity to cross-train into communications while serving in the Air National Guard. After more school and training, I got a job in the field.

I have always been blessed to work in nurturing environments. In fact, my hiring manager, Dr. Adrien Lang, was the inspiration for me pursuing my PhD. Adrien pulled me to the side one day and asked me, "What do you want to do when you grow up." Adrien managed several groups in our organization and was well-respected by everyone. He explained to me the importance of a PhD, particularly the obligations that come along with it. At that moment, I decided that I wanted to earn a PhD in the IT field.

I believe things happen for a reason. I was not meant to be a medical doctor. I was meant to become a PhD. As such, I found the right program for me, and as a result of hard work and dedication, I am now adding to this book as a contributor with a PhD. The gratitude and humility that I have gained over the years is overwhelming at times. Inspiration is a power force.

Doctoral Journey Best Practices

When I started on my doctoral journey, I did not know what to expect. I had fears that I could not write at the doctoral level. I also had fears that I would not get the big picture associated with a PhD. I feared not really knowing what I needed to know to talk about my research confidently. My approach to orienting myself to the doctoral process was rather simple. My focus in preparing for my journey included time management, support from individuals around me, and networking.

Time Management

Part of my success on my doctoral journey was due to being able to manage my time effectively. Time management is critical in almost everything people do. The doctoral process is no different. Balancing family, friends, work, school, and personal time can be a challenge to most people. The key to my success is technology. I stay connected to my iPhone, iPad, or any other device that helps me keep track of what I need to do. Having my own digital personal assistant is a stress reliever and keeps me operating effectively and efficiently. My dissertation chair and mentor, Dr. Walter McCollum, taught me that early in the process.

Gaining Support From Family, Friends, and Work

Before I started on my journey, I knew it would be demanding and time consuming. I talked to other graduates and read several articles about the demands of working on a PhD. All the books and articles I read and the people I talked to said the same thing: be honest with family, friends, and employers about school. I had several talks with my family and friends about the possibility of not being available or not being in contact with them like usual, which helped to reduce the stress of not being able to give them the kind of time I was used to providing. After several discussions, it got easier, especially when they realized the priority given to the PhD process.

Rethink My Networking

I received an excellent tip at one of my residencies in the PhD program. The faculty member suggested that we step outside our normal boundaries and start speaking to people we normally would not speak to. I began speaking to people in grocery stores or coffee shops just to initiate some type of conversation. Often the conversations lead to something surprising, such as that person knowing a family member or working in the same field.

I would even ask to sit next to a person I barely knew in the lunchroom. This technique is especially useful if you want to expand your professional network. You might be surprised about what you find out by just talking to someone. Exchanging information and building your contact list builds confidence and typically leads to new opportunities, both professional and personal.

Course Work Completion Strategies

I like to work when it is quiet around the house, and therefore I do my best work when everyone is asleep. I dedicated the hours of 10:00 p.m. to 2:00 a.m. as my official time to work on my doctorate. This was my time to conduct research, write, edit, and research some more. I kept that schedule throughout my journey, and I still keep late hours to get work done.

Dedicated Time for Study

Knowing that I have specific time set aside to do my work was a stress reliever. Unwanted stress can keep a person from having the focus needed to research topics or write certain sections of a particular chapter. Health is an important factor in the success of any doctoral program.

Medical setbacks can add years to a program if you are not careful and do not take care of yourself.

Embracing the Cohort Model

I was fortunate to be part of Dr. McCollum's revolutionary cohort model while working on my PhD. The model provided students with a vehicle to have most of their questions answered. Dr. McCollum's model was designed to help students learn from each other. The lessons learned were the foundation that made the model so successful. The students who embrace the process become empowered to take charge of their destiny. Seeing senior students in the cohort graduate each quarter was enough motivation for me.

I was blessed with the opportunity to lead the cohort for some time. I thank Dr. McCollum to this day for the opportunity. I had stellar cohort leaders before me that set the bar for how leaders should conduct themselves. Additionally, the cohort model provides instant motivation by allowing everyone to stay connected with other learners. The weekly calls, mock oral defenses, and guest speakers were instrumental in my success.

Essential Tools

The right tools are critical success factors in any doctoral program. Several tools were instrumental for helping me graduate. Taking advantage of technology helped me stay on schedule and provided me with instant feedback with regard to being organized.

Grammarly

Grammarly was instrumental in helping me develop as a writer at the doctoral level. Grammarly is a Web-based automated grammar tutor for students. The program helps to develop sentence-level writing skills and reinforce proper citation habits. Learners can upload drafts to Grammarly to receive immediate instructional feedback on over 100 different grammar rules and conventions. This tool helped me gain the confidence needed to write at the doctoral level. Practice makes perfect is particularly true for the doctoral process. The more you write, the more comfortable you become with writing. I still use Grammarly.

Copernic Summarizer

Copernic Summarizer is a tool that saved me hours of research time. Copernic Summarizer is a Web-based tool that summarizes text documents for you electronically. It provides the researcher with a synopsis in minutes that can be used to make comparisons or lists for other resources. This was especially useful for articles full of scholarly information but not good enough to be used as a reference. It was also useful for articles I used as references, as the software finds links between texts, group texts around topics, and contains all the facts from all the documents read. This is a very powerful tool.

Dropbox

Dropbox is a tool that has changed how I save and share my information. Dropbox is a company that provides online data backup. It allows you to store up to 2 GB of data free of charge. If you need to save more than that, there is a charge based on the amount of space needed. I use Dropbox because it allows me to sync my files across various work computers, home computers, and mobile devices. For example, while going through the doctoral process, I would write part of my dissertation at work on my PC. I would then save the file in my Dropbox folder, which backs it up. When I revisited my writing at home, I could then access my document from my Mac.

One great feature of Dropbox is that the document updates sync across all devices. There is no need to try to remember what version was saved. It also gives me an additional backup of my research that I would hate to lose. Lastly, the software allows me to share files for collaboration and to store and share video and photo galleries. All this is accomplished on the secure servers that Dropbox provides to safely keep track of my data.

Livescribe

Livescribe is one of my favorite tools. It was invaluable to me in class and in residencies that I attended while working on my research. Livescribe has a smartpen that records everything heard and written. There is also a special notebook required that helps capture words, diagrams, doodles, symbols, or anything else written on it. I never miss a word because Livescribe syncs everything heard and written. One of the great features of the software is that all I need to do is tap on my words and my smartpen will play back my notes. This saves a lot of time, especially when the session is note intensive. All my notes are conveniently accessible from my iPhone or iPad.

Personal Challenges

I experienced several challenges throughout my journey. Looking back, I can see that each of those challenges helped mold me into the scholar-practitioner that I am today. I highly recommend that you take some time and do a self-introspective assessment to make sure that you are spiritually, physically, mentally, emotionally, and financially ready to embark on your scholarly journey. You will definitely be tested throughout the entire process. Each test makes you stronger and helps mold you into the person you are destined to be.

Scheduling Conflicts

Unfortunately for me, I completed my proposal in December. I did not take into account the unavailability of committee members, editors, and other school officials. In December, some editors, reviewers, or even your chair may need to take more time to provide feedback to you. The school typically closes for the holidays, so be mindful of the holiday schedule and the turnaround times for committee members. Not doing so may have an impact on your graduation date. Several of my colleagues had to push back graduation plans because they did not consider multiple edits in their writing or additional time needed to research recommended perspectives by committee members.

Survey Participation

Another personal challenge I experienced was a major change with my survey participants. I planned to use a well-known IT organization for my study. I made the necessary phone calls and initial telephone calls to establish a connection with the organization. I was told that I needed to become a member to sample the members. So I became a member, as I followed them anyway. Weeks went by, and I completed my proposal. But before I reviewed university research reviewer (URR) approval, I wanted to make sure that the organization was still going to participate in my study. I contacted the organization and was told there had been some policy changes. The change included the fact that members were not to be asked to participate in any surveys from members or nonmembers. I was devastated. I had to change my proposal changed and then go through the entire approval process again. Fortunately, my committee chair had an excellent relationship with the committee members, which minimized some of the response times. If it were not for the dissertation cohort, I would not have planned for this type of roadblock. Instead, I had developed a list of back-up participants just in case an organization changed its decision.

Approval Processes

Even committees that work well together have differences of opinions sometimes. I had a major problem with my third committee member, the URR. My URR reviewed my proposal four times before finally approving it. Each time there was a different set of suggested changes that were unrelated to the previous suggestions. It got so bad during the last review that my chair had to schedule a meeting to make sure that they were both on the same page. The review time for a committee member is 14 days, so the four iterations of reviews took 56 days. Consequently, I missed my planned cut-off date for summer graduation with some of my colleagues, and I had to wait to graduate in winter.

Additional time was needed to get the proper approvals for instruments, diagrams, and other copyrighted material used in my dissertation. Using copyrighted material can be a nuisance. It may be difficult to find the owners of the copyrights. It may equally difficult to get approval. Fortunately, many copyright owners are lenient to students, as they know students are not trying to make a profit on their research, or at least not yet.

Each obstacle affected my graduation at some point. The final approvals can take some time as well. I defended in June. My degree was conferred in August. My graduation ceremony was the following January. It can be quite difficult getting through the process if the entire committee is not on the same page.

My Advice to Doctoral Learners

Although my doctoral journey is really just beginning, I am humbled by the fact that there are so many PhDs willing to help doctoral learners achieve their academic goals. I remember reaching out to several experts in my field of study for advice on emerging trends and research keywords. Each person I communicated with was open and inviting. They also provided some invaluable information about what to expect after graduation. So preparing for graduation needs to start as soon as you enroll in the doctoral program. The preparation includes thinking about social change implications, self-assessments, and branding.

Social Change Implications

After you begin your journey, a seed will forever be planted within you. That seed will allow you to grow into someone who has the capability to impact lives. Having a PhD provides many options. You may impact lives by teaching at a local university or school. You may be just as impactful working as a volunteer in your community or church. Your options are limitless, and you are only bound by your lack of imagination. So start thinking about how you can help others when you graduate. This journey is a humbling experience, and you will definitely need help along the way. So do not be afraid to give back.

Self-assessments

Another useful tool for new doctoral learners is a self-assessment. Take some time to look at yourself and take note of your strengths and weaknesses. For example, one of my weaknesses was public speaking when I started my journey. I worked with my mentor on my weaknesses. Dr. McCollum gave me speaking opportunities, which I graciously accepted. After time, my feelings about public speaking changed. I wanted to be a better public speaker, so I joined a local Toastmasters chapter. That experience was helpful as well. The self-assessment can be a very powerful tool if used properly. You can turn your weaknesses into strengths.

Branding

Your personal and professional qualities may start to change as you go through the doctoral process. The work ethic and relationships you build will help mold you into a new and improved person. What type of person are you? Are you dependable? Do you provide ethical and reliable counsel? These are just some of the questions that you may wonder about, but remember that your journey is a direct reflection of you. You are responsible for shaping and molding it to what you want it to be. Your chair, committee members, colleagues, family, and friends cannot make that decision for you. People will look at you differently when you graduate. Will they like what they see? Embracing the process early will help you determine the path you are destined to take. I hope I was able to help. Good luck!

20
Jodi M. Burchell, PhD

Educator

Education is not preparation for life; education is life itself.
—John Dewey

Is true success possible without great personal challenge? I reflected on this question as I wrote this chapter on maneuvering through the dissertation process. Success is the achievement of one's goals, but that is not the subject of this paper. This paper is about achieving life-altering success. This paper is about conquering the biggest challenges that one could willingly, purposively face. In this essay, I will share insights and experiences from my personal journey through the dissertation process. I will also discuss the main external force I attribute to my successful journey: involvement in a peer mentoring program. Specifically, I am referring to the peer mentoring model developed by my dissertation chair and mentor, Dr. Walter McCollum.

At What Expense?

For some people, success seems to come easy. For others, most of us actually, success is something conquered—something achieved through sacrifice and personal strife. In some ways, you and your loved ones may pay dearly to achieve your goal of earning your PhD. Payment may be rendered in the form of lost time with loved ones, lost sleep, lost time in church activities, lost personal time doing things you love, lost vacation activities, and so forth. I paid in the form of lost time with loved ones. I missed some of my nieces' and nephews' birthday parties. I missed parties at friends' houses. We all make choices in our lives, though. I made the choice to focus on my educational goals. Luckily, my loved ones understood and willingly sacrificed time spent with me. They were part of my support system, which is a dire need in a doctoral program. I cannot stress enough the importance of a support system. Support from your loved ones is essential, but so is support from your school, your mentor, and your fellow students. Support from loved ones may be given unconditionally out of love, but support from others is achieved through mutually offered support.

Inspiration

My initial inspiration to earn my doctoral degree came from a need to continue to learn and educate myself. I wanted to teach. I wanted to be an expert in something. At each step in my education and professional life, I wanted more. Don't we all want more of something? We all have our own reasons for wanting more—some internal need or hole to fill. I did my research and looked at several universities. As someone with a technical background, Walden University's model fit me best. I was also fascinated by Walden University's commitment to social change that permeates their philosophy and purpose. I never felt like I could affect big change, like solving world hunger, but it became clear to me that small change was entirely possible. My desire to teach could be a way to affect social change. Making a difference in someone's life is part of social change, and every time students thank me for helping them to achieve their goals, my soul smiles. My eyes were opened through Walden's commitment to social change, and now I see things differently.

How to Prepare?

Having made the decision to embark upon this doctoral journey, there are many ways to prepare yourself. I've already mentioned the need for a support system within your family and friends. Another way to prepare is to develop a learning mind-set. Many students have years of experience in their field. They may have had success in their professional lives, and they may be very confident. Confidence is important, although it should be in an "I can do this" way, not an "I already know everything" way. When I first started my journey, I had some level of confidence. After all, I'd achieved a master's degree, right? I had other accomplishments as well. What I really had, though, was faith that I could learn, that I could adapt, and that I could do what I needed to succeed. The doctoral process was a learning process. I had to learn better time management. I had to learn how to write like a scholar. I had to learn how to engage and how to be engaged. I had to learn how to network. I had to learn to get support and give it as well. I had to learn how to be critical. I had to learn to write at the doctoral level, which is very different from the master's or bachelor's level. All these lessons were not learned in the first month or even the first year. These lessons are learned over the entire course of the doctoral journey. Students should be open to receiving those lessons and be diligent about learning them.

Making It Through

There is also a certain mind-set shift that students go through to when moving from course work to the proposal/dissertation stage. Doctoral programs follow many models, depending on the university you attend. The majority of universities require a certain level of course work in the degree area. Once completed, the student moves to research- and statistics-based courses until it is time to work on their prospectus or concept paper. Then the proposal process starts. Walden University also have knowledge area modules (KAMs), which are 100-page research papers in specific topic areas. In this model, students had the advantage of learning to write in a scholarly manner. The KAM model drew me to Walden because I had a technical background. I did not have to write a thesis in my master's program. I was not entirely confident in my scholarly writing ability.

Regardless of the model, your mind-set changes as you advance through the stages of the program. It's not comparable to a lightbulb going off in your head, but it involves small, cumulative changes. I noticed the small changes as I transitioned through the stages of my doctoral program; toward the end of my dissertation and after some reflection, I could see how I had changed overall. I recognized the big picture changes. I could compare my first writings to my later writings and see the difference. I could see my writing had improved. I could see I had become more comfortable in my ability to be critical. I could see my thought process, writing, demeanor, and so forth had become more scholarly. Dr. McCollum, my mentor and chair, calls this process "learning to embrace your scholarly identity."

Another way to make it through your program successfully is to take advantage of every possible resource available. As others have mentioned, universities usually have a writing center and a dissertation center with many resources, including documents, videos, webinars, and support staff. Within the dissertation center, they are likely to have guides, rubrics, and other resources for effectively writing and formatting their dissertation. I highly recommend using the resources often, even before you start your proposal. To help with my writing skills, I hired a professional editor to edit one of my previous research papers, which helped me to learn the writing skills I needed to create a more professional document. Other tools my peers and I discussed included speech recognition software and text-to-voice software. One of my colleagues used the text-to-speech software to listen to journal articles on her drive to work every day. I highly recommend using every technology available that makes sense for you.

Many universities offer residencies and dissertation intensives for doctoral students. Residencies tend to last several days and provide students with the opportunity to meet faculty, network, meet other students within their program, and acquire resources. Residencies also provide students the opportunity to present their research and attend poster sessions. Some universities have moved their residencies, partially or fully, to an online forum. I believe students should attend on-ground residencies as often as they can for a chance to interact with students and faculty face-to-face. Another more recent addition to the resources available to doctoral students are dissertation intensives. These intensives provide doctoral students the opportunity to work one-on-one with faculty who are specialists in dissertation writing, statistics, and so forth. This type of program gives students the time to spend several days focusing on the formulation of their dissertation without any distractions from the outside world. I attended one of these intensives, and I wholly recommend them to any doctoral student.

Obviously, I can't explain everything a student needs to do to be prepared for the doctoral journey. Preparedness depends on the individuals, their program, their prior experiences, the tools they have already acquired, and so on. Individual experiences within programs also shape students' preparedness throughout the program. Most universities have a plethora of resources to support students, but students have to be self-aware enough to know that they need some sort of support or resource and be motivated enough to get the support they need. Thus, it is imperative for doctoral students to continue to reflect in order to anticipate and meet any needs that develop.

Obstacles

The potential for obstacles and setbacks in a doctoral program is high. Some obstacles may include family, work, and church responsibilities. These are not small obstacles such as not carving out enough time to write a paper, although several missed deadlines or papers is indicative of a larger issue. More important and potentially problematic obstacles may include a continual lack of time management or a lack of commitment to your course work. Time management is easily learned and practiced. Writing skills can certainly be improved through acquired resources or taking a course. Students just need to recognize the deficiency and act upon that need. It takes a higher level of self-awareness and self-discipline to manage your needs successfully.

More important, students may suffer a lack of support. There could be many reasons for this, but it is ultimately students' responsibility to reach out and get what they need. Universities have staff support, library support, writing support, and so on, but many times that is not enough. Students need to connect with their mentors and with other students. Students need to work within a cohort, either informal or formal, to exchange ideas and garner support from each other. Additionally, students may stall in their efforts, causing them to miss their deadlines. Students may not make even a minimal amount of progress. Delays are inevitable, but students have to be able to motivate themselves to get back on track. Support from a cohort or mentor can be the catalyst toward getting back on track. This discussion of support and cohorts leads to the topic of peer mentoring and its potential within doctoral programs.

Peer Mentoring

To understand the value of peer mentoring, it is important to understand how it is different from the value of mentoring in general. According to McCollum (2011), "Mentoring is a long-term, one-on-one relationship based on mutual trust that is focused on the mentee's professional and personal development" (p. xiv). Universities have long understood the value of mentoring, as their dissertation chairs have developed more of a mentor role over time. This is especially true in online programs. Models of mentoring have been implemented in many different settings, and the topic of mentoring has been well-researched in many areas (Quisenberry & Burchell, 2013). Some educational institutions have even implemented different forms of peer mentoring programs. Peer mentoring differs from mentoring in that peer mentoring involves more of a mutually beneficial, reciprocal relationship. Much of the literature on peer mentorship involves a singular focus on success such as its impact on student engagement and retention or specific benefits to either mentors or mentees. Additionally, much of the research is limited and approaches peer mentoring mono-directionally rather than as a reciprocal relationship (Quisenberry & Burchell, 2013). Implemented correctly, peer mentoring in doctoral programs can offer an additional level of mutually beneficial support.

While serving as dissertation chair for Walden University, Dr. McCollum developed a peer mentor program for his doctoral students. I was lucky enough to be part of that program and I attribute my peer mentoring experience as being at least partially responsible for my successful completion. Through that program, I networked, cultivated long-lasting professional relationships, and developed leadership skills. Dr. McCollum's peer mentoring program allowed me to participate in a system of structured support with other students. Dr. McCollum, my colleagues, and I have since had many conversations on the value and benefit of implementing cohort models in the doctoral process. We've discussed formalized peer mentoring programs, how to implement them, and how to manage the people and the processes. Regardless, I speak from personal experience on their value to me and my doctoral process. I would have likely, eventually, made it through the doctoral process whether I was exposed to a cohort or not; however, my education and my experience was made richer by my involvement in Dr. McCollum's peer mentoring program. I have no doubt that my time as a doctoral student would have been a lot longer without the benefit of support from my peer mentor and my mentees.

Not only did Dr. McCollum develop and implement a peer-mentoring program, but he also created a peer-mentoring model referred to as breakthrough mentoring (McCollum, 2011). Dr. McCollum's formula for breakthrough mentoring involves critical components such as Emotional Intelligence and a structured process. As previously discussed, success for students in doctoral programs relies on high levels of motivation, self-awareness, and the ability to self-regulate. These abilities are all part of Emotional Intelligence. Within a peer mentoring program, these abilities are especially important. A peer mentoring or cohort model also calls for a social skill ability, which is included in Emotional Intelligence. In other words, mentors and mentees need to be able to manage their interpersonal relationships and build networks; which is part of offering and accepting support. The second critical part of breakthrough mentoring is the structured process, which includes nine phases building on each other for a journey that supports the peer mentor–mentee relationship. The key concept is support, support, support. Get yours!

Your university, program, or dissertation chair may not have a peer mentoring program. You may not be in a cohort per se, but I have felt the effects of the support offered in these environments. In the absence of a formal peer mentoring program or cohort, I highly recommend cultivating relationships with your classmates and your dissertation chair. These are reciprocal relationships, so be prepared to offer support as well as accept it.

What Now?

Walking across the stage was one of the proudest days of my life. I had other proud moments while working on my degree such as my first book chapter, my first published peer-reviewed journal article, presenting some of my research at Yale University, and the first time I presented at a scholarly international conference. Since graduating, I have worked to continue publishing. From an educator's perspective, you have to maintain a scholar mentality. It's also important to grow as a scholar-practitioner. I have learned that you have to brand yourself continually, as challenging as that may be. Otherwise, you can become stale. I still struggle with branding myself. You also have to know your value and worth after you have earned your degree. Knowing your value is especially important if you plan to advance within your organization, become an expert consultant, or change professions. Knowing your worth is important in academia as well. As you apply for teaching positions, you have to be able to discern your subject matter expertise.

Earning a doctoral degree has different meanings for different people. For some, it is a means for advancing within their profession. For others, it is an opportunity to change professions or to move into a consulting role, for example. For yet others, like me, a PhD offers the opportunity to work in academia. My profession has been information technology for the past 16 years. I currently work as a senior database administrator. I also teach for three universities as an adjunct professor. I am on two dissertation committees and I am scheduled to go to Vietnam to be a guest lecturer for Vietnamese MBA students. It has been interesting mixing my professional and academic efforts as a scholar-practitioner.

Final Thoughts

The list of advice that I can offer regarding how to prepare for entering a doctoral program, how to maneuver and advance through the program successfully, and how to take advantage of tools and resources is long. The most importance bits of wisdom I can offer are as follows:

1. This is your program. You have to take charge of your program and your timeline. You have to follow your mentor's instruction, but the management of your project falls on you.

2. Take full advantage of every tool and resource available to you.

3. Treat your dissertation like a project. Create a project timeline.

4. Find someone to whom you are accountable. Form your own cohort if necessary. It's hard to report to someone that you haven't made any of the progress that you had planned to make.

5. Find someone to practice presenting with. Join Toastmasters. Practicing like this will help you practice for your orals.

6. Be open to all opportunities that come your way. Seek them out and take full advantage.

7. Know yourself! Be ready to make changes if something is not working for you.

8. Support, support, support!

Earning a doctorate degree is the hardest thing I have ever had to do, but the rewards I have received also surpassed any others. Earning my doctorate allowed me to grow as a person, to grow as a scholar-practitioner, to become a subject matter expert, to present at international scholarly conferences, and to publish in peer-reviewed journals. I have also been able to achieve my personal goal of teaching doctoral students. Earning my doctorate allowed me to create life-long relationships with people whom I have immense respect for, to become their colleagues, to be part of a peer mentoring program, and to be part of something that literally changed my life.

References

Quisenberry, W., & Burchell, J. (2013). Building collaborative learning communities: Support for peer mentoring models in online doctoral programs. *Mid-Continent Review, 2013*(2), 8-27.

McCollum, W. (2011). *Breakthrough mentoring in the 21st century: A compilation of life altering experiences.* Washington, DC: McCollum Enterprises.

21
Kim Tran, PhD

Wisconsin Department of Transportation
Urban and Regional Planner Advanced

My voice shalt thou hear in the morning, O Lord; in the morning will I direct my prayer unto thee, and will look up.
—Psalms 5:3

I had a dream to earn a PhD and to become a professor at a very young age. Even though I faced many struggles and challenges in my life, I always tried to keep my dream alive. When I was a teenager, I considered doctors intelligent, knowledgeable, and able to understand and explain things other people couldn't. I have admired all doctors I have met. I realized that they had great knowledge, were very thoughtful, and understood the needs of other people. More important, they were able to use their lives to impact the lives of others. I wanted to be like them.

My best practice for preparing for the doctoral journey and completing the doctoral experience was that, after being born in Vietnam, I had the great privilege of moving to the United States when I was young, which has one of the best educational systems in the world. So I thought I should take advantage of this opportunity to complete my higher education. I also told the Lord that my desire was to complete my higher education. I was willing to put aside my personal life to focus on earning my PhD in the United States, even though English is my second language. After leaving Vietnam and beginning a new life in the United States, I asked the Lord to help me stand on my own feet and overcome the many challenges I would face. I was willing to devote my time and energy to starting over.

To keep working toward my goal of completing my higher education, I worked full-time and caught a bus in the cold Wisconsin winter to go to Milwaukee Area Technical College in the evening. I vowed to complete my educational goal so I would be able to assist other people the best I could. With a strong determination and my family's support, I prepared to start my PhD journey. No one in my family line had ever earned a PhD. As one of six children, I learned to take care myself and tried to be a better example not only for my family but also for Vietnamese women.

I did not have many challenges completing my course work. My best practices were to follow the course work syllabus carefully. I made sure that I did not miss any deadlines. I participated in the discussion boards frequently and in a timely manner. I asked questions if I did not understand. After responding to other students' posts, I posted my own questions as well. This helped me to understand the material better. I communicated and learned from the experiences of other students I met at the residency, which helped me to understand the transition from course work to the knowledge area modules (KAMs). I also took courses in the summer to help me make better progress in getting to the proposal/dissertation phase. Another best practice was I usually found a quiet place such as a local library, where I could concentrate on my reading and writing. Before studying, I created a daily plan on what I would need to study and when I would need to finish. Then I would adjust my plan as needed.

One of the challenges I faced was that I did not encourage myself to communicate directly with my professors. I hesitated to ask questions. As a result, I had difficulty on an exam, and I did not have enough confidence to know whether my responses were correct. However, I was able to make adjustments to get back on task by learning from my previous mistakes. I learned to prepare and post my questions in the discussion board to ensure I understood the problems before the exam.

I did not embrace best practices for making the transition from course work to the proposal/dissertation process because I had unpleasant experiences working with my previous mentor, prior to working with Dr. Walter McCollum. When I was working with my previous mentor, I tried hard but I was not successful because I did not know where to start to write the dissertation correctly. So, I did it my own way. I did what I thought was right. I did not communicate with my previous mentor frequently. I discussed with my mentor what I planned to use from my course work in my dissertation, but my mentor's ideas were different from mine. I was not able to use anything from my course work in my dissertation because my mentor did not support my research topic. It wasn't until I began to work with Dr. McCollum that I understood more about the dissertation process. I learned that KAMs can relate to the dissertation. It was especially important that I align KAM 7 to my dissertation, and this helped me to prepare my prospectus and Chapter 1 of my proposal. Based on the challenging experiences I faced with my previous mentor, if I had to do it over again, I would discuss my possible dissertation topic with my prospective mentor before I ask him or her to be my mentor.

One challenge I experienced in the proposal/dissertation process was that it was difficult to start working on Chapter 1. Determining how to choose the topic and develop the research questions was hard. One of the most challenging parts was not knowing how to develop the research questions and how to define the dependent and independent variables. How do I choose a research topic I have passion for? How can my dissertation help other students find best practices to succeed in online education? Sometimes, I felt that I did not have enough motivation. I was frustrated. I learned that scholarly writing was different from writing on course work. The first three chapters took me a long time to complete. Chapter 1 was my most challenging chapter because I had to understand how to see the big picture of completing Chapters 1-5. I had to get used to scholarly writing. The school recommended that I take courses in scholarly writing and American Psychological Association style. After taking those courses, my writing became much better and I was able to continue with the rest of my dissertation process. I always asked the Lord to help me to be able to complete my dissertation step-by-step.

I overcame the challenges I faced by gaining self-control. I encouraged myself to continue. I believed I could complete my education. I got back on task by looking for other role models and I found Dr. McCollum, whose leadership style, care, and compassion toward his students and others I admired. I have learned through his instruction and from many of his previous students who were successful in their dissertation process. I kept revising my dissertation plan to refocus on what I did not complete on time. I sent my revised plan to Dr. McCollum and indicated the dates I had chosen to complete each task. After my proposal was approved, I was more consistent with my plan. Every day was one day closer to graduation day. I felt that I gained more motivation to complete my educational goal.

The greatest lessons learned in the proposal/dissertation process were that I needed to establish regular contact with my mentor to confirm what was not clear to me, I should not hesitate to ask questions, I must be consistent with my dissertation plan, and I must attend the cohort meeting regularly. I sometimes felt that I did not have anything good to share in the meeting. I felt that after a long day of work, my mind would not function well; I felt I did not have enough energy to join the meeting. I learned that my reasoning was not good. I needed to overcome these obstacles. I needed to join the cohort to learn from other students' learning experience. I needed to be there to encourage others and myself to complete the PhD journey. I needed to be a better listener and communicator.

A best practice for completing the course work in a doctoral program is to follow the syllabus and the guidelines from instructors. Post and respond to other students on the discussion board on time. Ensure you read carefully and understand the university's policies and procedures. With regard to the proposal/dissertation, find a topic you love. Search libraries to find the right resources to support your proposal. Read other dissertations related to your potential research. Use those sources as examples. Study the structure of a dissertation. Participate in scholarly writing and dissertation webinars. Store articles and other sources where you can retrieve them. Ask the writing center staff at your university to edit your writing. Join a student cohort or network group and bring up questions to discuss.

A problem I experienced in my doctoral process that kept me from making progress in the program was that I did not follow instructions and plan accordingly. I was not consistent in my planning. I tried to rewrite my plan but I did not completely focus on it because other things were affecting my schedule. I did not have enough commitment and discipline. I was hesitant to contact my mentor to confirm what I needed to do. I did not contact other students or exchange ideas to find best practices to complete the program.

Peer mentoring in the doctoral process consists of student peer mentors who are willing to share their experience to motivate other students to complete the program. Peer mentors are willing to help and motivate other students to collaborate with other learners. Peer mentoring can help students complete their dissertation successfully. Peer mentors feel a sense of gratitude after they realize that they can help other doctoral candidates reach their full potential. They feel they are paying it forward by sharing ways that previous doctoral students helped them to be successful in their own dissertation process. Peer mentoring is a continuing process that involves helping students to achieve higher educational goals and is an opportunity to show caring and support to each other, not only to complete the doctoral process but also in completing a life plan.

Cohort models in the doctoral process are an ongoing benefit to encourage students to communicate during the dissertation process and after graduation. In the cohort meetings, I loved to hear dissertation experiences from other students. They provided hints on how to be successful in online learning. I no longer felt alone when I joined the cohort, and I felt I had support and encouragement from other students. The cohort members were willing to listen and provide feedback on my oral presentation, which helped me to do better.

I felt great when my doctoral degree was conferred. When I walked across the stage to be hooded, I felt that I had completed a journey I didn't know I could complete. I felt that I was able to walk on the surface of the ocean with Jesus Christ reaching out to me. Walking across the stage to be hooded was the happiest moment in my life. I felt like I was able to breathe the air of freedom after my unforgettable experience of being thirsty and not sleeping for a week while crossing the ocean from Vietnam to a refugee camp in Malaysia.

While I have grown as a scholar-practitioner, I still need more growth and development after completing such an intense research-based program. I have had opportunities to interact with other scholars through the Walden Alumni Association, LinkedIn and other associations. However, I still feel that I need more motivation to participate. I need to understand and experience how these associations can help me to achieve my goals of growing as a scholar-practitioner. I understand that I need to build relationships with other scholar-practitioners so that I can learn how to put my degree to use. I am thankful to Dr. McCollum for giving me an opportunity to join the cohort so I can keep interacting with PhD candidates. I continue to share my dissertation experience with the students and learn from them as well. Also, I have demonstrated impacting positive social change by traveling to Haiti with Dr. McCollum, Dr. Sandiford, and Dr. Quisenberry. I have experienced how social change theory intercepted with real life in Haiti after the earthquake. Also, I understood more about the love of God being the same everywhere in the world. People can help and encourage each other wherever they live to impact social change in positive way. People can motivate each other to be successful and use their abilities to help others to achieve their educational goals. I will keep growing as a scholar-practitioner and will keep praying that my work is the will of God.

I am still learning how to be successful. I was chosen as one of 14 new doctors to attend the New Scholar Workshop at my January 2013 graduation. My research proposal on traffic forecasting methodologies and best practices is being used as a focus for peer exchange for several transportation departments in the United States. I feel that I have gained more confidence in my research. I have grown both personally and spiritually. I will gain more experience as a practitioner and learn how to use my degree to impact positive social change.

My scholarly identity includes learning how to use my degree to help others and myself. I want to apply my knowledge to make society better. I want to share my knowledge and experience, and I want to learn from others. I pray that the Lord gives me His wisdom and instruction so I can complete my daily tasks according to His will. I am still learning how to embrace my scholarly identity. I look at the work of other scholars, and I want to understand better how to work with other scholars, publish my work, and manage my life more effectively.

My greatest accomplishment after earning my doctoral degree was traveling to Haiti in July 2013. We visited an orphanage and taught youth between the ages of

14 and 25 John Maxwell's leadership and development principles. The work we did in Haiti intercepted with Walden University's mission of positive social change. Another great accomplishment after earning my doctoral degree was having my proposal of traffic forecasting methodologies and best practices approved by the research program at the Wisconsin Department of Transportation. I am excited to have opportunities to contribute my research knowledge and dissertation experience to the Wisconsin Department of Transportation. I am thankful that Dr. McCollum and his cohort have helped me to understand best practices from the dissertation process that I can use to contribute my research knowledge to the agency.

I still need to learn how to integrate into the sea of scholars and professional networks comprised of other doctors. I need to improve my communication and research skills by collaborating with other scholars. My interests are adult education, business, database management, long-range transportation planning, especially on the Traffic Analysis Forecasting Information System and the Travel Demand Model. In a joint cohort meeting, Dr. McCollum indicated that PhD students need to start branding themselves by publishing and presenting at conferences. I am grateful that I have had the privilege of leading an analysis for summer 2014 Traffic Forecasting Peer Exchange that provided me an opportunity to integrate with other scholars in the transportation professional network. I was glad the research program accepted my proposal and used it as peer exchange (peer review) for departments of transportation in several states, including Florida, Minnesota, Michigan, North Carolina, Ohio, Virginia, Washington, as well as the Federal Highway Association in Washington, DC to exchange ideas, review, report, and find the best practices to improve and implement in the short or long term of traffic forecasting methodologies. The peer exchange will also be the best resource for me to write the report to improve the traffic forecasting policy and procedure and be ready to submit another traffic forecasting proposal to the Transportation Research Board in 2015.

The most important piece of advice I would offer doctoral learners is to focus on the dissertation project plan they have created and then take action and adjust the plan as needed. Patience is important. Find ways to use the doctoral degree and continue to develop your life plan. Stay in contact with mentors, colleagues, and previous professors and engage with other professional organizations to continue learning from other scholars.

22
Verna L. Velez, PhD

Federal Acquisition Consultant

It is not fair to ask of others what you are not willing to do yourself.

—*Eleanor Roosevelt*

There is no feeling worse than being afraid to achieve, afraid to fail, afraid to ask a question, or afraid to say "I do not understand." My dissertation process involved all these feelings of fear. If I had an opportunity to take the journey again, I feel confident I would achieve my PhD within my originally established timeline of 3 years. Some of the lessons I learned throughout my dissertation process are (a) many of the elements that caused me stress could have been managed, (b) choose the committee wisely, and (c) give back to others starting the journey after completing this process.

The Inspiration to Pursue a PhD

It took me 10 years to complete my master's degree. To fulfill my master's degree program requirements, I was required to complete a directed research project. I completed the degree via an online program. The university did not have a formal research committee, and students were allowed to use secondary research material to complete the research project. While I was reading and reviewing the literature, I remembered thinking that it had taken me far too long to complete this 2-year degree, and I needed to stay in school and further my education. The literature I was reading was a challenge to understand, and I felt lost and alone. Prior to completing my master's degree research study, I had no other training or education in conducting academic research.

In reviewing the literature, I noticed many of the authors were PhD holders. I conducted an Internet search to learn more information about the doctoral degree. The more information I read about the PhD and its research and scholarly contributions, the more my interest grew in earning a PhD to increase my knowledge about the academic research process and to teach and make a difference. I was also motivated to continue my education to prepare myself for the next phase of my life. I knew I wanted to teach in higher education, and I felt earning a PhD would be a great way to prepare.

Preparing for the Doctoral Experience

Because of the Internet searches I conducted and talks I had with a colleague who holds a PhD, I decided to pursue the advanced degree. I first decided what I wanted to study and what I would do with the degree. Then I researched various universities in the local Washington, DC, metropolitan area, including Virginia and Maryland suburbs. I completed my master's degree in an online forum and decided that I preferred that method to an onsite environment. I then researched the various online doctoral degree programs in my desired field of interest, which was public administration. I was working in civil service and wanted to remain in the field but in a different capacity or area.

After I identified a school that offered the program of interest, I verified the school held accreditation by the certifying associations recognized by the U.S. Department of Education. The goal was to ensure I would not have issues with the quality of the education I earned. I also wanted to avoid signing on with a school that had financial gain as its goal rather than the quality of the education provided. After I chose the school, I set about trying to determine how I would manage the financial aspect of my decision. I was accepted for admission to Walden University and I paid tuition for the first two quarters, which was a financial strain. I then decided to apply for a student loan and received approval. I was excited to start my program, but I did not have a clear understanding of what to expect or what working toward a doctoral degree involved.

Best Practices for Completing the Course Work

I started the program by taking one course because I was also working and had a 4-hour round-trip commute to and from work. I knew my time for school would be limited. I also wanted to ease into the program because I was not sure what to expect. I quickly learned that it is an individual process and you get from the process what you put into it. The online forum did not offer much explanation or feedback on course assignments. The course requirement was to submit online discussion postings and any assignments by required deadlines. In an effort to be fair to the other learners, I tried to meet the timelines, but was late on several occasions. I would arrive home from work about 8:00 or 9:00 p.m., tired and not motivated to study.

I usually submitted discussion postings and assignments right before the deadline on Sunday at midnight. In an effort to improve this behavior, I found a fellow student who lived in the local area and asked if we could form a study partnership. She agreed and we would meet about once a month to discuss the lessons, and we attended the first required residency together. This also helped me to remain accountable and feel as if I was not alone in the process. Having someone to study with and exchange thoughts and ideas with helped to keep me motivated. It seemed that several of the professors for the course work I completed were not engaged with the students. They did not give a lot of feedback to prepare me for the dissertation process. Outside of class assignments, the professors did not offer much assistance.

It took me several years to complete course work that should have only taken me 2 years. I took as many as three classes one quarter in an effort to complete the required courses so I could move toward the dissertation process. Completing the course was fraught with the challenges of time management; lack of motivation; lack of interaction from the professors; and competing obligations at work, in my family, and at school. I focused on completing the course work and reached my goal 3 years after starting the program, when I realized how much money it was costing me the longer I took to finish the courses. If I had known at the start of my program how much it would cost me by not focusing, I would have focused and made the work, family, and school adjustments immediately. It was a costly lesson. However, I was finally able to move toward the dissertation process.

The Dissertation Process

One good decision I made was to decide on my dissertation topic during one of the research courses. This helped me when I transitioned to the dissertation forum. It was a good idea to decide and submit class assignments that related to my dissertation topic. Although I did not receive a great deal of feedback from professors, at least I learned the topic was achievable as a research topic. I remembered completing the qualitative research methodology course where the final assignment was a sample proposal. I used my dissertation topic and the information I gathered to draft the proposal. Although I later learned none of that information was useful in the actual proposal, it was good practice. I knew the dissertation process was going to be challenging, and I learned from my course that I would need to focus on effective time management and establishing realistic goals and timelines to complete the dissertation process.

Unlike the course work, the dissertation process did not contain a defined completion date. I learned from my experience of wasting time and money while completing the course work that I would need to be organized and dedicated to completing the dissertation process. I created a milestone plan and worked from that plan. I also made contact with a couple of people who lived in the area who were also working on their dissertations and asked if we could study together and share ideas and information. It seemed that because many people were working and trying to find the time for their studies, committing to a meeting and study session was a low priority. It is important to try and pair up with someone as committed to completing the process as you are, as this is likely to result in a greater commitment by you to keep scheduled study appointments.

I was asked to join the study cohort of a mentor, which I found both helpful and rewarding. This worked well and helped me achieve many of my dissertation milestones. Joining a cohort with liked-minded people who were also eager to complete the process gave me a forum to ask questions of those who were ahead of me in the journey. It also enabled me to learn from their experiences. Before joining the cohort, I was not getting much feedback or direction from my dissertation chair or the members in my dissertation forum. The quality of my initial dissertation documents was not high because I was unsure of what I was doing. Participating in the cohort outside of my dissertation forum helped me to gain a better understanding by helping me to create outlines and work with more focus and structure, which enabled me to improve my writing and obtain approval on my individual chapters and ultimately my proposal.

During the proposal process, I was often stressed and uncertain about completing the process. I was so stressed and frustrated that I would cry and give myself headaches. I learned that I had to ask questions, and if one faculty member was unable to help, I would keep trying, knowing I would eventually find someone who cared and would offer good insight and direction. I learned that the most important part of the dissertation process is selecting a chair. A chair can either make you or break you. It is also important to think and ask questions before you speak and create discontent among committee members. I had a nice chair, but my chair was not overly active in my process. My chair did not do anything to hinder my process, but also did not do much to help further my process. My best lesson learned was to be careful and smart about selecting a chair and committee members.

Tools to Help Achieve Dissertation Success

One of the best tools to achieve success during the dissertation process is to create a support network. The network could include two or more individuals capable of helping you stay the course and complete the program. Collaborating with other people in the program and sharing information is also helpful, although this could also be an interference if the environment becomes competitive. It was helpful to know that I was not the only person who did not understand the expectations or the process and we could share experiences to help each other move forward. Some faculty mentors establish boundaries, and many will share only what is required.

Another valuable tool was having a faculty mentor who cared, which helped a great deal. A successful mentor is beneficial when he or she takes an active role in helping students to navigate the dissertation journey. The knowledge, insight, and resources offered by a seasoned and giving faculty mentor were invaluable to the completion of my proposal process. I was able to experience firsthand the difference between a scholar-practitioner and a PhD holder. I found the scholar-practitioner could put into action the role of educating.

Doctoral learners can use numerous books, websites, and dissertation services, but the most sincere assistance I received during this process was the honest and open feedback from a seasoned mentor. This feedback helped me to understand what actions I needed to execute to complete the dissertation process. Not everyone involved in the process cared, but it was obvious this seasoned mentor cared and was committed to helping me complete the journey.

Having a great professional editor is also a good tool for successfully completing the dissertation process. Using friends or family members, unless they are professional editors, is not a good idea. Having access to a research library such as the Library of Congress or a university library that provides access to a variety of literature and journals is also important. Nothing is more frustrating than being unable to obtain an important article because you do not have access to the journal in which it was published. Reviewing other dissertations with the same research design is also helpful. Three books that were helpful for me during the dissertation process were *Practical Research: Planning and Design* by Leedy and Ormrod (2005), *Designing Qualitative Research* by Marshall and Rossman (2011), and the Bible. These primary resources helped to guide me through the process.

The dissertation process is challenging, and a student can get lost in the process for a long time. You have to pray, have faith, and do your part to complete the journey. It took me about six quarters to complete the process. Some students do not remain motivated because they do not receive encouragement from their chair. I have seen peers become stagnant because they do not establish hard deadlines and milestones. Students make other areas of their lives more important than the goal of completing the dissertation. Some students have questions about the expectations and do not know whom to ask. University faculty members have mixed feeling regarding the length of time it should take to complete the dissertation journey.

The inconsistency among committee chairs directly affects students.

Completing the Dissertation Process

The best way to complete the dissertation process is to establish realistic goals, to know your personal strengths and weaknesses, and to have a plan. One of the key aspects of completing the process was joining a cohort of students at various stages in the dissertation process. This helped me because I was able to learn information to which I would not otherwise have had access. Walden University treats the dissertation as a solitary process. Students log into the classroom forum and make a posting. It was rare to receive feedback from postings. Each student focused on trying to achieve his or her own goals. In the cohort group, there was a real sense of support and information sharing. If a student is interested in this type of setting, it should be available. However, I also found some students preferred to work individually and even though they were members of the cohort, they were not willing to share much information.

At this writing, I am about six steps away from completing the dissertation process. Although I wish I were done already, I understand where my setbacks occurred.

Understanding what you are doing, why you are doing it, and what will happen with the result is important. It took several rewrites to understand how my document should come together, and each element connects to the study and its importance. I learned by going through the process. Having more information on how to execute the process would have saved time and financial resources. Earning a doctoral degree is a costly endeavor, and it is important not to waste time or money. People can achieve the goal by learning from the lessons of others and choosing those elements that work well for them. Everyone has a story, but it is important to listen to what will work best for your individual situation.

References

Leedy, P. D., & Ormrod, J. E. (2005). *Practical research: Planning and design.* Thousand Oaks, CA: Sage.

Marshall, C., & Rossman, G. B. (2011). *Designing qualitative research* (5th ed.). Thousand Oaks, CA: Sage.

23
Lisa R. Brown, Doctoral Candidate

Diversity and Inclusion Consultant

Through hard work, perseverance and a faith in God, you can live your dreams.
—Benjamin Carson

The doctoral journey is arduous and requires perseverance and passion. Earning a PhD requires great sacrifice, and many are unable or willing to make a commitment. A person's willingness and ability to navigate through doctoral challenges determines whether he or she will be successful. Every day I remind myself why I embarked upon this journey, and I know that, despite the many challenges, I am fulfilling a lifelong dream. This chapter provides insight into the power of perseverance and collaboration.

Inspiration to Earn a Doctoral Degree

My passion for knowledge has fueled my desire to earn a doctoral degree. As a college freshman, I knew that I would one day earn a PhD. Over the years, my interest grew through my interaction with Dr. Nancy Baym. Dr. Baym was my first female professor. We often spoke of the benefits of working in academia. She was very encouraging and piqued my interest in the doctoral process.

Eventually, Dr. Baym and I developed a mentor relationship and often discussed my academic aspirations and passion for learning. Her invaluable guidance solidified my decision to one day pursue a doctoral degree. Because of her encouragement, I am fulfilling my dream of earning my doctoral degree.

Dr. Baym was a strong advocate for women in academia. She encouraged me to pursue a doctoral degree despite a decrease in the rate of U.S. enrollment (McIlveen, George, Voss, & Laguardia, 2006). Research has shown that women's rate of enrollment has increased greatly between 2004 and 2014 (McIlveen et al., 2006). Nevertheless, she did not want me to be misled about the doctoral process. She taught me about the challenges women encounter, such as "family responsibilities, job related pressures, financial concerns, the nonexistence of community support, and poor quality mentor relationship"

(Lovitts, as cited in McIlveen et al., 2006, p. 168; see also Maher, Ford, & Thompson, 2004).

Dr. Baym is an advocate for women in academia. She became my role model for women who pursued careers in male-dominated fields. Because of her, I have the confidence to earn a PhD that will allow me to contribute to positive social change in two male-dominated fields: academia and the automotive industry.

Best Practices to Prepare for the Doctoral Experience

To make consistent progress, it is necessary to adopt and adapt the best practices of other doctoral learners. Best practices are practices that contribute to specific outcomes. Three best practices have helped orient me to the doctoral experience. First, seek out current doctoral students and learn as much as possible about their doctoral experiences. Before enrolling in a doctoral program, I reached out to friends and inquired about their doctoral journey. It was irrelevant that none of them was in the same program; the key was to learn about the time commitment, program rigor, and financial aid options.

The second best practice was to make personal connections early in the program. I take every opportunity to meet new people at residencies and in the online forum. More important, I made a concerted effort to develop kinships that transcend the classroom. I now have a circle of friends with whom I speak to numerous times a week. We offer each other support, provide constructive criticism, and celebrate each other's accomplishments.

Last, it is important to make connections with faculty, and connecting with advisors, librarians, professors, and writing center staff has been advantageous. Building relationships early on will help students avoid the dreaded mentor crisis. Students often complain that it is difficult to find a chair for their committees. Thus, I recommend students cultivate faculty relationships during the first year of the doctoral program.

Best Practices for Completing the Course Work

Over 50% of students who enter doctoral programs fail to complete the course work (Maher et al., 2004; McIlveen et al., 2006). There are many reasons some students become all but dissertation (ABD). According to Maher et al. (2004), the biggest obstacles for students are increased time to complete the program, financial resources, and inexperience with research methodologies and preparation. Adopting a timetable for course work completion minimizes two of the aforementioned barriers. As for research experience, working closely with faculty members builds research confidence. I also recommend purchasing research methods resource books, which are useful in completing research course work.

Challenges for Completing the Course Work

My journey over the past 2 years has been exciting. In the beginning, I was afraid that I would have difficulty adjusting to the online classroom environment. Moreover, the notion of learning American Psychological Association (APA) style terrified me.

By the second class, I was comfortable with the online environment and was navigating the classroom with ease. As for learning APA style, Dr. Donna Brown, a Walden faculty member, was instrumental in my learning the fundamentals of APA style. She had a zero tolerance for APA mistakes. By the third week of her class, I was well on my way to mastering APA style. Her disciplined approach toward APA style improved my skills and lessened my anxiety regarding APA style.

Based on my personal experience, time management is problematic for most students. Many students have full-time jobs and have difficulty with work–life balance. For example, during the first 18 months in the program, I traveled 85% of weeknights, which consisted of extensive driving and over 100 hotel stays a year. The following year, I relocated two times within three states in 90 days. Despite this, I persevered, because I was committed to doing a bit of school work every night. This disciplined approach ensured I was not overwhelmed and allowed me time to complete assignments and tend to familial responsibilities.

Best Practices for the Transition From Course Work to Proposal

The transition from course work to proposal is delicate. Walden's doctoral curriculum schedule eases students into the proposal writing phase. The phase-out stage begins with the Writing the Proposal course, where students learn in detail about writing Chapters 1-3. During this class, students complete weekly assignments and simultaneously work on chapters of the proposal. Like most students, I was eager to complete the course work, as I felt it infringed upon the time needed for writing the proposal.

Making the transition from course work to the proposal process was seamless. I benefited greatly from participating in a weekly dissertation cohort. I have taken best practices shared during these calls and incorporated them into my proposal development plan.

Challenges and Setbacks Experienced During the Proposal Process

Time management continues to be my biggest challenge. I am now on my third relocation since entering the program in 2011 and I am struggling with time management. In March 2014, I started a new job in a new city, put my home on the market, and began the process of house hunting. I am mentally exhausted and find it difficult to stay on task. I rely on encouragement from my classmates to keep me motivated and focused.

As I am just beginning the proposal process, I do not have any setbacks to discuss. However, I would like to share a setback that I experienced while writing the prospectus. During the early stage of writing the prospectus, a faculty member noted that my topic might not be suitable for a PhD study. For two weeks, I was in a frozen state. The task of locating new articles was overwhelming. My independent research was fruitless, and I ultimately required the assistance of Walden's librarians.

Eventually, I was able to locate a sufficient number of articles using outside sources. The greatest lesson learned was to expand my search resources. In addition to Walden's library, I now use three public university libraries, which allows for broader access to more literature resources and databases.

Tools to Help Achieve Proposal/Dissertation Success

No one matriculates in a doctoral program with the intention of being ABD. In addition to the financial cost of completing a doctoral program, most students have made tremendous sacrifices. The goal is successful completion of the dissertation process in a timely manner. Success is contingent upon being equipped with the proper tools that aid in the satisfactory completion of the dissertation requirements. Although there are many tools to help achieve academic success, the foundation for success involves mentoring, purposeful writing, applicable knowledge development, and organizational skills (Downs & Morrison, 2011).

Research has shown that a student–faculty mentor relationship minimizes feelings of isolation (Downs & Morrison, 2011; Felder, 2010). Because doctoral programs require that students work in isolation, the students should strive to cultivate as many student–faculty relationships as possible. Faculty mentorship provides professional development and helps shape the academic identities of doctoral students.

According to Davidson and Johnson (as cited in Felder, 2010), faculty mentorship involves events and exchanges related to research, skill procurement, and social or emotive facets of the mentor–mentee relationship. It is essential to the doctoral experience and thereby increases the likelihood of degree completion (Downs & Morrison 2011; Felder, 2010).

Resource Management

Resource management is integral to the dissertation writing process. Students need a reliable and flexible management system that allows for the accumulation, consolidation, and management of reference resources. Cost-conscious students will most be attracted to the free resources management tools. These tools are available as desktop programs, Web-based services, and browser add-ons.

Zhang (2012) recommended sampling various tools to determine their strengths and weaknesses. I recommend sampling free management tools such as EndNote, Zotero, and Mendeley. According to Zhang (2012), each is useful for "accessing, collecting, organizing/managing, collaborating, and citing/formatting" (p. 46) literature. I will refrain from offering any recommendations, as this is a personal decision that involves experimentation.

Common Problems of Doctoral Learners

Doctoral learners experience numerous challenges throughout their journey. For many, delayed progressed often occurs due to time constraints, availability of funds, advising relationships, student preparedness, and personal concerns such as family, marital, and health challenges (Maher et al., 2004). Many of my peers say funding is the most common problem, followed by inadequate advising or poor mentoring relationships, which affects student development and motivation. Another challenge to program completion is the lack of research experience. Research shows that students are ill prepared and lack the aptitude to complete their studies (Maher et al., 2004; McIlveen et al., 2006). Students should plan for disruptions to their dissertation process that relate to finances, employment, family, and health issues.

From my experience, community support is favorable for overcoming barriers. I recommend students create a supportive environment that is conducive to decreasing stress and other impediments. Every student should strive to incorporate supportive people into his or her social network. Doing so provides the support needed to make it through challenging times.

Peer Mentoring

Students should take advantage of peer mentoring. Although Walden University does not have a formal peer mentoring program, I have formed several peer mentoring relationships. These informal relationships provide a supportive environment in which to collaborate and offer encouragement to one another.

The benefits of peer–mentor relationships and faculty–mentor relationships are different. Peer mentorship is a reciprocal relationship that must equally meet the needs of all parties. All parties must have a clear understanding of the relationship. My colleagues and I use peer mentoring primarily to share our experiences during the dissertation process and to build camaraderie.

Cohort Models

College programs have cohort models to build camaraderie and a sense of learning. Walden used cohort models in the classroom environments and during residencies. I have mixed feelings about the benefits of the cohort model in the online classroom environment. Online cohorts are supposed to be collaborative learning environments where students come together to learn and share. However, my experience has been lackluster due to lack of group structure and leadership, thus limiting the effectiveness of the group. I prefer not to participate in online cohorts, as there is too much variance in student motivation, competency, focus, and accountability. Insufficient classroom structure and the lack of peer discipline have sullied some of my learning experiences at Walden.

Conversely, I voluntarily participate in a dissertation collaborative cohort. Within the cohort are students at various stages of the dissertation writing process. I have learned a lot from my cohorts' experiences.

Members are willing to share their experiences for the betterment of the other members. The group's culture allows for increased learning through constructive feedback and collaboration. Holmes, Birds, Seay, Smith, and Wilson (2010) proffered that collaboration is effective in advancing students through the dissertation process. The dissertation cohort offers a communal environment where students can make connections in a supportive environment (Driscoll, Parkes, Tilley-Lubbs, Brill, Pitts-Bannister, 2009; Holmes et al., 2010).

Doctoral Process

The dissertation process is challenging, but through perseverance, faith, and indomitable determination, it can be a fulfilling journey. Preparedness and perseverance are key characteristics of successful doctoral students. Students interested in earning a doctoral degree should (a) select a program that has ample resources such as residencies, writing support, librarians, and writing intensives; (b) participate in mentoring relationships; (c) join or form a collaborative cohort; and (d) solicit support from family and friends. The more knowledgeable someone is about the doctoral experience, the more likely he or she will have a rewarding experience.

References

Downs, C., & Morrison, H. (2011). Beyond the PhD: Putting the right tools in your research toolbox. *Biological Research Nurse, 13*, 5-14.

Driscoll, L. G., Parkes, K., Tilley-Lubbs, G. A., Brill, J. A., & Pitts-Bannister, V. (2009). Navigating the lonely sea: Peer mentoring and collaboration among aspiring women scholars. *Mentoring & Tutoring: Partnership in Learning, 17*, 5-21.

Felder, P. (2010). On doctoral student development: Exploring faculty mentoring in the shaping of African American doctoral student success. *Qualitative Report, 15*, 455-474.

Holmes, B. D., Birds, K., Seay, A. D., Smith, D. B., & Wilson, K. N. (2010). Cohort learning for graduate students at the dissertation stage. *Journal of College Teaching & Learning, 7*, 5-12.

Maher, M., Ford, M., & Thompson, C. (2004). Degree progress of women doctoral students: Factors that constrain, facilitate, and differentiate. *Review of Higher Education, 27*, 385-408.

McIlveen, P. J., George, M. R., Voss, S., & Laguardia, A. (2006). Surviving the doctoral dissertation experience: The N. W. Sisters' study. *Journal of International Women's Studies, 7*(4), 168-185.

Zhang, Y. (2012). Comparison of select reference management tools. *Medical Reference Services Quarterly, 31*, 45-60.

24
Jennifer Perkins, PhD, MPH, CHES

Public Health Faculty

Until the lions have their own historians, tales of the hunt will always glorify the hunter.
—*African Proverb*

Successfully Navigating the Dissertation Process

I was born and raised in Gary, Indiana. I was a stellar high school student with the promise of a bright future. I entered Indiana University (IU) as a biology/premed major with hopes of pursuing a career in pediatric medicine. At the end of my freshman year, my grade point average was 1.9 and I was put on academic probation. I contemplated not returning, but couldn't bear to tell my parents after all they had sacrificed for me to attend college. I returned my sophomore year only to perform just as poorly as I had the previous semester. I received notification that I was being dismissed from the university and was emotionally destroyed. That moment forced me to ask myself a very difficult question: What do you want to be when you grow up?

Once I recovered from the gut punch of dismissal, I had to rally support from university leadership to gain admittance. This required me to change my major and obtain letters of support and signatures from faculty members in my new program of study. As I was going through this process, I not only had to justify my case to them, but I also had to make a promise that I would give my best and complete my degree. These faculty members gave me a second chance at education that many in my situation would never receive.

The applied health science program became my academic home for the next 3.5 years. I learned a lot about health education, but I learned even more about what it meant to be student centered. I successfully matriculated through the bachelor's program and began contemplating my next step. I often stopped and asked myself that same critical life question whenever I found myself at a crossroads: What do you want to be when you grow up? As I was applying for master of public health programs, my academic mentor at IU asked me what my plans were after graduation. When I indicated I was looking into graduate school, she asked me if I had applied to IU. After discussing the advantages and disadvantages of staying on campus, I was convinced that IU was the best place for me at that time. These interactions again reinforced the concepts of effective mentoring and student centeredness. It was nice to have someone take an interest in my future.

At each milestone of my academic and professional career, people have noted that we had a special gift to share with one another. These individuals were faculty members at all stages of my education, and they each left me with a lesson and a covenant for me to pass it along.

When I made the decision to pursue doctoral studies, I had worked in public health for 2 years in the Dallas area. I connected with local public health professionals in the area and extended my network to local faculty members within the two programs I was considering. I was deciding between the DPh, traditionally a practitioner's degree, and the PhD, traditionally more of an academician's degree. Both options had a concentration in community health but would prepare me professionally in very different ways.

After asking myself the question that was driving my career and life decisions, What do you want to be when you grow up, I decided on the PhD in health studies at Texas Woman's University. At the time I made this decision, I was also preparing for another major milestone: motherhood. I was expecting my first child, who was born just 2.5 months before I sat in my first doctoral class. This truly put my personal preparations into high gear, but it reinforced that I was making the best decision for our future.

Being a doctoral student takes time, dedication, discipline, and at times a good sense of humor—as does being a parent. These new challenges came in a wave of opportunity that led me to read, reach out, and read some more. Developing a strong work–life balance early on was critical to completing my program in 3.5 years. I was driven to succeed by the support of my family, friends, and professional network. Scheduling blocks of time for each component and responsibility can seem a bit overwhelming, but it can also provide moments of clarity during the times when we feel unsure of our next steps. Having an academic plan laid out in an easily manageable and accessible form decreases unproductive downtime. It can also foster a feeling of accomplishment when you complete items and move one step closer to your goal.

Given that I was completing a traditional brick and mortar program, I began my coursework knowing that I had limited time to dedicate to attending classes. I made the difficult decision to resign from my full-time community health job and focus on my classes. My next step was to meet with my academic advisor and plan the most effective strategy to complete my courses while I worked part-time for the university. Communication with my academic advisor and my instructors each term was critical for me to remain on schedule and meet my semester goals.

At the beginning of each term, I reviewed the course syllabus to identify major course assignments. Organizing my academic journey fed into my ability to have more organization in my home life. It was important to me for the two to work in concert with one another. We have all had the domino effect when work and home spiral out of control. The chaos causes frustration, but it also burns time.

Having a dedicated place to read, work, and store academic materials made the journey and the commitment seem more attainable. I opened and closed my studies each day, just like work offices open and close each day. My dining room became my refuge and escape for learning and privacy to connect with my internal scholar. It was large enough for me to spread out all of my work and books, but small enough to be contained as my personal sanctum of knowledge and writing.

After I completed my courses, my plan was to return to work full-time at a local health organization. This would coincide with the completion of my research and dissertation as another major milestone in the academic journey. As I was completing my prospectus, I was offered a full-time position at Dallas County Health and Human Services. The transition to full-time employment brought even more challenges, including my commute, child-care arrangements, and fewer hours that I could dedicate to reading and writing each day.

The best suggestion I was offered and am able to pass along is that, with each course I completed, I was able to add research articles to my growing collection to use for my dissertation. The idea of having to start from scratch would have been daunting given the schedule I laid out for myself when I started the journey in January 2001. I color coded and cataloged each article I reviewed into a specific category for future reference. Each week I would select a category and focus my time and attention on reading, highlighting, and making note of important information or gaps associated with the specific component of what was to become my dissertation proposal.

The area that was most challenging for me during the process was gaining institutional review board approval. My topic related to sexual attitudes, perceptions, and behaviors. My participants were adolescent girls. Although I was warned that this topic, and this age group, would be difficult, I felt that it was important to stay with my plan. Even though it took me 5 months to receive institutional review board approval, I wouldn't change my scope for anything.

At this point, I used both the university library for intense research sessions and the public library when I felt the need to have a more relaxing environment outside of the house. I used my home office for writing and any late night work I did when my family was asleep. I needed to respect my routine, so that others would follow suite. As I addressed each group of articles, I was able to see the big picture in my mind of how this large task of writing a dissertation became much more manageable one chapter at a time.

This transition was much easier during the proposal phase than it was in the results phase. As I was nearing the end of my proposal phase, I found we would be blessed with baby number two. The excitement of my then 3-year-old having a younger sibling was a bit overshadowed by the realization that I was becoming physically exhausted in a shorter period of time than before. I entered the final stages of writing with less energy but with more determination that the completion of this journey was on the horizon.

In an effort to regain balance, my 3-year-old became my study buddy. When I read, she read; when I needed to dedicate time to writing, she was treated to closed caption TV time. As a sidebar, this was very helpful in her development; at 13, she reads and comprehends at a college level. I had to take the opportunity to spend quality time with her before our new arrival but also complete my dissertation in a timely manner.

Although I faced a few small hiccups during the completion of my dissertation, key individuals and critical resources made the process go a little more smoothly than I could have hoped. Having a supportive peer network and a knowledgeable and compassionate chair were critical for me. My program had a relatively small cohort of students. We had a mutual respect for one another and an earnest desire for all of us to succeed. We commiserated together over meals when time were rough, and celebrated with each other when a milestone was achieved. We served as each other's informal reviewers and editors when deadlines were quickly approaching.

My chair was knowledgeable, firm, trustworthy, funny, compassionate, and most of all available. Dr. Mary Shaw welcomed me not only as a doctoral student but as an employee, a daughter, a friend, and a future colleague. I trusted her to be honest with me about my work, and yet nurturing when I was having "one of those days." She exposed me to her professional network and taught me how to brand myself as a professional in the field of public health. This relationship still exists today, 10 years later. This past October, I was able to introduce my doctoral mentees to her to complete the circle of mentoring.

My day planner was the keeper of all of my lists, impromptu dissertation notes, reminders, and inspirational quotes. With the introduction of so many technology advances, there are many methods to keep you organized. For me it was using pen and paper to write everything down and having the pleasure of literally crossing off the accomplishments from my to-do list. At the end of the day, I had a tangible record of what I had been able to accomplish and a list of tasks that were still before me. It was a realistic and accurate representation of my plan and kept me grounded in the work that lay before me. Two books that I would recommend for current doctoral students are *Writing for Publication* by Henson (2007) and *Surviving Your Dissertation: A Comprehensive Guide to Content and Process* by Rudestam and Newton (2005).

The day I defended my dissertation orally was one of the most nerve racking days of my life. I had come to know my committee well and I knew what their expectations were. As I went through my slides and graphs, a feeling of calm and peace came over me. I knew that the journey was coming to an end, and while my feet were swollen and my belly too big for my comfort level, I felt a sense of peace. At the end of my presentation and question-and-answer session with my committee, I stood proud. I had done it. The long hours, missed events, and stressful days were worth it and no one could take that away from me.

The day of commencement, I was a ball of nerves and very pregnant. I promised myself I wouldn't cry, but let's be honest, everyone knew that I would. I sniffled from the time I put my regalia on until it was time to walk into the ceremony. I managed to get through the entire ceremony without shedding a tear until they called my name and I walked on the stage. My daughter was standing at the end of the stage in a red and white seersucker dress waiting for me. She was smiling and clapping as if it were her own special day, and in a way I guess it was both of ours.

Immediately at work, I refocused my energy to settle into my new position, I had been promoted to a new department that I had little experience with. I had a new team to get to know and new content to master. I had worked in HIV/AIDS for 4 years and was now working in bioterrorism and disaster response. This meant I not only had to rebrand myself because of the academic achievement but also become a content expert in an emerging public health field. The doctoral journey had given me a renewed faith in my abilities, and my colleagues were taking notice. I hosted a few episodes of a local public access TV show and was becoming the go-to person on the team.

I remained in this department for the next few years before deciding it was time for a career move, again asking myself the daunting question: What do you want to be when you grow up. I had been working as contributing faculty for an online institution, was beginning to get the hang of the online environment, and was enjoying the student interactions and the flexibility it allowed me. I was receiving positive feedback from the university and was awarded Faculty of the Year. My students appreciated the real-world experience I brought to the classroom and felt that I created a stimulating learning environment.

Remembering all the faculty members who helped and supported me on my academic journey from Indiana University through Texas Woman's University, I finally was able to answer the question. I wanted to do for other students what had been done for me. I wanted to mentor public health students through their academic journey and provide the support that we all need at some point. I decided to take a leap of faith and transition to academia full-time. I was able to join Walden University as the practicum coordinator for the master of public health and master of health administration programs. This position gave me the best of both worlds, as I am working with students while they are completing their field experiences and working with doctoral students on their dissertation research. This position affords me the opportunity to remain current in the field I love so much as well as continue to develop my own professional skills, all while sharing it with future colleagues across various disciplines.

When I started the journey to complete my PhD, it was my backup plan to becoming a physician. What I came to realize is that this was God's plan for me all along. I didn't see it at the very beginning, but over the course of my career, each challenge was followed by great success. I have met wonderful individuals and developed meaningful relationships. At times, I felt that I wasn't cut out for this journey, but throughout the process, I have grown and become more confident. I am taking on new work responsibilities and exposing myself to areas professionally that I have always steered away from. It took me longer to prepare myself after earning my doctorate to truly identify myself as a scholar, but now that I am here, the sky is the limit.

So, when the roadmap to success is unclear, ask yourself the question, What do you want to be when you grow up, and then navigate yourself there one milestone, one speed bump, and one backup plan at a time.

References

Henson, K. T. (2005). *Writing for publication: Road to academic advancement*. Boston, MA: Allyn and Bacon.

Rudestam, K. E., & Newton, R. R. (2007). *Surviving your dissertation: A comprehensive guide to content and process*. Thousand Oaks, CA: Sage.

25
Victoria B. Buck, Doctoral Candidate

Principal/Administrator of Renal Consultants

Every great dream begins with a dreamer. Always remember, you have within you the strength, the patience, and the passion to reach for the stars to change the world.
—Harriet Tubman

Learning is a lifelong goal. It is a goal that defines, directs, and ignites the learner's desire for knowledge in all its realms of possibilities. Socrates said, "Education is not the filling of a vessel, but the lighting of a flame." As doctoral learners, we are more than empty vessels waiting for education to be poured liberally into our souls. Through our education, we become effectively equipped to illuminate transformational social issues that positively affect our families, communities, and nation.

Inspiration to Earn a Doctoral Degree

Learning has always been the seminal process by which I define and challenge myself. Who I am and what I am is continuously being reshaped through learning, the environment, my family, social relationships, and life experiences. I have diligently strived to acquire the knowledge and leadership skills to sustain the businesses and organizations to which I am committed. Additionally, I have sought unique opportunities to discover and embrace an emotional, cultural, and spiritual intelligence about the community organizations to which I serve.

The doctoral degree has always been a goal for my life, but one I delayed until each of my four children had successfully embarked in his or her field of endeavor. As my youngest child departed to college in 2011, I started my doctoral program. It was a life-fulfilling venture, timed perfectly to coincide with the mixed emotions of having an empty nest. As a lifelong learner, I sought to earn a doctoral degree as a means of enhancing the leadership, strategic decision making, and delivery of services of the local nonprofit organizations to which I respectively volunteer or serve on the board of directors. Leadership deficits are prominent among the nonprofit organizational sector. Community organizations need strategic leadership to guide them through the change processes that threaten their operational success. I drew my inspiration to earn a doctoral degree from a profound awareness of the needs of the nonprofit organizations I serve and witnessed the PhD consultants brought on to craft working solutions to the problems these organizations faced.

Best Practices to Prepare for the Doctoral Experience

I completed my master of business administration in a traditional brick and mortar environment. I enjoyed attending classes and having the opportunity to meet with fellow student and professors, but my life soon changed. Having to care for elderly parents, I needed an academic program that could accommodate the time flexibility that my life now required. I talked with a friend who had completed her PhD studies in 2010 through Walden University. While I was awestruck that she had seemed to have effortlessly completed a PhD, I had no inkling that she earned her degree through an online university. What was online learning? I had never considered online learning as a possible academic opportunity. She enthusiastically shared her area of concentration with me, which was organizational change management. It thoroughly resonated as the doctoral experience I had envisioned. I researched the benefits of online learning and decided it was an ideal fit with my current responsibilities.

To prepare for the onset of doctoral learning, I first talked with my family to explain the implications of a doctoral study and the challenges of setting new priorities. Later, I decided to adjust my work hours and volunteer commitments to accommodate the requirements of my doctoral study. Preparing for the doctoral program also included talking to my advisor to review the course schedule for my area of specialization, securing financial aid, purchasing course textbooks, and creating a mental roadmap for how to balance the coursework with family, work, and social responsibilities. I immediately sensed that embarking on a doctoral journey was going to unleash a mixed blessing of academic fulfillment and frustration. How could I manage this feeling of being constantly overwhelmed? Mujtaba, Scharff, Cavico, and Mujtaba (2008) posited that doctoral students have to deal with difficult feelings such as boredom, frustration, and loneliness and that these feelings are exacerbated when students are not fully able to identify the personal motivation for pursuing the degree, which causes added stress and ultimately results in dropping out of the program.

Practices for Completing the Course Work

Preparing to complete the course work generates a lot of insecurity as a doctoral student, as you do not know what to expect; you are not familiar with the course work, the field of research, or the instructor; you do not understand how to negotiate the university library or research center; and you do not know any of the students on your course roster. You feel like you are in a foot race without knowing the parameters of the racetrack. Pursuing a doctoral degree is often compared with running in a marathon. Tweedie, Clark, Johnson, and Kay (2013) noted there are implicit similarities between the two: the need in both for extensive preparation and focus, the very real and quite commonly occurring possibility of withdrawal before completion, and the extraordinary challenge presented by both. Tweedie et al. further asserted that though a long distance runner appears to be a solitary entity, in actuality, most long distance runners embrace a community of practice support. Similarly, to ensure success with course work, the doctoral student must embrace a community of support from family, advisors, instructors, and peers. Academic residency programs created a community of support for me through sponsoring the opportunity to meet instructors and peers face-to-face and share the doctoral learning experience. I have continued relationships with many of the students I met at past residency programs. Maintaining these relationships allowed me to sustain a shared learning experience throughout my doctoral program. Talking with students, listening to their stories of program challenges, and learning how they addressed their fears or concerns about the doctoral program, family, work, and social commitments provided an invaluable barometer to assess my feelings, concerns, and continued plan of action. Additionally, joining the cohort of a leading faculty member in the doctoral program provided weekly clarification of the doctoral process, a shared learning experience with fellow students, a realistic timeline for completing milestones in the program, and a working relationship with experienced faculty to navigate my steps through the process.

Challenges of Completing Course Work

Doctoral course work often presents challenges in unimaginable ways. During the earlier course work, I routinely submitted assignments early and without difficulty. As I entered the 6-week courses that required group presentations, my organizational efforts were often challenged by the irresponsible work ethic of one or more team members. Often, it required leveraging my best negotiation skills to ensure the group project was completed in a timely and exemplary manner. Toward the end of my course work, the demands of providing responsible care for my parents escalated. Where I was usually among the first students to turn in assignments or complete discussion posts, I found myself struggling to complete the work. I often left work to take a parent to the doctor or hospital. At the onset of the doctoral program, I believed that the academic work was the first priority; when my elderly parents required more assistance, I had to rework my plan.

Many of my classmates instantly recognized the change in my ethic, and they were immensely supportive upon learning about the circumstances. Several classmates encouraged me to reset my motivation and focus. Other classmates offered real-life solutions to manage the caregiving of my parents. Not one student suggested that I quit the program or delay my academic efforts; instead, they focused on possible solutions. Their nurturing and encouragement revitalized me and strengthened my resolve to finish the doctoral race. I began working between 3 and 7 a.m. each morning, before going to work to ensure I would complete the academic work. I was determined to continue completing the coursework as scheduled, so I reworked the time I allotted for studying to provide an increased opportunity to stay focused. While I do not see myself as a superwoman, I do recognize that the doctoral learning process requires a significant commitment from me that must be balanced by my personal commitments to family, work, and society.

Practices for Transitioning From Course Work to the Proposal/Dissertation Process

Nothing can truly prepare you for the transition from the course work to the proposal and dissertation. Are you a self-starter? Do you have effective time-management skills? Are you capable of setting goals and attaining them? Can you still stay on task amid challenging circumstances? If your are able to sustain self-motivation and stay organized in relation to your academic responsibilities, then there is a greater likelihood that you will survive the transition from the course work to the proposal/dissertation process.

As a self-starter, I was anxiously awaiting the conclusion of the coursework so that I could finally begin to work on my proposal and dissertation. The frustration for many students rested in the fact that we were required to continue to take course work while we crafted the prospectus. The commitment to completing assignments and discussion posts from two courses while working on the prospectus proved daunting for many students. The self-imposed competition among peers for research center approval on the prospectus raised the bar for potential frustration and feelings of inadequacy. Many students felt that they were not rising up to meet the demands of the program. As I shared with my closest friends in the program, this is not a race to turn in a deliverable. This is the beginning of the research process for a significant study for which we can truly be proud. Doctoral students should wisely invest time to ensure a meaningful research question and methodology is crafted that will yield a study with measureable learning outcomes that can be accomplished in a realistic time frame.

The selection of your dissertation committee is critical to your success in the doctoral program. I have been blessed with a conscientious chair who gently paces my work on a realistic timeline. I have shared my concerns about balancing the increasing commitments to my parents. While he still maintains timeline expectations, his timeline strikes a balance between completing the proposal and dissertation and managing my parents to afford me a little time to negotiate a setback and remain on course. Your dissertation chair and committee should provide guidance during each step of the dissertation process to ensure your investment of time, resources, and research is well organized and will result in a meaningful and completed dissertation in the allotted time frame.

Challenges and Setbacks Experienced in the Proposal/Dissertation Process

Challenges and setbacks are inherent in the doctoral learning process. The dissertation is an unpredictable process that involves uncertainty, ambiguity, and unexpected events (Mujtaba et al., 2006). Each milestone associated with the proposal and dissertation requires patience and diligence.

Doctoral students must prepare themselves for the process by remembering that the feedback and insights given by the chair, committee member, university research reviewer, advisor, or librarian is for their benefit to strengthen your dissertation. Affixing a how-great-I-am attitude to your proposal draft will simply set you up for a feeling of inadequacy when the committee feedback is returned. As doctoral learners, you should realize that though God has granted each individual special talents and capabilities, we do not know the answers to everything.

One of the most significant challenges and setbacks I have experienced during the doctoral program necessitated a topic change. My initial prospectus topic was to examine transformational leadership and the perception of readiness of federally qualified health care centers (FQHCs) amid the onset of the Affordable Care Act. It was to be a groundbreaking study that provided the world with information that could impact how FQHCs approach patient care, or at least I thought it would. I did not realize that FQHCs were adopting a cautious posture about the media or outside attention on their health centers.

I shared my concerns about gaining access to FQHCs to conduct research with my committee. I indicated that I knew three chief executive officers of FQHCs in my state very well. They advised me to take their pulse about conducting research in their centers without revealing the topic. To my surprise, each responded no. They had too much at risk as the date for enactment of the Affordable Care Act approached. I was devastated. I had researched this topic for 2 years, used my topic in every one of my courses to gain a fuller understanding, and accumulated a plethora of articles and resources for my literature review. My committee had approved the prospectus but were waiting for my final decision before sending it and the completed dissertation rubrics to the university research center for approval. The idea of giving up on my topic was not appealing. How could I start over? This was the topic I wanted to pursue, how could I make it happen? The answer was that I could not make it happen. FQHCs are health care centers administered by federal mandates and funding. I told my committee that I was starting over with a new topic and my committee supported the decision.

Overcoming Challenges and Setbacks in the Proposal/Dissertation Process

Upon learning that I would have to rewrite and reresearch my prospectus, I indulged myself in a self-satisfying grieving period. After a week of feeling sorry for myself, one of my closest friends in the program said it was time to move onward. She inspired me to begin anew, but to do it expeditiously as I had lost some time. I worked diligently and rewrote the new prospectus.

My chair set a new deadline to complete the prospectus 4 weeks prior to the end of the second dissertation mentoring course, which was a required course with the mentor/chair. He wanted to complete all changes and submit it in time to obtain approval before the start of the first doctoral dissertation course. My committee reviewed the new prospectus and made minor changes. They submitted it to the university research center for approval and it was approved by the second week of the doctoral dissertation course.

The experience of changing a dissertation topic is not unique. It is actually a common occurrence in a dissertation program. It's not about you—it's about the dissertation. It's hard not to take it personally when you are criticized for your dissertation or research. If your committee wants you to change some or all of your proposal or dissertation, it is because they want to ensure you will succeed. As doctoral students, we must realize that everything happens for a reason, and it is better to discover a required change early in the process and adapt to the requirements of that change.

Greatest Lessons Learned in the Proposal/Dissertation Process

Many of the greatest lessons I have learned about the proposal/dissertation process have come from conversations with my instructors and peers. I am sure that as I continue my tenure in the doctoral process, I will learn more lessons. The most important lesson is to take good care of yourself. You must build in time for mental health moments to exhale and ensure you are managing yourself, family, and circumstances well.

Emotionally check yourself to reassess if you are sustaining a positive feeling about the doctoral process and ensuring the work you are doing and making sacrifices for is indeed meeting your expectations. I never said no in my past. Now, I routinely say no and have communicated to everyone I know and care about that I do not have as much free time and cannot do many of the things that I used to undertake. If you do not nourish yourself emotionally, physically, and spiritually, you will not have the stamina or the resiliency to finish the journey.

Create a doctoral sanctum as your place of study, as it will provide the necessary spiritual direction to guide your progress. Identify a tranquil area where distractions are kept to a minimum and your research can be organized and readily accessible. In my home, I moved from a desk in my adult son's room to the kitchen table, so that I can look out the doors into the woods that back our home. The serene setting provides constant inspiration. I use the adjourning butler's pantry as a library and resource center to hold all of my research and important information.

This was a special sacrifice that my family extended to allow me the continuous use of the kitchen table. They take their meals at the kitchen island countertop. Honesty is always the best policy. If you do not know how to do something, you must be willing to let someone know and ask for help. If you do not allow others to know that you are drowning, they cannot save you. Do not be afraid to venture in new directions with your research study. Faith in taking new steps is often perceived as blindly venturing down an unknown path, but in researching the unknown, leaps of faith often yield dynamic and groundbreaking results.

Goal setting is an important part of the doctoral journey. As the architect of your doctoral process, break down tasks into small, manageable pieces. Take time to celebrate the small successes on your doctoral journey. I love that my cohort acknowledges every accomplishment that every student achieves. Seeing 10-15 congratulatory e-mails is an empowering experience that propels you toward the next milestone.

It is important to surround yourself with a community of support. Whether it is family, instructors, student peers or friends, each individual act of support ensures you will become stronger and more focused to achieve the next milestone. Keep focused on the big picture, but remember the devil is in the details. As researchers, we can overlook a fact that will dramatically alter the results of our study.

Keep a notes-to-self list of important things to add to your proposal or dissertation or of research to conduct. This will limit memory overload and frustration. Doctoral students feel quite capable of managing their writing process, but resist the urge. Use resources at the writing center or through an editor to help relieve some of the stress from proofing for grammatical and American Psychological Association style errors.

Finally, enjoy your doctoral journey. This is your time to pursue your academic dream. Relax and relish each accomplishment you attain toward that goal.

Tools for Completing the Course Work, Proposal, and Dissertation

Each doctoral student should assemble a toolkit for ensuring the successful completion of the course work, proposal, and dissertation. Special toolkit items should include developing organization skills; setting realistic goals; gaining the skills to conduct research of scholarly resources; creating or selecting a literature review software system; building a community of support from among family, dissertation committee members, instructors, and peers; constructing and maintaining a task review list; determining an excellent editorial system; and setting aside appropriate time to address personal, family, social, and work-related issues. Each toolkit may offer additional tools as deemed necessary by the individual student or the student's unique circumstances. Sakurai, Pyhalto, and Lindblom-Ylanne (2012) posited that students' engagement with their studies and their persistence in pursuing them have been identified as key factors in ensuring the completion of their doctoral studies.

Problems That Constrain Progress in the Doctoral Program

Factors that caused the most dissatisfaction in my doctoral program and that threaten to hinder my performance or progress are family commitments, lack of support or feedback from course instructors, low group-member contributions, and uncertainty of financial aid funding. While I have not listed these experiences in any priority order, I was most disappointed at experiences where the instructor provided little or no direction or feedback and low group-member contributions.

As a self-starter, I proceeded to complete assignments, even group assignments, to the best of my ability. However, I felt immensely ill-equipped to complete the course work when the instructor rarely commented or retroactively commented about what should have been done when sharing the course grade for the assignment. I also felt deeply conflicted about group members not doing their fair share of the work. Another group member and I would often do most or all of the work. I could have turned the individual student into the instructor but chose not to do so. In the real world, when a team must prepare a deliverable, there is no rationale to justify not having it prepared due to someone dropping the ball. Sakurai et al. (2012) noted that most situations where students considered dropping out of their doctoral programs were associated with lack of supervisory experience from instructors and inherent problems with the department.

Peer Mentoring in the Doctoral Process

Peer mentoring is a viable means of enhancing the value-added experience of doctoral learners. The opportunity is enhanced when students are paired with students of varying progress levels in the doctoral process. Shared learning promotes a deepened understanding of program expectations, broadens awareness of learning outcomes, builds a community of support, and heightens students' confidence in their ability to negotiate the doctoral journey. Sakurai et al.'s (2012) findings emphasized promoting the broader scholarly community as a safety net, especially for international students.

Benefit Realization of Cohort Models

Cohort models strengthen the confidence of students to negotiate their doctoral process through creating a shared learning model. Teitel (1997) further asserted that academic cohort models promote strong bonds among students and enhance student retention. The opportunity to participate in a cohort model during the doctoral journey has provided me with an enriched understanding of the process from the perspective of peers as well as the faculty member who directs the cohort. The faculty member also contributes to the cohort learning through informative talks and guest lecturers. It would be beneficial for all doctoral mentors to provide a cohort model that would enjoin their respective students.

References

Mujtaba, B., Scharff, M., Cavico, F., & Mujtaba, M. (2008). Challenges and joys of earning a doctorate degree: Overcoming the "ABD" phenomenon. *Research in Higher Education Journal, 1,* 10-26.

Sakurai, Y., Pyhalto, K., & Lindblom-Ylanne, S. (2012). Factors affecting international doctoral students' academic engagement, satisfaction with their studies and dropping out. *International Journal for Research, 3*(2), 99-117.

Teitel, L. (1997). Understanding and harnessing the power of the cohort model in preparing educational leaders. *Peabody Journal of Education, 72*(2), 66-85.

Tweedie, M., Clark, S., Johnson, R., & Kay, D. W. (2013). Reflection: The "dissertation marathon" in doctoral distance education. *Distance Education, 34*, 379-390.

About the Author

Walter Ray McCollum, PhD

Dr. Walter McCollum is an educator and international consultant. He has been employed by some of the top companies, including Lucent Technologies, Booz Allen & Hamilton, Lockheed Martin, Science Application International Corporation (SAIC), Capgemini, and Sodexo.

Prior to working in the private sector, Dr. McCollum, a Desert Storm veteran, served 13 years in the U.S. Air Force, where he held various Air Force specialties in the areas of information management and communications.

His military awards and medals include Air Force Commendation Medal w/1 Oak Leaf Cluster, Joint Meritorious Service Medal, Air Force Achievement Medal w/2 Oak Leaf Clusters, Southwest Asia Service Medal, Humanitarian Service Medal, National Defense Service Medal, Distinguished Graduate Noncommissioned Officer's Academy, Military Citizenship Award Noncommissioned Officer's Academy, and the Office of the Secretary of Defense Junior Enlisted Member of the Year.

As a scholar-practitioner, Dr. McCollum has authored and published five books: *Process Improvement in Quality Management Systems: Case Studies Analyzing Carnegie Mellon's Capability Maturity Model*, *Applied Change Management: Approaches to Organizational Change and Transformation*, *Strength of a Black Man: Destined for Self-Empowerment*, *Breakthrough Mentoring in the 21st Century: A Compilation of Life Altering Experiences*, and *How to Use Emotional, Cultural and Spiritual Intelligence to Mentor Doctoral Learners*.

Dr. McCollum is also an adjunct professor at several universities, including New York University, Walden University, Northcentral University, Capella University, Central Michigan University, and Colorado State University—Global. He holds a PhD in applied management and decision sciences with a specialization in leadership and organizational change from Walden University, an MA in management from Webster University, and a BS in psychology from the State University of New York, Albany.

www.ingramcontent.com/pod-product-compliance
Lightning Source LLC
Chambersburg PA
CBHW021826220426
43663CB00005B/146